Teaching Social Studies:
A Methods Book for Methods Teachers

Edited by
S.G. Grant
John Lee
Kathy Swan

INFORMATION AGE PUBLISHING, INC.
Charlotte, NC • www.infoagepub.com
Co-published with C3 Teachers

Library of Congress Cataloging-in-Publication Data

The CIP data for this book can be found on the Library of Congress website (loc.gov).

Paperback: 978-1-68123-884-5
Hardcover: 978-1-68123-885-2
E-Book: 978-1-68123-886-9

Printed in the United States of America

Teaching Social Studies:
A Methods Book for Methods Teachers

CONTENTS

PART 2

TEACHERS AND TEACHING

PART 3

SUBJECT MATTER

PART 4

CONTEXT

CHAPTER 1

INTRODUCTION

The Task of Teaching Social Studies Methods

S. G. Grant, John Lee, and Kathy Swan

Like our colleagues in other school subjects, we teach methods courses intended to prepare students to become teachers. Below that surface similarity, however, social studies methods courses have a crazy quilt quality. Many of us teach an elementary or secondary methods course, but some courses run the K–12 gamut. Many of us teach stand-alone courses in social studies, but some courses are combined with literacy and still others combine attention to science and mathematics as well. Many of us teach classes designated for undergraduate or graduate students, but some courses put both groups of students in the same class. The generous interpretation of all the above is that we are a flexible group.

Also like our colleagues in the other school subjects, we can choose from a number of methods texts. That said, a peek behind the curtain reveals some startling differences. A quick search on Amazon netted the following results: Although there are 23,912 references to social studies teaching texts, science leads the way with 55,435. By comparison, literacy and mathematics methods books yield totals of 40,755 and 29,627. We know—we were surprised too!

There are differences among the texts in our field and others but, in many ways, methods texts display a strong conventionality—a soup-to-nuts, every-

Teaching Social Studies: A Methods Book for Methods Teachers,
pages 1–5.

thing-including-the-bathroom-sink narrative covering a wide range of generic and subject-specific instructional topics. David Cohen (1989) has called teaching an "impossible profession" due to the complex, nuanced, and contextual relationships at hand. Little wonder, then, that the methods books we academics write and use try to anticipate and respond to as big a swath of teachers' lives as possible.

We make this point not to be critical, but to acknowledge the challenges of trying to help prospective teachers build a repertoire of knowledge and skills that will well serve them in the classroom. We have used these books to good advantage. As we have done so, however, we have wondered if the methods book genre might profit from a different kind of text.

Many possibilities arose. Coming off our leadership of the effort to develop the *College, Career, and Civic Life (C3) Framework for Social Studies State Standards* (National Council for the Social Studies, 2013), we entertained ideas about a methods books highlighting questions and sources, disciplinary knowledge and evidence in a variety of combinations. In the end, we were drawn to the notion of a book focused on the tasks that we assign to our students. Tasks represent both formative and culminating experiences in that, as they respond to tasks, students demonstrate their capacity to do something with the ideas and resources we put in front of them. Because there are many things that we methods professors want our students to demonstrate, the kinds of tasks offered in this book vary considerably.

To bring some measure of coherence to the 42 tasks described, we organized the chapters loosely around Joseph Schwab's (1978) *commonplaces of education*—learners and learning, teachers and teaching, subject matter, and milieu or context.

Although Schwab defined his commonplaces in terms of curriculum building, we find them equally useful as a heuristic for helping teacher candidates think about the range of issues likely to confront them across a school day. As they plan lessons and units, we expect candidates to think about questions such as the following:

- What do I know about my learners that will enable them to complete tasks that both support and challenge them?
- What do I do in order to represent the ideas such that all of my learners can embrace them?
- What do I understand about the subject matter that will honor both the content and my learners' knowledge and experience?
- What do I know about the school and community contexts that I can bring to bear in the preparation of my instruction?

Questions highlighting the individual commonplaces are useful, but equally useful is encouraging candidates to think about the commonplaces in interaction. That is, how does what I know about my learners' lives outside of school influence what I want to highlight in the content I teach and in the instructional representations I create? For example, when teaching about geographic distance, an urban teacher might draw on her students' lived experience and use the term "block" as a unit of measurement, while a rural teacher might use "mile." Social studies teachers likely will want their students to understand that there are many ways of representing distance; knowing one's students' initial understandings, however, can prove invaluable.

The challenge that we posed to our colleagues was straightforward: In something less than 2000 words, describe a task, assignment, or project that teacher candidates complete as part of their methods classes. Other than the word count, the only other requirement was that authors indicate which of Schwab's (1978) commonplaces was most apparent in the tasks they described.

In *Teaching Social Studies: A Methods Book for Methods Teachers*, we use Schwab's commonplaces as a general approach to categorize and present the authors' suggested tasks. The Learners and Learning section features chapters that promote teacher candidates' understandings of themselves as learners and as prospective teachers. For example, Scott Wylie's chapter asks candidates to use their teenage recollections in order to think about the ideas and issues that might engage their students. The Teachers and Teaching section offers a range of tasks intended to help teacher candidates realize the full palette of instructional approaches they can use as they build their pedagogical practices. Brian Girard and Bob Bain, for example, describe a task where their candidates participate in an exercise in which they practice grading student essays. It will likely surprise few readers that the Subject Matter section is the larger of these first two sections by about a third. The scope of the social studies curriculum has always been one of the biggest challenges for new teachers, so the subject matter chapters present a collection of tasks designed to push teacher candidates' content understandings across all the social studies disciplines. History (including local history) gets considerable play (e.g., Jenifer Hauver's and Michael Marino and Margaret Smith Crocco's chapters) as does economics (e.g., Cheryl Ayers' and Jason Harshman's chapters), and civics (e.g., Jeff Passe's and Paul McHenry's chapters). Finally, the chapters in the Context section highlight the several ways that teacher candidates can better know their students and the communities in which they teach (e.g., Nick Bardo and Barbara Cruz's and Alexander Pope's chapters) with several authors explicitly addressing the issue of social justice (e.g., Alexander Cuenca's and Erik Jon Byker, Amy Good, and Nakeshia Williams' chapters).

Organizing the chapters in this fashion offers readers the chance to hone in on a particular kind of task. However, those designations are offered only as an initial entrée into the tasks described. Therefore, while, Rebecca Mueller, Lauren Colley, and Emma Thacker's chapter "What Should I Teach?" is part of the subject matter section, it has clear implications for the other commonplace elements. Thus, we invite readers to enter the chapters with an initial commonplace perspective in mind, but to stick around to see how the others emerge.

In order to get the maximum number of chapters into this volume, we limited the authors to 1750 words in the text and references and allowed only those appendices that amplified a particular element in the chapter. To streamline the reading of the chapters, we asked authors to follow a narrative template. That template features the following elements:

1. **Background**: A brief description of the author(s), intended audience, title of the course taught, commonplace featured, and the relevant National Council for the Social Studies teacher education standard.
2. **Task Summary**: A one-sentence summary of the task.
3. **Description of the Task**: A narrative description of the goals, activities, resources, timeframe, and assessment relevant to the exercise.
4. **Candidates and the Task**: A short report of how students respond to the activity.
5. **The Task in Context**: A concise account of how and when the task occurs during the course.

Although we did not ask the authors to address the *C3 Framework* in their chapters, many did so explicitly. For example, Jason Endacott's methods students use the Inquiry Arc as the basis for their instructional planning and Mark Pearcy's candidates use it to "problematize" the social studies curriculum. Other authors describe tasks that reflect an implicit nod to the *C3 Framework*. For example, Todd Dinkelman speaks to the broad nature of inquiry and the specific use of questions to help his candidates think through and express their emergent ideas.

We know that many teacher candidates struggle to break free of the apprenticeship of observation (Lortie, 1975) that delimits their instructional potential to craft inquiry-based practices. They come to us passionate about the content and about the chance to do something noble and good with their students. Our teacher candidates sit in our classes because they love social studies; they have already seen how the content can inform and enrich their lives. Translating their passion into practices that will engage and encourage *all* of their students, however, is a steep challenge. It will surprise no one, then, to learn that each of the tasks described pushes teacher candidates' existing ideas about teaching, learning, subject matter, and context. The bad news is that they need that push; the good news is that invariably they respond well.

Ultimately, then, *Teaching Social Studies* is a success story: The inquiry-based practice evident in the *C3 Framework* is intended to get under students' skins; these chapters do the same for our teacher candidates. We invite readers to have fun playing with the ideas in this book.

* * * * *

We would like to thank the over 60 social studies educators who participated in this project. Writing to a template is no easy task, nor is writing to a severely limited word count. With those challenges in mind, we much appreciate the authors' thoughtful contributions and the grace and good humor they exhibited in response to our editorial nagging. More importantly, however, we would like to thank the authors for their willingness to share this terrific set of instructional tasks. Doing so is huge contribution to the teaching of social studies methods and suggests to us that the care and feeding of prospective social studies teachers is in good hands.

REFERENCES

Cohen, D. (1989). Practice and policy: Notes on the history of instruction. In D. Warren (Ed.), *American teachers* (pp. 393–407). New York: Macmillan.

Lortie, D. (1975). *Schoolteacher*. Chicago, IL: University of Chicago Press.

National Council for the Social Studies. (2013). *The college, career, and civic life (C3) framework for social studies state standards: Guidance for enhancing the rigor of K–12 civics, economics, geography, and history.* Washington, DC: National Council for the Social Studies.

Schwab, J. (1978). The practical: Translation into curriculum. In I. Westbury, & I. Wilkof (Eds.), *Science, curriculum, and liberal education* (pp. 365–383). Chicago, IL: University of Chicago Press

PART 1

LEARNERS AND LEARNING

CHAPTER 2

RAISING YOUR VOICE

Engaging the Social Studies Through Spoken Word Poetry

Lauren Bagwell and Brooke Blevins

Name: Lauren Bagwell and Brooke Blevins	Audience: Undergraduate students
Affiliation: Baylor University	Length: Three hours
Course Title: Secondary Social Studies Curriculum	Commonplace featured: Learners/Learning
NCSS Teacher Education Standards: Standard 4. Candidates plan and implement relevant and responsive pedagogy, create collaborative and interdisciplinary learning environments, and prepare learners to be informed advocates for an inclusive and equitable society. Standard 5. Candidates reflect and expand upon their social studies knowledge, inquiry skills, and civic dispositions to advance social justice and promote human rights through informed action in schools and/or communities.	

Teaching Social Studies: A Methods Book for Methods Teachers,
pages 9–14.
Copyright © 2017 by Information Age Publishing

TASK SUMMARY

This task engages teacher candidates as they incorporate spoken word poetry as a culturally relevant and meaningful method for student engagement and learning in the social studies into a series of lesson plans.

DESCRIPTION OF THE TASK

Through participation, design, and implementation of spoken word poetry in the social studies classroom, teacher candidates experience and employ a pedagogical practice that values student voice and alternative perspectives. This assignment provides the opportunity for candidates to examine a unique way to cultivate a democratic and culturally relevant classroom.

The Task: Teacher candidates participate in several spoken word poetry activities during their methods course including watching performances, constructing a list and a two-voice poem, analyzing famous speeches from a poetic perspective, and constructing and performing their own spoken word poetry. After participating in these exercises, they design lessons that utilize spoken word poetry for use in their classrooms. Several of the activities we use follow.

Introducing Spoken Word Poetry: We begin by showing our students Steve Colman's piece, *I Wanna Hear a Poem* (https://www.youtube.com/watch?v=tRsITgjBsLs). After the performance, candidates engage in a short debrief of the performance, around questions such as:

- What stood out to you in the piece?
- What does this piece say about spoken word poetry as a whole?
- How did the poet's performance influence the overall meaning of the poem?

Establishing Expectations & Rules for Sharing: Because sharing is an important part of spoken word poetry, we work together to set classroom expectations for sharing. In this process, candidates describe what rules and expectations they think are important in creating a safe space for sharing. Some of these expectations include: listen when someone is speaking, avoid laughing when not appropriate, encourage one another, be vulnerable, and be truthful. We remind candidates that positive feedback is an integral part of creating a safe space for students to share. In the poetry world, positive feedback is often expressed in the form of snaps in the middle of the poem and claps at the end of a performance.

This is My America: Candidates watch a YouTube performance of *America in Four Minutes* (https://www.youtube.com/watch?v=GZDNUGMMxLk). In this clip, the poet considers alternative perspectives to what defines America, offering that America is a mosaic of the positive and the negative. Prior to watching the clip, candidates take note of the various issues that are addressed in the performance, including how these issues are persistent across time. We ask them to consider questions such as: In what ways has the U.S. seen progress in regards to these issues? In what areas do we still have work to do?

Candidates then create a list poem by composing a list of 10 things they know to be true about being an American or about America as a whole (either concrete examples or abstract ideas). Candidates share their lists, including reading the numbers and each item on their list aloud.

Candidates then create another list poem using the pre-described sentence stems below.

I am from...
I like...
When I am older I will be...
Poetry is...

After completing their lists, candidates share their poems with the class. Throughout this process, we remind them that poetry can be as simple as making a list. We emphasize that these poems are meant to help them voice their unique stories and perspectives. Finally, we underscore that spoken word is poetry that demands to be heard and thus sharing is an important part of the process. (See the Appendix for an example of a list poem).

Poem for Two Voices: A two-voice poem provides a unique way to compare two things or demonstrate two distinct perspectives on an issue or event. Usually written in two columns, the two voices go back and forth to create a dialogue or conversation. Sometimes the voices come together as one and are written in the center of the page or on the same line in each of the two columns. Utilizing an example of a rich and poor woman found in Christensen & Watson (2015), candidates explore how to write a poem for two voices by thinking about opposing perspectives and voices that might have been present during the Civil War (i.e., Grant and Lee, North and South, slave and freeman). From that list, candidates pick one pair to use in their two voice poems. They later share their two-voice poems with the entire class. (See the Appendix for an example of a two-voice poem).

Prose Poetry: We also introduce students to the notion of prose poetry. Prose poetry is written in paragraphs, but contains characteristics of poetry such as poetic meter, imagery, repetition, and rhyme. To introduce this concept, we show students a YouTube performance entitled *Please Don't Steal My Air Jordan's* by Lemon Anderson (https://www.youtube.com/watch?v=WT7VMrxTPPA). We ask candidates to consider how the style of this poem is similar to or different from others we have watched, including how the poem draws the reader into the narrative.

From here, we discuss how many famous speeches are written as prose poetry. Before presenting the Gettysburg Address as an example, we guide candidates through a series of questions, about the purpose of the speech and how it represents a turning point in the Civil War. We then read/perform the Gettysburg address as a spoken word piece.

We debrief the Gettysburg Address together, drawing attention to the poetic elements used including repetition, metaphor, and imagery. We then ask candidates to think about a turning point in their own lives and what changed at that moment. Using the template below, teacher candidates write about that event:

_____ years and _____ months ago, something _____happened.
A turning point like Gettysburg things changed from _____to_____.
(Describe the event in 4–6 lines; you may choose to use repetition, imagery, figurative language, or rhyme)
Old Abe would agree _____changed my history.

Candidates then consider if their poems would read like one from a Confederate or Union soldier after the Battle of Gettysburg. For example, if things went from really bad to really good, then it would be similar to the experience of a Union soldier.

Assessing the Task: We assess candidates through their planning and teaching of at least two lessons that utilize spoken word poetry as a pedagogical tool. The lessons must include examples of spoken word poetry and writing activities that help students connect the material to their own lives. After teaching the lessons, candidates reflect on the outcome of the lesson including examining student work.

CANDIDATES AND THE TASK

At first, teacher candidates are apprehensive about writing poetry and leading lessons that utilize spoken word poetry. Once they participate in writing activities such as the list poem and watching YouTube performances, however, they see that the task is doable. After examining examples of various types of poetry, they typically recognize the potential of spoken word poetry to connect to students' lived experiences and offer alternative perspectives in the classroom. Once candidates create and teach their own lessons, they generally realize how willing students are to interact and engage with spoken word poetry. Finally, the spoken word poetry activities and subsequent lessons usually lead to further discussion about engaging students in a democratic classroom that prioritizes student voice.

THE TASK IN CONTEXT

Prior to learning about spoken word poetry, teacher candidates engage in discussions and activities about the purpose of the social studies, how to create a democratic classroom, and pedagogical strategies to increase student voice and perspective taking. They have learned about planning for instruction and lesson design, including assessing student learning. This activity asks them to integrate multiple concepts they have learned about in the methods class in order to create lessons around spoken word poetry that they can utilize in their field experience placements.

APPENDIX

What follows are examples of list and two-voice poems.

REFERENCE

Christensen, L., & Watson, D. (2015). *Rhythm and resistance: Teaching poetry for social justice*. Milwaukee, WI: Rethinking Schools.

Example of List Poem

Ten Things I Know to Be True About America

1. I've sung Francis Scott Key's Star Bangle Banner more times than I can count.
2. We were once a part of England, but broke away. There is rebel blood running through our veins. We are the descendants of Patriots.
3. Our first president had wooden teeth.
4. We are the land of the free because of the brave sons, daughters, best friends, siblings, mothers, and fathers who fought with everything they had so why is it that I've seen more veterans living in a cardboard cutout of the American dream?
5. Our nation was founded by drug dealers…and by drug dealers I mean tobacco saved Jamestown.
6. The turning point of the American Revolution was the Battle of Saratoga.
7. There will be days that you feel like you're about to be blown to pieces on the front lines of whatever obstacle is standing in your way and on that day I want you to remember life is full of Saratogas.
8. We forget too often that the freedom of speech must always be complemented with a willingness to listen.
9. We were born with the right to constantly pursue happiness. Pursuing happiness will bring you life. Life will bring you liberty.
10. We have work to do.

Lauren Bagwell

Example of a Two-Voice Poem

A: I am the Union, I live in the North.
B: I am the Confederacy, I live in the South.
A/B: I love my home but my country is fighting.
A: At my home I see factories and tall buildings.
B: At my home I see farms and open land
A: I am against slavery
B: I support slavery
A: Where I live there's rock soil
B: Where I live there's rich soil
A/B: I love my president.
A: My president is Abraham Lincoln.

B: My president is Jefferson Davis.
A/B: I am fighting for my way of life.

Lauren Bagwell

CHAPTER 3

USING CURRENT SOCIAL PROBLEMS TO CONFRONT PRE-SERVICE TEACHERS' DEFICIT ORIENTATIONS OF THEIR CANDIDATES

Emilie M. Camp and Prentice T. Chandler

Name: Emilie M. Camp and Prentice T. Chandler	Audience: Undergraduate students
Affiliation: University of Cincinnati	Length: Two hours
Course Title: Methods of Teaching Social Studies	Commonplace featured: Subject Matter
NCSS National Standards for the Preparation of Social Studies Teachers: Standard 1. Candidates demonstrate knowledge of social studies disciplines. Candidates are knowledgeable of disciplinary concepts, facts, and tools; structures of inquiry; and forms of representation. Standard 2. Candidates plan learning sequences that draw upon social studies knowledge and literacies to support the civic competence of learners	

Teaching Social Studies: A Methods Book for Methods Teachers,
pages 15–19.
Copyright © 2017 by Information Age Publishing

TASK SUMMARY

This task asks teacher candidates to use their content knowledge to develop a lesson plan that addresses a social problem and to collectively reflect upon the expectations they hold of their students and the possibilities of applying this content in their field experience classrooms.

DESCRIPTION OF THE TASK

The primary goal of the task is for teacher candidates to articulate the relationship between the content knowledge required to address social problems and the Ohio social studies standards through the development of a lesson. Further, the task aims to disrupt candidates' deficit models of thinking with regard to their students through the reflection on the imperative of developing such knowledge in *all* candidates (Gorski, 2013).

The Task: In a social studies methods course, candidates are tasked with making connections between various current events and the *Ohio Learning Standards for Social Studies*. The two-semester methods sequence focuses on developing candidates' philosophies of social studies, particularly related to the nature of the content and to the purposes for teaching social studies (Parker, 2012). To help candidates move beyond a singular focus of "social studies as history," they examine current social issues and the connection to standards and purposes for teaching social studies. Candidates do so within the context of developing the knowledge, skills, and dispositions of democratic citizenship (Parker, 2012). They report a realization that current issues are important to teach and that they do connect to the state standards.

During the second semester, candidates apply their new understandings of social studies to the classroom context as they enter their first field experience placement. The task described below reflects insights into candidates' struggles to connect the pedagogy learned in class to their field experience classrooms, particularly around their expectations of students. Although "social problems" are not specifically identified as key social studies content in the state standards, they are embedded in those standards through the language of civic participation, analysis and interpretation of data, and the evaluation of multiple perspectives. This task asks candidates to extract key concepts and goals from the standards that function to develop understandings of the nature of social problems and possible solutions to them and develop a related lesson.

Throughout the second semester, candidates examine a specific method of instruction in social studies, experiencing those methods as both the student and teacher, with opportunities to reflect on and constructively critique each approach. The instructional methods (e.g., role-play, various discussion strategies, effective source work approaches) are inquiry-based and framed through a lens of critical pedagogy (Agarwal-Rangnath, 2013). The week prior to this task, candidates participate in a Socratic Seminar using *Decolonizing the Mind for World Centered*

Global Education (Merryfield & Subedi, 2006) as the central text. Each year, we find that candidates express enthusiastic support of this discussion strategy in social studies, yet there is a clear skepticism that *their* students could successfully participate in a Socratic Seminar. Candidates' low expectations of poor students and students of color is unsettling and in need of disruption. Thus, the task is designed to help candidates interrogate their lingering deficit orientations of students of color and poverty.

For the class activity, we identify four current issues as the appropriate context: 1) rising sea levels, 2) growing food in space, 3) the Zika virus threat, and 4) the heroin addiction crisis. We organize candidates into four groups and assign to each one of the topics. Their first step is to examine multiple sources of information (including their own background knowledge) related to the assigned issue. As the instructors, our role is to clarify questions and recommend additional on-line resources for this stage of building background knowledge. Next, candidates brainstorm the social studies content knowledge needed to address these issues. They typically compile a robust list on the board (e.g., knowledge of coastal demographics, local community public health needs). Each group then locates at least one related social studies standard at the middle grades level and uses the *Inquiry Design Model* (Grant, Lee, & Swan, 2014) to develop a lesson on the topic.

At this point in the semester, the lessons are generally well developed; candidates are accustomed to writing and engaging in peer-critique of lesson plans each week, and they typically have a solid grasp on lesson planning. Each group then presents their lesson design to the class. Through this sharing process, candidates offer constructive feedback in the form of questions, particularly aimed at the alignment between the social problems context and the relevant standard.[1]

The final stage of the activity is a structured whole-class discussion, centered on the question, "when you look at your students in your practicum classroom, do you look at them with the expectation that *they* may very well be the people who will solve these problems?" This question quiets the room as candidates confront their own deficit thinking, their own racism and classism, and the adverse pedagogical implications of such thinking. What follows is a discussion of their expectations of students and lingering deficit orientations (Paris & Alim, 2014; Valencia, 1997) and the implications for their pedagogical decisions. The discussion concludes by revisiting of the purposes for teaching current issues (Evans & Saxe, 2007) and an opportunity to think beyond the commonsense purpose of

---

[1] Examples of connections made to the Ohio Learning Standards in Social Studies (Ohio Department of Education, 2010) include: 1) "individuals can better understand public issues by gathering and interpreting information from multiple sources. Data can be displayed graphically to effectively and efficiently communicate information" (p. 20), (fifth grade, government), 2) "the ability to understand individual and group perspectives is essential to analyzing historic and contemporary issues" (p. 24), (seventh grade, government), 3) "cultural biases, stereotypes, and prejudices had social, political, and economic consequences for minority groups and the population as a whole" (p. 26), (eighth grade, history).

developing knowledge, skills, and dispositions of democratic citizenship (Parker, 2012). For social problems to be solved, the problems themselves must be taught to those who will hold the solutions; if not *their* students, then who?

Assessing the Task: Candidates engage in peer assessment of the alignment between the stated standard and the content knowledge the presenters deem to be essential to addressing the selected social problem. Through the group presentation of their lesson plans, peers offer immediate feedback on strengths and areas for improvement on such alignment. Through the discussions, we probe and listen for evidence that candidates are applying the general frame of "asset models" of thinking (Paris & Alim, 2013) explored theoretically during the first semester to the specific context of their field experiences in socioeconomically and racially diverse urban schools. Although this approach represents an informal, formative assessment of candidate learning, it serves as a foundation for remaining assignments that require theoretical framing of teaching and learning around these broad concepts.

CANDIDATES AND THE TASK

The immediate response to the activity is positive. Teacher candidates raise important questions, connect their own schooling experiences of privilege to the development of their low expectations of their students, and begin to acknowledge that solutions to problems should involve all of those most affected by them, including poor students and students of color. What stands out is the prevalence of authentic connections between real-world problems and the content of their discipline. The four group lessons are engaging, rooted in inquiry, and reflect a philosophical stance toward the content tightly connected to democratic citizenship.

Additionally, some candidates refer to this class session as a formative moment in their development as social studies teachers. One candidate immediately transformed her instructional plans for her field experience, planning lessons for fourth graders on racism and sexism. Although somewhat nervous to bring such complexity into her teaching, she took that important step, and came back with a positive reflection on the lessons. She continues to take such an approach during her yearlong student teaching placement. Another candidate used this particular class activity as the foundation for her final project on her social studies philosophy, in which she explained how significant the class was in re-shaping her expectations of all children.

Finally, six months after this activity, a candidate approached us to discuss her ideas on developing a service-learning program led by the students and community. She named this class activity as one that she routinely revisits when confronted with the question of who she is as a teacher and what her social and ethical responsibility is to her students living the realities of racism and poverty.

THE TASK IN CONTEXT

The two-semester methods sequence begins with a focus on developing teacher candidates' philosophies of social studies, particularly related to the nature of the content and to the purposes for teaching social studies (Parker, 2012). A critical element of the course is the examination of current social issues and their connection to the standards and purposes for teaching social studies. Candidates explore the content of current issues within the context of developing the knowledge, skills, and dispositions of democratic citizenship (Parker, 2012). During the second semester, candidates begin to apply their new understandings of social studies to the classroom context, as they enter their first field experience. This task occurs midway through the second semester to so that candidates can connect the pedagogy learned from our class to their field experience classrooms.

REFERENCES

Agarwal-Rangnath, R. (2013). *Social studies, literacy, and social justice in the Common Core classroom: A guide for teachers.* New York: Teachers College Press.

Evans, R. W., & Saxe, D. W. (Eds.). (2007). *Handbook on teaching social issues* (NCSS Bulletin 93). Washington, DC: National Council for the Social Studies.

Gorski, P. (2013). *Reaching and teaching candidates in poverty: Strategies for erasing the opportunity gap.* New York: Teachers College Press.

Grant, S. G., Lee, J., & Swan, K. (2014). The inquiry design model. Retrieved from http://www.c3teachers.org/inquiry-design-model/

Merryfield, M. M., & Subedi, B. (2006). Decolonizing the mind for a world-centered global education. In E. W. Ross (Ed.), *The social studies curriculum: Purposes, problems, and possibilities* (pp. 283–295). Albany, NY: State University of New York Press.

Ohio Department of Education. (2010). Ohio's new standards: Social studies standards. Retrieved from http://education.ohio.gov/getattachment/Topics/Ohio-s-New-Learning-Standards/Social-Studies/SS-Standards.pdf.aspx

Paris, D., & Alim, H. S. (2014). What we are seeking to sustain through culturally sustaining pedagogy? A loving critique forward. *Harvard Education Review, 84*(1), 85–100.

Parker, W. C. (2012). *Social studies in elementary education* (14th ed.). Boston, MA: Pearson.

Valencia, R. R (Ed.). (1997). *The evolution of deficit thinking: Educational thought and practice.* London: RoutledgeFalmer.

CHAPTER 4

PRACTICING DELIBERATIVE DISCUSSION

A Supportive Protocol

Todd Dinkelman

Name: Todd Dinkelman	Audience: Undergraduate and graduate students
Affiliation: University of Georgia	Length: 60–90 minutes
Course Title: Methods in Secondary Social Studies	Commonplace featured: Learners and Learning
NCSS Teacher Education Standard: Element 4d. Candidates select, create, and engage learners with a variety of social studies instructional strategies, disciplinary sources and contemporary technologies, consistent with current theory and research about student learning.	

Teaching Social Studies: A Methods Book for Methods Teachers,
pages 21–25.
Copyright © 2017 by Information Age Publishing

TASK SUMMARY

The Final Word is a group discussion protocol that provides opportunities for teacher candidates to engage in a scaffolded group activity in which they listen deeply, develop ideas, and circle back for the "final word."

DESCRIPTION OF THE TASK

Course readings and texts are common features of social studies methods courses and student teaching seminars. Instructors assign readings for various reasons. One is the belief that readings convey important information teacher candidates benefit from knowing. Another is that readings provide a foundation for subsequent seminar activities, such as whole class discussions—a version of "flipped learning" well before that term was coined.

The Task: I use course readings to set the stage for the kind of shared deliberative inquiry I hope to both teach about and model. This sort of collaborative engagement with powerful, often controversial, and generative ideas grounded in written texts stands at the heart of social studies education. Yet a set stage only represents potential; tapping into this potential is another matter. In classroom settings, bringing a group of teacher candidates together to collectively and productively explore texts can be a considerable challenge.

One approach to help candidates construct meaning around course texts is to structure interaction through a Final Word protocol (Fischer-Mueller & Thompson-Grove, n.d.). The National School Reform Faculty deserves recognition for this protocol and for the rich repository of teaching ideas they make freely available, including over 200 protocols for facilitating group discussion and learning (See http://www.nsrfharmony.org/free-resources).

I begin by asking candidates in advance of class to highlight a particular selection or two of course readings that leave them with "burning questions." Burning questions are inquiries centered on important ideas and issues candidates encounter as they read a text, questions they most would like to raise for consideration with others in the class. Candidates bring their highlighted text passages, along with the texts, to class prepared to discuss the significance of their selections with others. The Final Word is a scaffolded group activity that has them listening deeply, developing ideas, and circling back for the "final word."

Before we begin, I find it helpful to share my intentions regarding the use of this protocol. In an effort to make my own pedagogical decision-making visible, I describe the kinds of intellectual engagement and collaborative inquiry I hope will result from the activity. The protocol works as follows:

- Candidates sit in a circle of groups of four or five participants.
- One member of the group is identified as a timekeeper whose role is to watch the clock and facilitate the process. Strict adherence to time limits is encouraged.

- Participants only speak when it is their turn. Cross talk is strongly discouraged.
- One person begins a round by reading the highlighted passage from the text, and is given no more than three minutes to explain why that passage is important, what insights it prompts, the questions it raises, and the like. The other members of the group listen closely, jot down notes, and consider their reactions to what the first speaker shares.
- Each member of the group then has no more than 1.5 minutes to respond to the first person's contribution. The goal here is to identify assumptions, extend interpretations, and provide the first person with different perspectives on the highlighted text and explanation.
- As group members provide their responses, the first person attends to and jots notes about the group members' responses.
- After each group member has responded, the turn circles back to the original speaker who then has 1.5 minutes for the final word. This brief response offers a chance to address new understandings prompted by the cycle of peer responses.

The initial speaker's final word completes a round. Taking turns, and adhering to the same discussion rules, each group participant gets a chance to share her or his quotes, receive feedback, and weigh in with the final word.

At the conclusion of all rounds, I ask the groups to debrief the activity by discussing key questions and ideas about the reading raised in the sharing. Since I typically use this activity in teacher education courses, I also ask candidates to discuss the activity itself. How did the protocol influence the nature of the dialogue? How did the sorts of engagement and discussion in this activity compare with other forms of group discussions they have experienced?

Assessing the Task: As with most class activities, the Final Word protocol offers opportunities for both informal and formal assessments. Informally, when underway, the rounds allow me to stand back from the activity to gauge the quality of candidate preparation and engagement. Without exception, I see candidates listening closely to the ideas of the peers, taking notes, responding to peers, and sharing their own ideas. In my experience, the task creates a lived example of the kind of careful listening, student-to-student engagement, and perspective taking I hope future teachers will try to make possible in their own classrooms. Sometimes, the quality of intellectual experience made possible by the Final Word satisfies my interest in assessment.

At the same time, the Final Word offers more formal opportunities for evaluation. I have asked candidates to produce brief records of the citations and ideas shared during the rounds. A simple chart suffices on this account. As an extension, I have candidates write reflections on the debriefing sessions that follow the completed rounds. These reflections might address deeper understandings developed about a particular course reading. In a social studies methods course, candidates might produce lists of reasons why they might wish to employ this method in their own teaching, as well as reservations they may have. I work to create opportunities for candidates to unpack the very methods I use in my classes. Such evaluation approaches serve my interest in assessments of my own teaching, as well as prompts for candidates to consider how they might assess deliberative discussion in their future practice.

CANDIDATES AND THE TASK

I have used this method for a variety of texts and found that the Final Word seldom fails as a powerful means of achieving at least three aims. First and most directly, teacher candidates report that the protocol prompts learning about the burning questions posed by themselves and their peers. The task offers entrée into course texts that spring from the questions candidates have about a reading. The meanings they bring forward from their encounters with class texts center the group discussions. Deeper understandings develop in a manner of discussion that engages virtually every candidate and for substantial stretches of time. Judging from both the traces of spoken conversations and written records made available by the activity and its debriefing, candidates find the Final Word a method that leads to deeper understandings of the text.

Second, the Final Word helps candidates see how instructional scaffolds can be used to lessen the burden teachers often feel when leading whole class discussions. As Brookfield and Preskill (1999) suggest, "creating the conditions for democratic discussion and realizing them to the extent possible are deliberate, intentional teaching acts" (p. 34). Productive group discussions do not just happen. Setting the conditions for, and then leading, large group discussions characterized by such widespread and sustained participation is challenging work for even the most accomplished teacher. Of course, beginning social studies teachers find this work especially daunting. The Final Word provides an example of a well-designed framework to facilitate rich discussions.

Finally, the Final Word enables candidates to live and experience some of the deliberative competencies at the center of social studies inquiry. Methods instructors cannot assume that candidates have a long enough history in other classrooms with mutual, engaging, and focused discussion of course texts. Candidates may not have ever known what it feels like to be a part of this sort of engagement. They may not have lots of experience with practicing the competencies required for democratic discourse. Among these competencies, one outcome that stands out for many candidates is *listening*. For all the value placed on talking in deliberative discussions, deep listening to the ideas of others sometimes is easy to overlook. Many candidates find that classroom discussion is mostly about figuring out what they might say if and when it is their time to contribute. The pressure means that it can be difficult to listen attentively to the words of others. The Final Word design structures careful listening in ways that other forms of classroom discussion do not.

Related, the Final Word fosters widespread participation in a focused discussion—discussion grounded in give and take among participants, and not just back and forth with the instructor. Therefore, it is not only that candidates get a chance to experience careful listening; they attend and respond to each other. I often participate in a Final Word group, sometimes because my inclusion balances the group sizes, but also because the experience is a striking reminder to me that powerful collaborative discussions do not always rely on the skilled work of a teacher interpreting and redirecting each comment a participant makes. With support and practice, I hope candidates more and more come to see each other as important sources of ideas and meaning making.

THE TASK IN CONTEXT

The Final Word is one approach toward the aim of a seminar discussion, a type of discussion and shared inquiry with the purpose of "enlarged understanding of ideas, issues, and values in or prompted by the text" (Parker, 2003, p. 131). Since seminar discussions are a mainstay of my teaching, I tend to use this task early in my courses to set the stage for work that follows. My aim is to provide teacher candidates with an early experience in collaborative engagement with texts. Yet the Final Word works well any time I hope to engage candidates in the process of generating understanding, clarifying insights, and exploring thinking about participant-generated questions regarding a class or seminar text.

REFERENCES

Brookfield, S. D., & Preskill, S. (1999). *Discussion as a way of teaching: Tools and techniques for democratic classrooms*. San Francisco: Jossey-Bass.

Fischer-Mueller, J, & Thompson-Grove, G. (n.d.). The final word. National School Reform Faculty Harmony Education Center. Bloomington, IN. Retrieved from http://www.nsrfharmony.org/system/files/protocols/final_word_0.pdf

Parker, W. C. (2003). *Teaching democracy: Unity and diversity in public life*. New York: Teachers College Press.

CHAPTER 5

IT'S IN THE BAG

Alternative Assessment and the Brown Bag Exam

Jeremy Hilburn and Denise Ousley

Name: Jeremy Hilburn & Denise Ousley	Audience: Graduate candidates
Affiliation: University of North Carolina Wilmington	Length: One hour
Course Title: Middle Grades Social Studies Methods	Commonplace featured: Learners and Learning
NCSS Teacher Education Standards: Element 3a: Candidates design a range of authentic assessments that measure learners' mastery of disciplinary knowledge, inquiry, and forms of representation for competence in civic life and demonstrate alignment with state-required content standards. Element 3b: Candidates design coherent and relevant learning experiences and engage learners in disciplinary knowledge, inquiry, and forms of representation for competence in civic life and demonstrate alignment with state-required content standards.	

Teaching Social Studies: A Methods Book for Methods Teachers,
pages 27–30.

TASK SUMMARY

We designed a Brown Bag Exam (Ousley, 2008) to assess and enrich teacher candidates' understanding of a required course text titled *Guns, Germs, and Steel: The Fates of Human Societies* (Diamond, 1997).

TASK DESCRIPTION

I (Jeremy Hilburn, first author and methods instructor) selected *Guns, Germs, and Steel* as a required reading because the sixth-grade curriculum standards in my state require the teaching of world history up until 1450. I realized that this content area was the weak link in my teacher candidates' content knowledge. *Guns, Germs, and Steel* provides a well-argued macro-theory (though admittedly with limitations) that explains why Europeans were the ones who did the colonizing, rather than, say, Australians. Thus, this text addresses much of the content in the sixth-grade curriculum.

As I attempted to design an assessment of candidates' understanding of the text, however, I used traditional assessments. I found this to be problematic since much of the course is dedicated to alternative methods. In order to develop a stronger, more authentic assessment that was more in line with the spirit of the course, I collaborated with my colleague (Denise Ousley, Content Area Literacy instructor) to utilize an assessment she developed for her candidates, the Brown Bag Exam.

The primary aims of the task are for candidates to demonstrate and deepen their understanding of the subject matter by identifying connections between the content of the text and the brown bag items. In this sense, the Brown Bag Exam is both an alternative assessment and an enrichment activity.

The Task: The Brown Bag Exam has five steps, which are completed individually and in collaboration with peers. First, candidates select a brown lunch bag that contains an instructor-selected item symbolically or literally connected to the content of the book. In Step 1, candidates have 10–12 minutes to individually identify connections between the item and the content of the text. To illustrate, the candidate who selects the bag with an apple in it may choose to connect the apple to plant domestication (a major topic of *Guns, Germs, and Steel*) and how plants such as apples are much more difficult to domesticate than others (e.g., wheat). These connections are written in a bullet-point format on Brown Bag Exam form.

Although Step 1 is left to chance—the bags the candidates select influence the connections they are able to make—the second step allows them considerable choice in the item and connections. For Step 2, candidates offer their own items that they believe connect to the text. For instance, a candidate may bring in a compass to reflect the axial orientation of continents and technological and flora and fauna diffusion. Step 2 is also completed individually (about 8–10 minutes) in bullet-point format.

In Step 3, the Brown Bag exam moves from an assessment to a deeper enrichment activity. For this step, candidates work in triads to help each other make additional connections. For instance, one group member may connect the apple to the concept of global exchange; while apples were previously confined to North America, they are now available throughout the world due to the same advances that spread disease and technology. These extra connections are bullet-pointed in the third section of the form. I allocate 12–16 minutes to this step, as it is often the most productive portion of the Brown Bag Exam.

For Step 4, candidates return to *Guns, Germs, and Steel* to identify two passages that support their connections with textual evidence. Since this step asks candidates to re-examine the text with a specific purpose, they have 10–12 minutes for this task. This step often leads to deeper examination of the subject at hand because the Brown Bag items inspire a more purposeful reading of the text.

In the final step of the Brown Bag Exam, each candidate notes one significant aspect of the experience and shares it with the class. That aspect might be a thoughtful connection, a new idea emerging from a peer conversation, a surprise discovery from the text, or an alternate consideration from a previously overlooked perspective or voice. The focused discussion derived from the final step drives the classroom discussion for as long as the instructor desires.

The resources needed to complete the task are lunch bags, the preselected items, and the Brown Bag Exam form on which candidates can record their responses. Printed images can be used instead of concrete items; however, we believe that actual items create a more powerful experience.

Like any task, there are strengths and limitations. One major strength of this alternate assessment is its flexibility. For instance, Denise created the Brown Bag Exam for classroom teachers to generate candidate conversation about fictional texts. It has also been applied to multiple content areas, to team teaching and special education (Dieker & Ousley, 2006), and to non-fiction texts. Another strength of the task is that it extends learning beyond the assessment. As the final step requires candidates to identify and report one item for further discussion, candidates continue to talk about the text even after the assessment has ended. This experience stands in contrast to more traditional assessments in which the end of the assessment is often the end of candidates' thinking. Another strength is that the task can be used either as a summative assessment or as an activity to continue learning about the text. For instance, the connections identified during the Brown Bag Exam can actually be used to frame an essay about the text. Finally, because I do not dedicate much class time to *Guns, Germs, and Steel*, I find that the dual purposes of the task (assessment and enrichment) are an effective use of limited time.

Despite these strengths, the task has its own set of limitations. One is that candidates can limit their learning opportunities if they have not completed the reading or read well. Since candidates give and receive a great deal of support during the experience, it is possible to receive a passing grade on the assessment even if they have not completed the reading. Another limitation of the task is that the emphasis is on making connections rather than other skills such as forming arguments.

Assessing the Task: There are many ways to assess the Brown Bag Exam. Denise and I grade it holistically. Others might assess the task by allocating an equal number of points to each of the sections or by varying the number of point allocations, such as giving more weight to the individually completed sections when compared to the cooperatively completed sections.

CANDIDATES AND THE TASK

Teacher candidates respond very positively to the Brown Bag Exam; in fact, it was candidates who brought the assessment to my attention. I had shared my frustration with traditional assessments for the text and asked them what type of assessment they would prefer. In small groups, they brainstormed different assessments. Candidates who had taken the Content Area Literacy course with Denise shared the Brown Bag Exam. This idea was unanimously selected as the preferred assessment model. After the assessment, I conferred with several candidates about its effectiveness and was encouraged to continue using the task as it was an engaging, interesting, and authentic way to demonstrate their understanding of the text.

THE TASK IN CONTEXT

This task occurs at the end of the course. Generally, I focus the bulk of our methods class time on the foundations of social studies and pedagogy rather than on content acquisition. As such, I do not spend much in class time on the text. Instead, candidates read the text throughout the semester and demonstrate their understanding of the text on the Brown Bag Exam. In sum, the Brown Bag Exam offers a useful combination of enrichment and assessment that demonstrates a novel form of assessment that future teachers can replicate.

REFERENCES

Diamond, J. (1997). *Guns, germs, and steel: The fates of human societies.* New York, NY: W.W. Norman Company.
Dieker, L. A., & Ousley, D. M. (2006). Speaking the same language: Bringing together highly qualified special education and English teachers. *Teaching Exceptional Children Plus, 2*(4), 1–13.
Ousley, D. (2008). Alternative assessment and the brown bag exam: What does assessment have to do with lunch? *English Journal, 97*(6), 113–115.

CHAPTER 6

IMAGES OF AFRICA

The Influence of Culture and Experience on Perceptions of Place

Hannah Kim

Name: Hannah Kim	Audience: Undergraduate students
Affiliation: University of Delaware	Length: 60–75 minutes
Course Title: Planning a Course of Instruction (Secondary Social Studies Methods Course)	Commonplace featured: Learners and Learning
NCSS Teacher Education Standard: Element 5b. Candidates explore, interrogate, and reflect upon their own cultural frames to attend to issues of equity, diversity, access, power, human rights, and social justice within their schools and/or communities.	

TASK SUMMARY

This in-class assignment asks teacher candidates to address their preconceived notions of Africa and to consider how these conceptions can influence the ways in which they teach Africa.

DESCRIPTION OF THE TASK

Advocates of both global education and multicultural education encourage students to view a subject from different perspectives and to take a more worldly approach to problem-solving. In order to achieve these goals, teachers must do more than merely relay content. They must help students consider the construction of knowledge, who controls that construction, and the subtext of the message (Merryfield, 2001). By deconstructing knowledge or "decolonizing the mind," we begin to construct narratives more culturally responsive to the global community and less Western focused.

An important step in achieving this goal is to help candidates understand how their own cultures and experiences influence their perspectives on peoples and regions. I chose Africa as the subject of the activity because the region conjures strong images and impressions. As much as educators have incorporated Africa into the social studies curricula, it continues to be an area prone to misconceptions and misperceptions. African regions and cultures are still taught using Eurocentric sources, often reinforcing rather than breaking down myths and stereotypes (Schmidt, 1990). Hence, the goal of this activity is to address the cultural baggage that candidates bring to the classroom, their preconceived notions of Africa, and how their perceptions influence the ways they teach Africa.

The Task: I begin the task as an anticipatory set. I give candidates a blank piece of paper and instruct them to draw an image of Africa. They are not allowed to discuss what they draw and I provide no other instructions or guidelines. They can draw anything they want, including stick figures or symbols. I give the class five to eight minutes for the activity.

Next, I have candidates compare their images with a neighbor and list the commonalities and differences across their drawings. As they make their lists, candidates can usually see patterns beginning to emerge. Many portray climatic regions, political boundaries (most are inaccurate), human suffering, and safari animals. I give them a handout of common images that I have noted in past years and ask them to check off the images that they included in their own drawings. I project this same list on the board and have candidates come up and make tally marks next to the images that they checked off so that the students can see how the class did as a whole. We then talk about what these trends indicate collectively, rather than individually. I try to draw their attention to subtle trends such as:

- The preponderance of deserts and rainforests even though savannas are the largest climatic regions in Africa.

- Historical and contemporary images that portray Africans as victims.
- Cities in South Africa with rarely a reference to Cairo, the largest city in Africa.

Candidates begin to see that their images depict Africa as a primitive and dangerous place valued merely for natural resources or exotic animals. They can see that their pictures imply that Africans are less advanced and are passive actors in their own history. I ask them to consider how these cultural impressions could influence power dynamics in the region, U.S. immigration policies, travel and tourism, and international conflict resolution.

I emphasize that the point is not to embarrass them for falling prey to these stereotypes, but instead to consider why negative images overwhelmingly come to mind when they think of Africa. As teachers, we struggle against a powerful narrative, one that holds more influence over our perceptions than academic knowledge. If this is true for my students and me, then what can we expect from our secondary students? Who will help young people overcome these stereotypes of Africa and Africans and offer alternatives to the vision presented in the media and popular culture?

To provide concrete examples, candidates examine two short movie clips and describe the natural and built environments in both movies. The first clip I show is from the 2003 Bruce Willis movie, *Tears of the Sun* (53:00–57:00). Willis plays the commander of a Special Forces unit that is sent to Nigeria to rescue an American doctor. The team comes across a village under brutal attack from a rebel unit. Defying their orders, Willis's soldiers decide to rescue the villagers. I ask candidates to describe the scenery in the clip and how it helps set the mood for the segment. They note the heavy, wet foliage, dark lighting, and thatched huts with dirt floors and crude wooden fences that comprise the village. The setting emphasizes the savagery of the rebel units, which is punctuated by screams in the background.

The second clip is from the 2004 Don Cheadle film *Hotel Rwanda* (7:30–9:00). In this scene, the main character, Paul Rusesabagina, returns home from his job as the manager of the Hôtel des Mille Collines in Kigali, Rwanda. Again, I ask for descriptions of the scenery in the clip and how it sets the mood for the segment. They note the wide roads, low-storied buildings, and tree-lined streets of the neighborhood. Rusesabagina's gated house has a manicured lawn, shrubbery, and a play area for his children. Candidates are often surprised when I point out that *Tears of the Sun* was filmed in Hawaii whereas *Hotel Rwanda* was primarily shot in South Africa with secondary units in Kigali, Rwanda.

Over the years, I have also gathered photographs of Kigali, which disrupt candidates' preconceived notions of Africa, particularly Rwanda. I show pictures of mansions, modern shopping areas, and golf courses in Kigali as well as pictures of poor housing areas and dingy urban centers. The object is to have candidates examine alternative images of Africa, ones that they would not normally imagine, and to have them consider the power of using such images and materials in helping their students gain a richer, fuller perception of Africa.

Last, we examine a sampling of state standards for world history and global studies. New York, New Jersey, Texas, and Virginia are good standards to use in addition to our Delaware standards. I ask candidates to determine if the standards either support new ways of thinking about Africa or reinforce old stereotypes. The discussion varies depending on which states are used, but the standards typically provide little or no guidance, which is an interesting contrast to the specific guidance and details given for European or American history. In their study of state curriculum standards, Marino and Bolgatz (2010) showed that very little has been done to remove world history standards from its Euro/Ameri-centric core. This activity helps reinforce the point that candidates must be resourceful in finding alternative sources and materials to use in their classroom in order to disrupt students' perceptions of Africa.

Assessing the Task: A few days after the initial task, I have candidates revisit our discussion by asking them to write a reflection on how culture and experience influence their perceptions of Africa and how those perceptions could affect their teaching. I also ask them to reflect on what they might do to change those perceptions. It is important to allow a few days to pass before asking candidates to reflect on what learned.

CANDIDATES AND THE TASK

In their in-class reflections, most teacher candidates recognize the influence of the media and popular culture as well as the shortcomings of their own academic knowledge. Many write that they need to be more aware of their own biases and to be selective about the content they teach and the materials they use in the classroom.

I was curious about the impact of the task and so interviewed three of my former methods students a few years after they had graduated and began teaching. All three commented that class discussions and activities about moving world history away from a western perspective made an impact on how they teach. Two remembered vividly the drawing activity and incorporated the activity in their own classes. All three commented that the course and activity led them to take particular care with the lessons and materials that they use in their Africa units, to supplement class materials with outside sources, and to directly address stereotypes. The teachers felt it was important for them to discuss with their students why their knowledge of Africa was so limited and one-sided and to try to help their students understand the construction of knowledge. All three teachers said that they need to be more knowledgeable themselves in order to address misperceptions and stereotypes, and so recognized the need to constantly improve their own content knowledge about not only Africa but also other areas and regions.

THE TASK IN CONTEXT

The task usually occurs during a series of classes when we examine the multidisciplinary ways to address the social studies in their teaching. I use this task when we discuss how to incorporate geography standards, especially Standard 6 of the National Geography Standards, which asks teacher candidate to think about the influence of culture and experience on their perceptions of place. The task also serves to expose candidates to comprehensive geography standards, which guide them in learning and practicing the content and skills germane to the discipline.

REFERENCES

Bryce, I., & Fuqua, A. (2003). *Tears of the sun.* United States. Columbia.

George, T., & George, T. (2004). *Hotel Rwanda.* United States. United Artists.

Marino, M., & Bolgatz, J. (2010). Weaving a fabric of world history? An analysis of U.S. state high school world history standards. *Theory & Research in Social Education, 38*(3), 366–394.

Merryfield, M. M. (2001). Moving the center of global education: From imperial world views that divide the world to double consciousness, contrapuntal pedagogy, hybridity, and cross-cultural competence. In W. B. Stanley (Ed.), *Critical issues in social studies research for the 21st century* (pp. 179–207). Greenwich, CT: Information Age Publishing.

Schmidt, N. J. (1990, November 3). *Africans as primary actors in their own lives and lands: Validating African curriculum materials.* Paper presented at the African Studies Association Meeting, Baltimore, Maryland. Retrieved from http://www.africa.upenn.edu/K-12/African_Curriculum_16166.html

CHAPTER 7

BECOMING CRITICAL READERS

Analyzing Authorship in Texts

Kimberly R. Logan, H. James Garrett, and Avner Segall

Names: Kimberly R. Logan, H. James Garrett, and Avner Segall	Audience: Undergraduate and Graduate
Affiliations: The University of Georgia Michigan State University	Length: 3–6 hours
Course Title: Social Studies Curriculum and Methods	Commonplace featured: Learners and Learning
NCSS Teacher Education Standard: Element 2e. Candidates use theory and research to plan learning sequences that integrate social studies content, disciplinary sources, digital learning, and contemporary technologies to foster inquiry and civic competence. Element 5b: Candidates explore, interrogate, and reflect upon their own cultural frames to attend to issues of equity, diversity, access, power, human rights, and social justice within their schools and/or communities.	

Teaching Social Studies: A Methods Book for Methods Teachers,
pages 37–41.
Copyright © 2017 by Information Age Publishing

TASK SUMMARY

In this activity, teacher candidates use Werner's (2000) eight cultural studies concepts to examine commonly used social studies curricular objects, particularly textbooks, in order to practice modes of questioning that invite critical readings of texts.

DESCRIPTION OF THE TASK

So many of the textbooks we use, films we show, and documents we engage are presented to students as author-less. Every text we read and use, however, has an ideological stance, and engages particular issues in some ways and ignores others. A foundational claim embedded in this task is that teacher candidates become familiar with the idea that all texts are produced, authored, and are arguments that make claims about the world rather than simple statements of fact.

This assignment asks candidates to engage with texts of various kinds by using Werner's (2000) eight cultural studies lenses. These reading strategies invite candidates to shift from asking questions about *what* a text means to *how it comes to have meaning.* The concepts outlined in the article—*representation, gaze, voice, absences, author(ity), intertextuality, mediation,* and *reflexivity*—help readers think about questions such as what section headings were chosen and how do they influence our understandings? What photographs, maps, and primary sources are pulled and what is, as most information and source material necessarily is, omitted from the text? What happens if we think of textbooks as "exclusive" constructions?

Avner originated the assignment in 2006 and we have each given a version of it to our candidates over the last 10 years (Jim adapting it from Avner; Kim from Jim) at the graduate and undergraduate levels spanning K–12 contexts. The goal is not to develop fluency with Werner's eight concepts, but rather to:

- Introduce candidates to a critical vocabulary they can use to analyze texts.
- Conceptualize what else might be done with commonly found classroom texts (a textbook, news article, photograph or film) aside from glean content.
- Practice identifying authorship and the ways that all texts are partial, and that this partiality is in inherent in all representations. There are no objective representations.

The Task: The task begins with independent reading of Werner's article and an accompanying textbook chapter on British imperialism. We ask that teacher candidates read the article first and then use the eight lenses to analyze the chapter. To exemplify this process, we utilize Werner's (2000) term, "the gaze," which attends to the "implied attitude, value stance, or power relationship towards the people, place or event depicted" (p. 199). In the textbook chapter is an image depicting a white colonial family being served by Indian workers. An apparently

British child is held by a dark-skinned, robed individual. Another apparently Indian servant holds an umbrella, and a third serves drinks and food. The two white adults are reading and reclining. The caption describes the British family celebrating Christmas in India. Students could interpret this image as a "Eurocentric" or "romanticized" or "imperial" gaze due to the ways that the image and caption center the colonizers and portray the native population as docile servants. Omitted are the stances and experiences of the Indian individuals. These elements come together to construct particular meanings open for interpretation. The initial reading of Werner's article alongside the textbook chapter is meant to illustrate the concepts and questions we then discuss in class. We do not expect candidates to have a well-developed understanding of these concepts before our class activity, but we want them to engage with and (attempt to) apply these lenses to the text prior to class.

With students in class, we discuss Werner's eight concepts—representation, gaze, voice, absences, author(ity), intertextuality, mediation, and reflexivity. Although we have initiated this first discussion in different ways, we all review the concepts with our classes, asking candidates to provide definitions and examples from the accompanying textbook. In addition, candidates develop a sequence of 3–5 questions that engage these concepts in reference to the textbook that are appropriate to the level of students with whom they work. Candidates often need to be guided toward the idea that these questions are best asked in directed ways toward specific aspects of the text such as the relationship between a caption and a particular image, what is included/excluded from a timeline, and the like. We suggest our own versions of questions to facilitate this process, such as "What would happen if we renamed the chapter Westward Expansion to Westward Takeover?" or "Encroachment from the East?" In reference to the first example, we offer, "How might a different caption change the interpretation of the image?" and "What if the caption was written as 'Indian servants forced to serve and take care of a colonizing family'?" These activities and associated discussions generally take the better part of a three-hour class session as students define, question, and revise their understandings of the terms in relationship to the textbook chapter.

Finally, candidates must find their own texts to analyze and use for the assignment. The limiting factor we put on is that the texts they analyze must be common to the social studies classroom. That is, they ought not to be considered a controversial choice. This assignment is about learning how to critically engage with what is already there rather than adding new objects to an already crowded curriculum. After they have selected and analyzed their texts in formal writing, candidates explain whether or not, how, and why, they imagine using these ideas with their future students.

Assessing the Task: We assess these written assignments by giving feedback on candidates' interpretations of ideas and often make suggestions as to how they might deploy these ideas in their classrooms.

CANDIDATES AND THE TASK

Some of our teacher candidates struggle with their initial reading of Werner's article and need to be cautioned that it is not a piece that they can read quickly or simply scan for comprehension. For this reason, it is typically the only assigned reading for that class session, as the additional step of applying the concepts to the accompanying textbook chapter also requires time and consideration. We do not expect candidates to become experts regarding these concepts in such a short amount of time. We do expect them, however, to understand how these concepts differ from the questions they typically initiate toward a text.

Most candidates do not have difficulty understanding the concepts of representation, gaze, voice, absences, and intertextuality. But many have a harder time understanding author(ity), mediation, and reflexivity. With author(ity), we focus on the storyline of the text and how author(s) use various techniques to create and support the chosen narrative. For mediation, we ask candidates how the medium affects our understanding and interpretation of the events depicted. We also use the analogy of how the word medium signifies something that is between at least two other locations. Regarding reflexivity, candidates typically understand the first part that focuses on how "authors help readers understand and query authorship" (Werner, 2000, p. 212), but often overlook the second part of reflexivity that focuses on the reader. In this section, we guide candidates to examine their prior experiences and beliefs that influence how they engage with a text. This prompt includes using one of Werner's questions: "To what extent are you taking your own experiences, tradition, role, or social location as normative, and unreflectively reading them into this text?" (p. 214)

Lastly, many candidates have difficulty understanding that partiality is not inherently negative, but is a fundamental aspect of any representation. They have been trained, it seems, to understand bias as something that makes a source limited or "bad." If this is the case, then all sources are bad, which is not the case. The point is not that a source is biased, as all are, but instead to inquire as to the differences that those biases make to the interpretation of what is being represented. In the end, the challenge is less about getting candidates to identify these lenses in the texts and more about the consequence these differences makes: what groups or ideas are advantaged and which are not?

THE TASK IN CONTEXT

We assign this task at different points in our courses. Kim uses it after weeks of teaching about historical inquiry. Jim typically uses it toward the beginning of class to introduce candidates quickly to critical vocabularies upon which they can draw for the remainder of the semester. Avner, too, uses it early in the semester as candidates begin to take on more responsibilities in their classrooms, and actually begin engaging their own students in analyzing texts.

REFERENCE

Werner, W. (2000). Reading authorship into texts. *Theory and Research in Social Education,28*(2), 193–219.

CHAPTER 8

STARTING THEM EARLY

The Social Studies Needs Assessment Assignment

Starlynn Nance

Name: Starlynn Nance	Audience: Undergraduate students
Affiliation: University of Central Missouri	Length: Semester-long
Course Title: Methods of Teaching Social Studies and Mid-Level Field Experience	Commonplace featured: Learners and Learning
NCSS Teacher Education Standard: Element 4b. Candidates use knowledge of theory and research to plan and implement instruction and assessment that is relevant and responsive to learners' socio-cultural assets, learning demands, and individual identities.	

Teaching Social Studies: A Methods Book for Methods Teachers,
pages 43–46.

TASK SUMMARY

The *Social Studies Needs Assessment* (SSNA) assignment gives teacher candidates the opportunity to collect and analyze contextual factors (i.e., community, district, school, classroom, and candidate) for the creation and implementation of lesson plans particular to students' needs of that district.

DESCRIPTION OF THE TASK

Teacher candidates use the *Social Studies Needs Assessment* (SSNA) to collect and analyze contextual factors in order to create lesson plans particular to their students' needs. The contextual factors are separated into main categories like community and subcategories such as socioeconomic status and census data. The candidates complete the chart to gain knowledge of the community, district, class, and candidates assigned to them in their mid-level field experience. The five goals of the SSNA ask candidates to:

- Recognize contextual factors and resources for the district placement site.
- Collect and analyze the contextual factors to address student need.
- Research instructional strategies and activities according to the contextual factors analysis.
- Create, implement, and reflect on lesson plans made for the needs of the students in a particular district.
- Make adjustments to the lesson plans after the evaluation and reflection.

The Task: The SSNA assignment is completed through the methods course and mid-level field experience. I offer the candidates feedback on the data, analysis, and implementation of the lessons taught. After supervision, candidates reflect on their lessons and, with my assistance, make adjustments to instructional strategies, activities, and assessments for future lessons.

The assignment begins with candidates explaining the statement, "know your audience" and wrestling with the question, "what does a high school classroom look like?" This discussion leads to the physical aspects of classrooms and the students enrolled in the class. Candidates explain, usually from personal experience, their ideal of high school student characteristics, values, learning styles, and the like.

To provoke continued reflections and discussion, I pose the questions, "what if it is opposite of what you just described? How will you then teach the students? How can a teacher know about their students before he or she starts school and why is this important?" Candidates brainstorm responses to the questions by creating a list on a shared Google document. I guide candidates to place the items are into categories and choose category names. The category names reflect the contextual factors the candidates complete in a graphic organizer handed out at the end of the class period. With the list of contextual factors (i.e., community, district, school, class, and students), the candidates use their personal devices to research each factor and locate reliable websites and other information to help focus on their specific school district placements. For example, the factor "school" includes subcategories such as enrollment and percent of students receiving free and reduced lunch. The candidates find that the state education website holds this information according to district and each school in that district. With the research findings in hand, candidates respond to the question, "why are contextual factors important to collect?" in a whole-class discussion. At the end of the discussion, candidates receive specific directions and a graphic organizer focusing on contextual factors, resources, and student interest inventories.

The SSNA is conducted in three sections with due dates throughout the semester. My coaching takes place during class time and I encourage candidates to meet with me during office hours if needed.

First, the candidates collect and record data on the graphic organizer that consists of contextual factors, community resources, and student interest inventories. After the graphic organizer is completed, candidates collect qualitative data during the mid-level field experience. The qualitative data include interviews with the cooperating teachers, counselors, principals, and students to corroborate the quantitative data found. Candidates make notations of similarities and differences from the qualitative data. I assign candidates to cohorts (usually paired in the same district) to assist each other with data collection. They have eight weeks to collect the data and interview the different stakeholders.

The second section of the assignment is to analyze the data collected from the contextual factors, community resources, and student interests. From this data, the candidates research instructional strategies, activities, and assessments that are appropriate for their students' needs and interests. Having researched and written their lesson plans, candidates receive coaching from me. They individually present their lesson plans explaining how and why they wrote what they did on the contextual factors chart. The coaching focuses on questions so that candidates can reflect on and revise (if necessary) their lesson planning decisions. If a candidate is not on track or feels she or he needs more coaching, a second session is scheduled during office hours.

The last section of the SSNA is to implement the lesson plan in the classroom assigned during the mid-level field experience. I am present to supervise and evaluate the lesson. After the lesson, the candidate writes a reflection and schedules a meeting with me to review the evaluation and discuss the reflection. From the reflection, adjustments are made to the lesson plan focusing on the contextual factors and student needs for future lessons.

Assessing the Task: Assessing the SSNA includes (1) the completion of the contextual factors/resource charts, and student interest inventory page, (2) the completion of the lesson plan and coaching session, and (3) the supervision evaluation and reflection session. Each of these assessments receives a separate grade and feedback is given so candidates can adjust before and after teaching for the district placement site. Each assessment is intended to help candidates realize that preparation for lessons is more than designing fun activities and that understanding contextual factors will help them create lessons that allow instruction to be focused on the needs of the students.

The charts and candidate interest inventory are graded for accuracy and completion. The interest inventory is assessed on its connection with the contextual factors and how the data are used in the lesson plan. The lesson plan is evaluated on how well the candidates explain the reasons for choosing the instructional strategies, activities, and assessments and also how well they connect their research to the specific contextual factors. Finally, the supervision evaluation is graded from a state-mandated rubric and the reflection is graded on how well the candidate focused on the contextual factors and made adjustments as needed.

CANDIDATES AND THE TASK

This class is usually the first course in which teacher candidates use contextual factors to create lesson plans. At first, the candidates seem confused with how this information can help them construct their lessons. But as they participate in the mid-level field experience and complete the contextual factors chart, candidates begin to make more connections. Throughout the progress of the SSNA, they learn to collaborate, research, reflect, and make adjustments for student needs. When pairing this assignment with the mid-level field experience, candidates begin to practice what they are learning in the classroom.

The most helpful part of the assignment is the coaching sessions and reflections made for adjusting a lesson. The coaching sessions are very similar to a think aloud where the questions raised are intended for guidance and feedback. Candidates typically respond to the coaching sessions in a positive manner and, through that modeling, start to ask each other questions in the cohorts rather than tell each other what to do. Overall, candidates report appreciating this assignment after they begin their student teaching and complete a certification assessment required by the state.

THE TASK IN CONTEXT

The SSNA occurs throughout the semester. It is assigned the first week of class and is usually concluded one month before the semester is completed. It is the first topic of the semester and includes due dates throughout the semester, though it remains a theme throughout the entire course. When discussing new topics, I ask, "how can this certain topic relate to the data collection or your contextual factors?" Doing so typically sparks a conversation that helps the candidates with the SSNA assignment

CHAPTER 9

SOCIAL STUDIES THROUGH A STUDENT'S EYES

Collaborative Action Research for Teachers and Students

Tony L. Talbert and Brooke E. Blevins

Name: Tony L. Talbert and Brooke E. Blevins	Audience: Undergraduate students
Affiliation: Baylor University	Length: Four to six hours
Course Title: Secondary Social Studies Methods and Curriculum	Commonplace featured: Learners and Learning
NCSS Teacher Education Standard: Standard 2. Candidates plan learning sequences that draw upon social studies knowledge and literacies to support the civic competence of learners. Standard 3. Candidates design and implement instruction and authentic assessments for social studies that promote learning and competence in civic life. Standard 4. Candidates plan and implement relevant and responsive pedagogy, create collaborative and interdisciplinary learning environments, and prepare learners to be informed advocates for an inclusive and equitable society.	

Teaching Social Studies: A Methods Book for Methods Teachers,
pages 47–52.

TASK SUMMARY

The purpose of this action research assignment is to engage teacher candidates and their students in critical historical inquiry as a way to expand their knowledge and understanding of perspectives that are divergent from the official historical narrative.

DESCRIPTION OF THE TASK

This project encourages teacher candidates to investigate the official curriculum, examine how historical positionality informs what is taught in social studies classrooms, find alternative perspectives, and determine how best to incorporate these perspectives into their classrooms. Candidates collect data from students in an effort to plan and/or modify their instructional practice so that it is most meaningful to students. The intended result is to reveal both the depth and breadth of candidates' social studies knowledge and their ability to provide student-centered instructional strategies that facilitate cognitive and affective connections in their students.

The Task: In the *Social Studies Through a Student's Eyes* project, candidates explore, design, and implement differentiated and culturally responsive curriculum. This action research project draws on work by Kathy Swan (2010) and Linda Levstik and Keith Barton (2005).

The project has three phases; 1) a photograph sort and think-aloud instructional activity, 2) an interview, and 3) a reflective paper. We outline each of these elements below.

Phase One—Social Studies Knowledge and Perspectives Photograph Sort and Think-Aloud Instructional Activity. Candidates select and print a total of 12 photographs, illustrations, or paintings from any social studies source (e.g., Zinn Education Project, the National Archives, Library of Congress) and then conduct a think-aloud exercise with three-five students from their field experience using these images. The images are divided into two groups; they should evoke opportunities for students to demonstrate prior knowledge, knowledge of what they are currently learning, misconceptions, and perspectives based on beliefs and experiences. The selection of the images should reflect:

- Distinctive eras, geography, cultural representations such as clothing, architecture, and groups.
- Multiple knowledge-based clues and indicators (e.g., fashion, technology, social roles, geography, culture).
- More than highly recognized characters and provide diverse representation of women, men, and children from multiple races, ethnicities, gender identities, nationalities.

Candidates choose six images representing distinctive historical eras, events, or issues that can be used to elicit students social studies content knowledge (e.g.,

1865 U.S. Civil War photo, 1920 U.S. Oklahoma Dust Bowl photo). Candidates begin by showing students images with which they may be more familiar (e.g., a photograph with cars or other modern technology and one without) and asking them questions focusing on what they see and/or know about the scenes depicted.

Candidates also choose three topics, themes, or ideas they want students to explore (e.g., Internment) and then select two photos that depict these themes in differing contexts (e.g., Japanese-Americans in WWII and Middle Eastern detainees at Guantanamo Bay). The purpose of this phase is to evoke students' understandings of and perspectives on the issues, ideas, and events presented in the images. Candidates show students one pair of the images and ask them to explain what they see and how each image is similar and different from one another. During this process, the candidate takes note of how students describe these relationships and what processes they use to engage in critical historical thinking. After students have viewed each group of images, they compare and contrast all of the images expressing their perspectives and offering the opportunity to demonstrate how their content and prior knowledge informs or misinforms their perspectives about the themes and contexts revealed in the images.

During the think-aloud, candidates ask students to provide as much information about the images as possible ranging from explicit prior knowledge to speculative clues. They guide students using probing question to help them use familiar social studies knowledge based clues and historical thinking skills to analyze unfamiliar images. During the image sorting exercises, the candidates record precise descriptive and reflective notes of students' responses, particularly noting students' content knowledge, historical thinking skills, and historical perspectives.

Phase Two—Student Interview. In this phase, candidates conduct an interview after the image sort in order to gather narrative data as students describe their prior and emerging knowledge and perspectives on the themes and events depicted in the images. For example, in both the think-aloud and interview activities candidates might ask:

- Did you think this was easy or hard to do? What things made it easy or hard?
- What era/time period do you think each photograph represents? Why?
- What ideas (beliefs, philosophies, values) do you think each image represents? Why?
- Which images do you think are the most interesting? Why?
- What messages do you think each of the images is conveying? Why?
- Do you see similarities and differences in the photographs within each era/circumstance…between the eras/circumstances? What are they?
- What do you think your life would have been like had you been a person in the photograph?

Phase Three—Action Research Report. Following the interviews, candidates write an action research report detailing their findings from the photograph sort, think-aloud, and interview. A series of questions guide candidates as they examine students' prior knowledge, students' historical positionality and perspectives, and students' knowledge and perspectives around social studies content. Through this process, candidates think critically about their instructional and pedagogical decisions and how the learners in their classrooms inform these decisions. All data should be carefully transcribed, read, analyzed, and interpreted based on student responses to the interview questions and experience during the image sort and think-aloud. The action research paper is designed to help candidates analyze important student data, data that is often not reflected in standardized tests, in order to engage in instructional planning and assessment that is more meaningful to students.

CANDIDATES AND THE TASK

Teacher candidates find the process of action research to be both informative and surprising. Most often, they express surprise at the lack of content knowledge their students possess regarding the themes and context that are presented in the curriculum. Thus, their awareness grows of a need to provide constructivist-based, student-centered instructional strategies that start with the students' experiential knowledge and connect it to the new knowledge being presented. In addition, the experience provides candidates with a sense that even when students do possess content knowledge they do not always make connections across contexts and eras on such themes as internment, casualties of war, and persecution of the other.

THE TASK IN CONTEXT

The action research task occurs in the second semester of a two-semester methods course. In the first semester, candidates experience ideas such as the official curriculum, alternative perspectives, planning for instruction, constructivism, and data-driven decision-making. In the second semester, they engage in endeavors that promote a transformational and empowering pedagogical praxis. This action research project serves as the capstone project for this year-long methods course.

APPENDIX: SOCIAL STUDIES THROUGH A STUDENT'S EYES ACTION RESEARCH OUTLINE

Your action research paper should include an introduction describing the action research experience, the participants (pseudonyms), demographic description, and the setting where the action research took place. All data will need to be carefully transcribed, read, analyzed, and interpreted based on student answers to the interview questions and responses to the photographs/illustration sorting activity. The body of the paper should identify 3–4 main conclusions reached from the interviews and student responses. Each of the conclusions will be supported with the use of specific examples from the interviews as connected to the questions asked. All conclusions should be generalizations that identify patterns in students' responses, not a description of students' responses to every question asked. You will also need to provide instructional implications from your research. Please see the framework and the evaluation criteria for more detail on how the paper will be graded.

1. Introduction
   a. Title
   b. Problem Statement
   c. Purpose Statement (What are you hoping to accomplish?)
   d. The purpose of this action research is to _____ (fill in blank with a verb such as test, understand, develop) the _____ (fill in blank with a central concepts, problems) of/about _____ (fill in blank with the unit of analysis/participants) using a(n) _____ (fill in blank the method of inquiry) through _____ (fill in the blank describing the data collection methods)
   e. Context and setting
   f. Where is the setting that you will be conducting this research and why?
   g. Who will be participating in this research and why?
   h. What are the estimated results? Why?
   i. Significance of the research
   j. Why is this research important for social studies?
   k. Aims and objectives
   l. What is the overall driving force of the research (Aims)?
   m. What are the means by which you intend to achieve the aims (Objectives)?
   n. Research question(s)—Pose two to three questions that you wish to examine/answer in this research
2. Literature Review
   a. Relevant literature that provides a theoretical framework for the study.
   b. The particular perspective that you will use in this action research.
      i. What do other researchers say about the problem you are going to analyze?
      ii. What is so important about the chosen sources?
   c. Definitions and terms
3. Method
   a. Participants and how the sample is selected (i.e., with whom will you conduct your intervention/evaluation
   b. Restate research questions
   c. Data Collection—Describe in detail so that someone else could replicate your study.

          i.   How will you collect the data?

          ii.   Why did you choose the data collection procedures?

    d.   Data Analysis—Describe in detail so that someone else could replicate your study.

          i.   How and why did you analyze the data you collected in this way?.

    e.   Timeline: Provide a detailed timetable scheduling all aspects of the research. This will include time taken to conduct background research, questionnaire or interview schedule development, data collection, data analysis and report writing.

4.   Results (Narrative or Outline form)

    a.   Research Question 1

          i.   Describe the results of the analysis of the data from Data Source 1

          ii.   Describe the results of the analysis from Data Source 2

          iii.   Describe the results of the analysis from Data Source 3.

          iv.   Answer Question 1

    b.   Research Question 2

          i.   Describe the results of the analysis of the data from Data Source 1

          ii.   Describe the results of the analysis from Data Source 2

          iii.   Describe the results of the analysis from Data Source 3.

          iv.   Answer Question 2

5.   Conclusions

    a.   Summary of Findings

6.   Were the results consistent with what the literature predicted or not (explain thoroughly)?

    a.   What are the implications for your own teaching and what are the implications for others?

    b.   What are the implications for additional research (i.e., what type of additional research should follow-up on the results of your study)?

7.   References

8.   Appendices

REFERENCES

Levstik, L., & Barton, K. (2005). *Doing history: Investigating with children in elementary and middle schools*. Mahwah, NJ: Lawrence Erlbaum Associates.

Swan, K. (2010). *Social studies pedagogy in the secondary school syllabus*. Department of Curriculum and Instruction, University of Kentucky, Lexington, KY.

CHAPTER 10

RECONNECTING WITH YOUR TEENAGE SELF

Scott Wylie

Name: Scott Wylie	Audience: Graduate students
Affiliation: Chaminade University of Honolulu	Length: 100 minutes
Course Title: Secondary Social Studies Methods	Commonplace featured: Learners and Learning
NCSS Teacher Education Standard: Element 4b. Candidates use knowledge of theory and research to plan and implement instruction and assessment that is relevant and responsive to learners' socio-cultural assets, learning demands, and individual identities.	

Teaching Social Studies: A Methods Book for Methods Teachers,
pages 53–57.
Copyright © 2017 by Information Age Publishing
All rights of reproduction in any form reserved.

TASK SUMMARY

In this activity, teacher candidates use their reflections on the popular culture of the day to write brief descriptions of their teenage selves and imagine going back in time to talk with their teachers about making the curriculum interesting, engaging, and relevant to their lives.

DESCRIPTION OF THE TASK

Dewey (1897) believed that "only through the continual and sympathetic observation of childhood's interests can the adult enter into the child's life and see what it is ready for, and upon what material it could work most readily and fruitfully" (p 15). This activity asks teacher candidates to turn that "sympathetic observation" to their teenage years and reconnect with the interests, concerns, and experiences of their high school selves. Ultimately, it allows them to see these interests as "the sign of some power below...[and] to discover this power" in their own students (Dewey, 1897, p. 15).

The Task: Candidates read *My Pedagogic Creed* (Dewey, 1897) before coming to the first class session. This essay introduces Dewey's beliefs about education and sets the tone for the work we will do over the course of the semester. I begin the activity with a brief discussion about the word "interest" and ask candidates to brainstorm the types of things that might interest high schoolers. As graduate students, they all finished high school at least five years ago (most of them longer ago than that), and I suggest that their life experiences in the intervening years have left them far removed from their teenage selves. The goal of the exercise is to recall how it felt to hear, see, or experience these things for the first time.

First, candidates use the Internet Movie Database to find the top grossing movies from their junior year of high school (http://www.imdb.com/year/). They write down the titles of these films and then go to YouTube to watch the trailers. The cacophony of multiple film trailers playing at once helps set the tone for an energetic and entertaining activity. In addition, as most candidates were in high school at about the same time, hearing all the film trailers helps recreate the atmosphere of that time period.

After watching a few trailers, candidates locate the top songs from their junior year in high school. Many different websites provide this information, so I leave it up to the candidates to locate the list that works best for them (e.g., pop, hip-hop, country). A simple Google search using the phrase "top songs in <year>" is usually all the candidates need to find the information they want. Again, I direct candidates to YouTube to play some of the songs they have identified.

While the music plays in the background, candidates open a new browser window and begin reading about the events that made the news during their junior year of high school. A number of websites provide this information, but I ask them to use InfoPlease as a starting point (http://www.infoplease.com/yearbyyear. html). This site includes short summaries of world and U.S. news, economic data, scientific achievements, and lists of award winners in literature, film, and music. I ask candidates to think about which of the stories they remember caring about in high school and to note why those particular events were important.

Finally, candidates write a brief description of their teenage selves, focusing on the following questions: What were your interests and concerns? What were you excited to learn about? If you could go back in time and talk with your social studies teacher, what would you want them to know about you? What could that teacher have done to draw connections between the curriculum and your interests and experiences? These descriptions are an important part of the lesson so, I give candidates 20 minutes or so to write their reflections.

With the reflections in hand, candidates turn back to *My Pedagogic Creed* and consider the following excerpt in light of their own interests as high school students:

> I believe that these interests are neither to be humored nor repressed. To repress interest is to substitute the adult for the child, and so to weaken intellectual curiosity and alertness, to suppress initiative, and to deaden interest. To humor the interests is to substitute the transient for the permanent. The interest is always the sign of some power below; the important thing is to discover this power. To humor the interest is to fail to penetrate below the surface and its sure result is to substitute caprice and whim for genuine interest. (Dewey, 1897, p. 15)

I ask candidates whether or not the movies, music, and news stories they researched constitute transient or permanent interests. I play the devil's advocate in this conversation, challenging all of the ideas put forth and requiring candidates to defend their positions. I encourage them to grapple with Dewey's (1897) argument that "the social life of the child is the basis of concentration, or correlation, in all his training or growth. The social life gives the unconscious unity and the background of all his efforts and of all his attainments" (p. 10). I ask how their interests as high school students represented the background of all their efforts and attainments and to think about how that background could be incorporated into the social studies curriculum.

These are difficult questions, and I do not expect solid answers in our first class meeting. Instead, I want candidates to begin thinking about a curriculum that emerges from their students' lives rather than the state-mandated curricular scope and sequence. That is not to say that we will ignore the learning objectives and course content that we are expected to teach, only that those requirements are not where our lessons will begin. This activity encourages candidates to ground their lessons in students' lives, drawing out connections to the larger curriculum in a way that honors students' interests and experiences.

Assessing the Task: There is no formal, summative assessment of this activity. There is, however, an informal assessment that takes place as candidates discuss the excerpt from the text. My purpose is not to ensure that candidates can faithfully summarize Dewey's arguments or to verify that they can define the role of student interest in the social studies curriculum. Instead, the goal is to challenge their thinking on these issues by asking them to explore the curricular possibilities offered by this approach.

It is important that candidates understand that the takeaway from this lesson is not that teenagers are only interested in movies and music. This is a stereotypical and grossly oversimplified generalization of high school students and would be to "substitute the transient for the permanent" (Dewey, 1897, p. 15) with regard to students' interests. Instead, I want candidates to ask questions about their own interests (and later, their students' interests) in an attempt to identify the power below these interests. Why these films and songs? What is it about the current social milieu that led these films and songs to become popular at this time and in this place? How might the answers to those questions be reflected in and/or related to the larger curriculum of the course? Candidates will not yet have answers to these questions, but the important thing is that they are being asked.

CANDIDATES AND THE TASK

As a lighthearted introduction to a semester-long conversation, there is a great deal of energy in the room when teacher candidates begin researching the movies and music from their teenage years. Frequently, they remark that they have not seen a particular movie in years and share stories about the first time they saw the film or how many times they saw it in the theater. As the music starts to play, there is laughter and a great deal of singing along. Candidates playfully argue about which songs are the best and reminisce about the parties and proms where this music played.

Candidates' reactions are more varied when they begin reading the news stories from their teenage years. Occasionally, those who were deeply engaged in current events in high school can recount discussions with friends and family about the issues of the day. Most candidates, however, recall only a passing understanding of the events in the news during their high school years. For candidates who are acutely aware of world events as adults, the emerging understanding that this was not always the case is eye-opening.

As candidates write their reflections, they are quick to point out that their teachers could have done more to connect the curriculum with their interests and experiences. Ideas about how those connections might happen, however, are slower to come. This is the first lesson in a semester-long instructional methods course, so this activity does not result in a light bulb moment where candidates suddenly understand how to approach the curriculum. Instead, the activity helps candidates see their role as one who helps students draw connections between their lives, the social issues of the day, and the social studies curriculum as a whole.

THE TASK IN CONTEXT

Taking place during our first class, this in-class activity serves as an icebreaker that helps teacher candidates begin to form relationships based on shared memories and as an introduction to the importance of connecting the curriculum to students' interests and experiences.

REFERENCE

Dewey, J. (1897). *My pedagogic creed.* New York: E. L. Kellogg & Co.

PART 2

TEACHERS AND TEACHING

CHAPTER 11

INVITATION TO A DINNER PARTY

Learning About Social Studies Leaders

Chara Bohan

Name: Chara Bohan	Audience: Graduate students
Affiliation: Georgia State University	Length: Four to six weeks
Course Title: Social Studies Concepts and Issues	Commonplace featured: Teachers and Teaching
NCSS Teacher Education Standard: Element 3c. Candidates use theory and research to implement a variety of instructional practices and authentic assessments featuring disciplinary knowledge, inquiry, and forms of representation for competence in civic life.	

Teaching Social Studies: A Methods Book for Methods Teachers,
pages 61–66.
Copyright © 2017 by Information Age Publishing

TASK SUMMARY

In the *Invitation to a Dinner Party* project, teacher candidates explore the work of important social studies leaders by asking them to engage in a group presentation about a particular leader and theory and develop an imagined dinner party where 4–5 social studies leaders discuss an important question in the field of social studies education.

DESCRIPTION OF THE TASK

The *Invitation to a Dinner Party* project is grounded in the understanding that most preservice and inservice teachers lack historical understanding of the field of social studies education. Learning about social studies leaders' theories and pedagogical practices should enable teachers to implement instructional practices that promote disciplinary knowledge and inquiry learning in their own K–12 social studies classrooms. To that end, the goals of the task are:

- Learn about several important social studies curriculum leaders and their theories and methods.
- Analyze and explain these social studies curriculum theories and methods in a small group.
- Plan, present, and implement an instructional strategy(ies) based upon the theory(ies) of the social studies leaders.
- Write about several of these social studies theorists in a creative, authentic, and engaging intellectual format.

The Task: In this course, teacher candidates focus on the application of historical and social science concepts, skills, and processes in the social studies curriculum. One of the primary goals is for candidates to learn about the history of the social studies field and the leaders of social studies curriculum movements.

In order to facilitate a complex understanding of social studies curriculum, candidates read several books on the history of the field: Ron Evans, *The Social Studies Wars,* Margaret Crocco and O.L. Davis, Jr.'s *"Bending the Future to their Will": Civic Women, Social Education, and Democracy,* and Christine Woyshner and Chara Bohan's *Histories of Social Studies and Race, 1865–2000.* Evans' book provides a succinct overview of the field from the formation of the American Historical Association in 1884 and the founding of the National Council for the Social Studies in 1921 through the World Wars and New Social Studies movement up to the current standards-based era; candidates read Evans in its entirety. In contrast to Evans' book where the actors are primarily white males, Crocco and Davis' and Woyshner and Bohan's books augment the traditional social studies narrative with women and African-American trailblazers in the field. Both *"Bending the Future to their Will"* and *Histories of Social Studies and Race* consist of edited chapters and candidates read a sample of the total 22 chapters in these two books.

Candidates learn about social studies curriculum leaders in a general chronological order, so that they develop a sense of the ebb and flow of various educational movements over time. Some of the early leaders include individuals such as Albert Bushnell Hart, Charles Kendall Adams, Lucy Maynard Salmon, and Mary Sheldon Barnes. In the late 1800s, Hart and Adams were advocates of a traditional approach to teaching history, which comprised considerable recitation of historical fact. Salmon and Barnes, on the other hand, advanced the idea of teaching history with primary source material foreshadowing the process of "doing history" Levstik and Barton (1997) describe a century later.

In the early part of the 20th century, social studies curriculum leaders Harold Rugg and George Counts promoted social reconstructionism along with new courses, such as problems of democracy, and new textbooks. Carter Woodson founded and advocated for Negro History Week, whereas Nannie Helen Burroughs sought to teach students about prominent African Americans through pageants and school plays. Credited with founding intercultural education, Rachel Davis DuBois dedicated her career to helping teachers and students learn about different racial, ethnic, and religious groups through dialogue, performances, texts, and radio shows. Lucy Sprague Mitchell, founder of Bank Street College of Education, promoted geographical awareness through exploration of the physical world around the students. Throughout this time period, many of these education leaders advanced more child-centered approaches to learning.

Social studies leaders in the later part of the 20th century include Shirley Engle, Donald Oliver, James Shaver, Edwin Fenton, Hazel Hertzberg, Diane Ravitch, Gary Nash, and Molefi Asante. The new social studies movement, a response to Sputnik, advanced hundreds of inquiry-based learning projects around the nation. Other recent social studies curriculum movements embraced issues—centered approaches, enduring historical questions, and African-centered education. Of course, most recently, social studies curriculum has been impacted by advocates of standards-based learning and assessment (Grant, 2006).

The three to four weeks of reading about social studies curriculum leaders and their pedagogical approaches begin with candidates placed into groups of 3–5. Each group receives a historical education leader and a social studies method to research and present to the class. Each candidate presentation takes approximately 20–30 minutes of class time. Candidates are expected to participate actively in the learning activities. In their presentations, candidates include content from the readings, create materials to support the learning, develop an active learning strategy for classmates, communicate clearly and promote student interest, and assess how they worked together as a small group. A presentation expectation guide, distributed in advance of the presentations, clearly delineates these requirements.

After the presentations of leaders and curriculum, the culminating project is the *Invitation to a Dinner Party* project. The project pushes candidates to focus on important social studies education leaders in order to further their understanding of education leaders, theories, and curriculum options for social studies teaching.

I encourage candidates to use their imaginations in designing the party of 4–5 living and/or dead social studies leaders. Candidates name the individuals whom they invite and their reasons for extending an invitation. They create a menu for the party and develop an imagined dialogue among these educators where they discuss an important question in the social studies curriculum. Finally, candidates answer questions about these social studies leaders: What are points of agreement and disagreement between these individuals? What lessons do these leaders advocate that can be implemented in a contemporary social studies classroom? Candidates must use evidence from the class readings to support their dinner party narrative.

Assessing the Task: I assess candidates on the presentations and the final project. During the presentations, I record notes on an observation sheet that includes five criteria: 1) content from the readings, 2) active learning activity, 3) teamwork, 4) materials, and 5) presentation. (See Appendix). The document has specific questions, but allows for open-ended feedback to be recorded. Groups also self-assess in written form. The self-assessment and my assessment are combined for a presentation grade.

The final dinner party writing project is evaluated on a 4-point rubric (see Appendix) that includes several criteria: 1) originality and creativity of ideas, 2) use of evidence from readings, 3) writing flow and sentence structure, and 4) grammar and mechanics in writing. In addition to the rubric, I record general thoughts about the overall project and the writing. The comments section allows for individual assessment of candidates' work.

CANDIDATES AND THE TASK

Most teacher candidates enjoy working in groups to develop their presentations. They typically have no prior knowledge of the social studies curriculum leaders, their theories, or their pedagogies. Since candidates can determine their individual roles within the group, no one is required to perform and can select a supportive role if desired. However, most of the candidates have field experiences in local area schools and are accustomed to teaching in front of a class. Sometimes, it is a bit more challenging for the candidates to develop a lesson where they are required to actively engage their classmates in a learning activity.

The dinner party writing project leads to some remarkably creative thinking. As the instructor, I enjoy reading these assignments and have kept a few in my records. For example, one candidate hosted a party where she invited James Banks, John Dewey, Pierre Bourdieu, Harold Rugg, and a 10th-grade student in her school. She developed a menu that included school lunch luxuries such as Doritos potato chips, frozen pizza with Ranch dressing, Caesar salad, and Coke Zero. She developed a script where the guests discussed whether public education should play a role in changing the power structure in society. Another candidate called his dinner party the Scholars of Pedagogy Supper Society or SOPSS where guests met monthly at Rhodes Hall on Peachtree Street. Invitees included Lucy

Sprague Mitchell, Diane Ravitch, Cheryl Craig, and Todd Dinkelman. At SOPSS, guests discussed the importance of reflection in social studies teacher practice.

THE TASK IN CONTEXT

This presentation and dinner party writing project occur in the first half of the semester, as the history of social studies education serves as a foundation for the remaining topics in the course. Further exploration of standards and assessment in social studies follow these two activities.

APPENDIX

Presentations Feedback Document

1. *Content from Reading(s)*: How was content presented?
2. *Active Learning*: Were candidates in the class active participants in learning the lesson?
3. *Team Work*: Did the candidate presentation group share in lesson preparation and work well together? How does the group believe they worked together?
4. *Materials*: Visual aids, documents, papers, manipulatives, other items to facilitate the learning process?
5. *Presentation*: Communication style, organization of presentation, articulation, eye contact, command of candidates, attention and interest—were these clear to audience?

Writing Rubric

Candidate Name: **Dr. Goodprofessor**

Grade	Exceptional	Excellent	Very Good	Good	Average	Failure
Category	A+/A	A-	B+	B/B-	C+/C/C-	D/F
1. Logic & Originality						
2. Mechanics						
Spelling/ Grammar						
3. Writing Style & Prose Clarity						
4. Critical Insights & Research Evidence						

General Comments:

REFERENCES

Crocco, M. S., & Davis, O. L. Jr. (1999). *"Bending the future to their will": Civic women, social education, and democracy.* New York: Rowman & Littlefield.

Evans, R. W. (2004). *The social studies wars: What should we teach the children?* New York: Teachers College Press.

Grant, S. G. (2006). *Measuring history: Cases of state-level testing across the United States.* Greenwich, CT: Information Age Publishing.

Levstik, L. S., & Barton, K. C. (1997). *Doing history: Investigating with children in elementary and middle schools.* Mahwah, NJ: Lawrence Erlbaum Associates.

Woyshner, C., & Bohan, C. H. (2012). *Histories of social studies and race, 1865–2000.* New York: Palgrave Macmillan.

CHAPTER 12

LESSON PLAN MENU

Daniel T. Bordwell and Christopher H. Clark

Name: Daniel T. Bordwell and Christopher H. Clark	Audience: Graduate students
Affiliation: University of Minnesota	Length: Fall Practicum (8 weeks) Spring Candidate Teaching (12 weeks)
Course Title: Advanced Methods of Teaching the Social Studies	Commonplace featured: Teachers and Teaching
NCSS Teacher Education Standard: Element 3c: Candidates use theory and research to implement a variety of instructional practices and authentic assessments featuring disciplinary knowledge, inquiry, and forms of representation for competence in civic life.	

Teaching Social Studies: A Methods Book for Methods Teachers,
pages 67–72.
Copyright © 2017 by Information Age Publishing
All rights of reproduction in any form reserved.

TASK SUMMARY

The Lesson Plan Menu enables teacher candidates to use pedagogical tools learned in their methods courses and themes relevant to diversity, social justice, and other traditionally underrepresented topics (e.g., gender, race, social class) throughout their field experiences.

DESCRIPTION OF THE TASK

Being a teacher candidate is tough; in addition to their own expectations, they must manage a host of demands from supervisors, cooperating teachers, schools, and districts. With all of these expectations, many adopt a survival strategy of "don't rock the boat." They avoid sanctions (Evans, Avery, & Pederson, 1999) and do not challenge the official curriculum (Salinas & Castro, 2010; Segall, 2002). As placement supervisors and course instructors, we understand, but are not happy with our candidates being overly reliant on lectures and hesitant to experiment with the authentic instruction and assessment (Newmann, King, & Carmichael, 2007). Therefore, with our faculty advisors, we designed the Lesson Plan Menu to create common expectations for candidates and ensure that candidates apply learning from their university courses during their field experiences.

The Task: At the start of their placements, teacher candidates are given the Lesson Plan Menu (see Appendix) to guide their lesson planning and assessments. During their fall practicums, they submit four lessons from the Menu. In the spring, candidates submit eight lessons, a pre-unit survey, a reflection of how they used that data, and an authentic assessment. In previous years, candidates turned in two to five lesson plans per week to their supervisors. These plans were evaluated for quality, with more authentic lessons receiving higher grades than more traditional lessons. Ultimately, however, candidates were not required to include specific pedagogical strategies or methods. Now, they design all lesson plans from the Menu and teach at least one lesson from each of four categories: Discussion, Group Work, Skills, and Source Analysis. All of the pedagogies in the Menu are demonstrated at some point in their program coursework. In addition, candidates must incorporate our university's curriculum priorities. These priorities call for inclusion of issues related to diversity, social justice, and other traditionally underrepresented topics in the social studies classroom. A single lesson can address both a pedagogical category and a theme. For example, a Structured Academic Controversy on racial reparations would count toward the Discussion category and one of the required themed lessons. Candidates can talk with their university supervisor to suggest other pedagogies and themes that can meet the requirements. For example, one candidate facilitated thoughtful discussion through a four corners activity and was allowed to use that lesson for the Discussion category requirement.

Assessing the Task: Candidates submit the lesson plans to their supervisors who evaluate the quality of each lesson and provide suggestions. Feedback is intended to be formative, though the scores on the lesson plans count for a portion of the candidates' course grades. Candidates are responsible for keeping track of which Menu categories they have completed, but supervisors create and share a Google Doc with candidates to help them keep track of the pedagogies and themes they use. By requiring a variety of pedagogical methods, the Lesson Plan Menu gives supervisors a better understanding of a candidate's strengths and weakness. They practice with a wider variety of tasks than prior to the Menu and build a broader pedagogical skill-set during their teaching placements.

CANDIDATES AND THE TASK

Overall, teacher candidate response to the Menu has been positive. With fewer lesson plans to turn in, candidates are less stressed than they have been in previous years. Further, many appreciate having the list of tasks available to them when doing their lesson planning. One candidate noted, "it gave me a clear reminder of some of the things we had learned and that I could use them in the classroom. I also appreciated the flexibility in what was accepted for the various options." Another candidate responded, "it was great to have a reminder of different activities to try out. We learned so many different techniques and approaches...that it became very easy to forget about them."

During our first year implementing the Menu, we realized improvements were needed. Many candidates requested more clarity about expectations for each type of lesson. For example, one candidate had difficulty with an image analysis exercise: "I would have liked the strategies...explained a little further. My first image analysis, for example, was not completed the way my supervisor wanted. Some quick directions and expectations on the Menu itself would clear up any possible confusion." The next semester, we added brief directions and expectations for each pedagogy. The discussions between supervisors and candidates about how to try out different pedagogical methods offered a latent benefit of this process.

The Lesson Plan Menu has facilitated better conversation among method instructors and supervisors about teacher candidates' strengths and areas for growth. Looking at the candidates' work led us to see which pedagogies needed clarifying and more modeling in our courses. Further, the Menu has helped us to identify some of the reasons why candidates are confused regarding certain pedagogies. For example, we realized each methods instructor in our program facilitates Socratic Seminars in a slightly different manner. We now acknowledge these differences in our courses and openly embrace the fact that there is often more than one "right" way to enact any lesson strategy. Doing so allows us to frame the differences as multiple options for the candidates to put in their "toolbox."

The Menu also helped clarify university expectations for cooperating teachers. We hope to place candidates with teachers known for their authentic instruction, but that is not always possible. Sometimes, candidates face resistance when they attempt to branch out pedagogically. Requiring the use of specific pedagogies gives candidates license to try new approaches in the classroom regardless of the host teacher's preferred pedagogies. Still, several candidates found it difficult to incorporate the required number of tasks into their host teachers' classrooms. Many also struggled to find space for the University's themes or to incorporate them in a way that felt like a good fit for the courses they were teaching. One candidate commented, "it was hard at times fitting in the themes, with the options available for lessons, combined with the types of lessons (skills, discussion, etc.). Some lessons felt a bit forced for this reason." Here again, the Menu offered candidates an opportunity to discuss with their supervisors and cooperating teachers how to include underrepresented, but necessary, topics within the social studies.

Cooperating teachers also like the Menu. One teacher who has worked with candidates prior to and after the Menu's development said, "I thought it was a good way for a teacher candidate to explore many different strategies, some of which made them uncomfortable. I especially liked the emphasis on teaching with equity and diverse perspectives in mind."

Comments from supervisors indicate that using the Menu resulted in a wider variety of pedagogies used in the lesson plans they evaluated and observed. Further, supervisors found that the Menu allowed them to be clearer in their communications with their teacher candidates. Prior to the Menu, supervisors hoped candidates would try out new pedagogies and address themes of diversity and social justice. Now these expectations are clear and assessed. As supervisors, we believe that making these pedagogies and themes a requirement sends a strong message to candidates about the teaching we value and want to see.

The Lesson Plan Menu is updated at the end of each semester to ensure that it meets the needs of candidates, cooperating teachers, and the university supervisors. By requiring fewer lesson plans, but mandating higher quality, the Menu provides better evidence of candidates' growth as emerging practitioners.

THE TASK IN CONTEXT

Candidates complete a one-year, intensive program to obtain their teaching certification. During this year, they complete two field experiences: an 8-week practicum in the fall and a 12-week candidate teaching in the spring. Candidates use the Lesson Plan Menu during these field experiences.

APPENDIX: LESSON PLAN MENU—SPRING SEMESTER

Directions: You will be submitting 8 lesson plans to your University Supervisor during your spring teaching experience and 2 assessments. During your teaching, you must teach <u>at least one lesson</u> from each of the following categories: Discussions, Group Work, Skills, and Source Analysis. You must also draw on at least <u>four</u> of the seven themes listed below the table. The two assessments are required.

Discussions	Group Work	Skills	Source Analysis
Fishbowl (Optional: Backchannel)	Inquiry (Teacher presents problem for inquiry, along with pieces of evidence for candidates to consider— look at Stanford History Project [sheg.stanford.org]for models and ideas)	Enhancing Reading Comprehension (think of pre- during-, and after-reading strategies)	Current Events Source(s) (e.g., video clip; blog; newspaper—op-ed, news, editorial; twitter)
Interactive Lecture (describe in some detail the lecture and how and when it will be interactive)	Jigsaw (key here is choosing material well-suited to a jigsaw)	Teaching Vocabulary	Film (lesson to assist candidates in reading the language of film)
Online Discussion	Stations (again, key here is choosing material well-suited to stations)	Developing writing skills	Graphic Organizers
Socratic Seminar			Image Analysis (e.g., photograph, painting, drawing, political cartoon)
Structured Academic Controversy			Primary Sources (analyzing one or more primary sources)

Key Themes (choose 4):

Gender	Race
Global Perspectives	Religion
LGBTQ	Social Class
Marginalized Identities	

Assessments (Both Are Required):

Pre-Unit Survey, Analysis of Results, and Implications for Teaching. You are required to design and administer a pre-unit survey to your candidates. You should include at least 3 different types of close-ended items. Administer the survey to at least one class, then write a 3–4 page paper that displays the results of your survey (bar graphs, tables, pie charts, etc. are appropriate for close-ended items) and describes the implications of your results for your teaching.

Summative Assessment. You are required to design one summative assessment. This will most likely be an end-of-unit assessment, and may be a project or a more traditional test with items such as multiple choice, matching, short answer, essay. If you are giving a project as a summative assessment, you need to include all directions and a rubric (it is not acceptable to say that you gave some directions orally). If you are giving a more traditional test, your items should reflect wise practices (e.g., items should reflect your learning outcomes, not trivia; do not use "all of the above," "none of the above," "a and c," etc. for MC options; the stem of the item should not give away the answer [for example, ends in "a" or "an"]). Other ideas for summative assessments should be discussed with your supervisor in advance.

Our goal is to have Teacher Candidates pull from these categories and themes over the course of the 12-week candidate teaching experience. Note: Teacher Candidates will be teaching at least 10 of the 12 weeks of their placement. A theme can be embedded within another lesson to meet the requirements. For example, the Structured Academic Controversy lesson plan can center on the theme of Race and this would count toward the Discussion category and one of the four required themed lessons.

Also, note that while candidates will be creating lesson plans for each day and share these with their Cooperating Teachers on a schedule that fits both of them, supervisors will *only* assess submissions from the above categories, themes, and assessments. All eight lesson plans that will be graded must come from the categories and themes above. If you have other ideas that are not included on the chart but fit the above categories, talk with your supervisor.

ACKNOWLEDGEMENTS

The authors would like to acknowledge Patricia Avery and J.B. Mayo, for their leadership and work on developing the Lesson Plan Menu, as well as their feedback on an early draft of this chapter.

REFERENCES

Evans, R. W., Avery, P. G., & Pederson, P. V. (1999). Taboo topics: Cultural restraint on teaching social issues. *The Social Studies, 90*(5), 218–224.

Newmann, F. M., King, M. B., & Carmichael, D. L. (2007). *Authentic instruction and assessment: Common standards for rigor and relevance in teaching academic subjects.* Des Moines, IA: Iowa Department of Education.

Salinas, C., & Castro, A. J. (2010). Disrupting the official curriculum: Cultural biography and the curriculum decision making of Latino preservice teachers. *Theory & Research in Social Education, 38,* 428–463

Segall, A. (2002). *Disturbing practice: Reading teacher education as text.* New York: Peter Lang Publishing.

CHAPTER 13

PEDAGOGICAL TOOLBOX ANALYSIS

Jonathan Ryan Davis and Maureen Connolly

Name: Jonathan Ryan Davis and Maureen Connolly	Audience: Undergraduate and graduate students
Affiliation: The College of New Jersey	Length: Series of assignments that take 30 minutes outside of class
Course Title: Secondary Education Methods	Commonplace featured: Teachers/Teaching
NCSS Teacher Education Standard: Element 3e. Candidates engage learners in self-assessment practices that support individualized learning outcomes related to disciplinary knowledge, inquiry, and forms of representation for competence in civic life.	

Teaching Social Studies: A Methods Book for Methods Teachers,
pages 73–77.
Copyright © 2017 by Information Age Publishing

TASK SUMMARY

For the *Pedagogical Toolbox Analysis* assignment, teacher candidates highlight effective pedagogical strategies they observe, reflect on obstacles to implementation, identify ways to differentiate the strategy, and explain how they might integrate the strategy in their lessons.

DESCRIPTION OF THE TASK

Teacher candidates consistently ask for concrete strategies they can take with them into their classrooms, though they want to see them in action and try them out. Therefore, we designed the *Pedagogical Toolbox Analysis* assignment to help candidates: 1) learn a range of tried and tested teaching strategies they can use in their future classrooms, 2) reflect on their practices and adapt their strategies, and 3) open up conversations between candidates and their cooperating teachers so that candidates do not pass judgment on a strategy without understanding their cooperating teacher's pedagogical decision-making.

The Task: Before candidates enter the field for their first practicum experience, they are introduced to the "Strategies for Your Teaching Toolbox" graphic organizer and assignment (see Appendix). The graphic organizer asks candidates to:

1. Describe the pedagogical techniques used/attempted
2. Give a brief narrative of the implementation of the strategy (with attention to effectiveness of and obstacles to implementation)
3. Add differentiation strategies for the English Language, Special Education, and advanced learners
4. Anticipate adaptations to the technique in the future
5. Provide handouts to implement the strategy

We push candidates to reflect on multiple elements of each strategy. Doing so is critical because it challenges candidates to reflect on each strategy in a meaningful way. It also helps candidates engage in dialogue with their cooperating teachers around each pedagogical strategy rather than judging cooperating teachers' pedagogical choices without understanding them.

Additionally, we provide candidates with a long list of strategies they might see in the classroom. We do this in a couple of ways. First, we model strategies daily for our candidates—from creative ways to engage students in a "Do Now" to strategies for facilitating an effective discussion. Second, we provide texts that outline various strategies (e.g., Lemov, 2015; Tanner, 2013). In preparation for their first week in the field and their first Toolbox assignment, candidates should have several strategies in mind when they begin observing their cooperating teachers. Doing so helps them make the transition from classroom student to teacher candidate.

Each week candidates complete a "Strategies for Your Teaching Toolbox" graphic organizer. They complete the organizer based on specific pedagogical techniques they witness. Once they begin teaching, they complete the organizer based on strategies they try to implement.

To complete the organizer, candidates take notes on the observed strategy during class time. Later, they reflect on the complexities of the strategy using the graphic organizer to facilitate that reflection. If the strategy was observed, candidates should attempt the strategy once they begin teaching so they can revise the organizer after they attempt implementation. After completing the organizer based on their own implementation, candidates attempt the strategy again based on their adaptations and record any differences in students' responses.

The next step is to have candidates share and compare their strategies with one another in a structured way. We do so in a couple of ways. One is to have candidates compare and contrast their analyzed strategies in groups of three to four taking turns sharing the details of their strategies and then allowing for an open dialogue about how the other candidates have tried the strategy. Candidates also explore possible challenges to using the strategy and how the strategy can be modified to work for all students. This same type of discussion can also take place online through a course website/blog/discussion board, allowing candidates to give constructive thoughts and feedback when it is most convenient for them. We then participate in the discussion and use class time to highlight key points raised in the online discussions.

Finally, to ensure candidates have access to as many strategies as possible, we compile all of their graphic organizers into the Class Book of Teaching Strategies that exists on online with search capacity.

Assessing the Task: Candidates submit anywhere from 5–8 toolbox reflections over the course of the semester. At the start of the semester, candidates typically submit one reflection per week based on their cooperating teachers' use of particular strategies. We review these submissions for completeness and critical thinking, differentiation, and changes for the future. As noted above, we provide feedback on online submissions, often encouraging candidates to solicit feedback from their cooperating teachers on each pedagogical strategy and to make connections with theory and research presented in class. Though we provide some feedback, assessment of the assignment is also based on how candidates respond to one another during class sessions or online. Candidates share their toolbox reflections with one another and we assess responses regarding adaptation of a peer's strategy into their own classroom and/or insightful questions that candidates pose or insights/connections to theory that they make.

CANDIDATES AND THE TASK

Teacher candidates enter our class eager for practical ideas about what to do in the classroom. They have strong theoretical knowledge from their adolescent psychology and educational foundations courses. They are eager to see how these initial courses support what they will do when they work with their own classes. Thus, they engage with this assignment eagerly because they are excited for the practical knowledge. The template itself helps candidates to know what to look for when they observe and prompts them to think critically about what they are observing.

When candidates are first becoming familiar with the toolbox template, an area that seems particularly challenging is differentiation. Although many have ideas about how to differentiate for struggling learners, some have not given much thought to enrichment for advanced learners; candidates typically suggest heterogeneous grouping so that advanced students can support struggling students. By the third week, we no longer accept this approach to differentiation. Rather, we ask candidates to focus on other aspects of process, along with readiness, product, interests, and learning style.

Candidates focus on instructional strategies and on strategies for classroom management as well. The samples below represent each category. It is interesting to see that candidates can note challenges to implementation, but struggle to suggest what they would change. This awareness opens discussion about how much of the teaching profession involves decision-making that is specific to classroom context.

THE TASK IN CONTEXT

We introduce this task when teacher candidates begin their field observations. They utilize this tool to reflect on their cooperating teacher's pedagogical choices and then apply the tool to their own teaching. After the practicum experience in which this Toolbox Reflection is used, candidates move on to student teaching with multiple strategies to choose from when they plan. They also engage in an action research course in conjunction with their candidate teaching. The kinds of reflective practice and consideration to how to adapt instruction that are supported by this tool are utilized throughout the action research experience.

APPENDIX

Strategies for Your Teaching Toolbox

After beginning your fieldwork, each week you will complete a "Toolbox" analysis/reflection on specific pedagogical techniques you witness your Cooperating Teacher use or techniques you have tried. Your analysis/reflection must include:

Strategy Name:	Basic Description:
Parking Lot	A small whiteboard on the side of the classroom where students can record questions for the teacher

Brief Narrative of Strategy's Implementation:

The parking lot is a strategy used by Ms. Haley to field unnecessary questions from students. 6th graders love to ask questions and most of the time they are irrelevant. The parking lot offers students a means to ask questions (whether relevant to history or not) in a way that is not disruptive to the class. The students are allowed to get up and write a question at any point during class as long as the teacher is not giving direct instruction. The teacher will respond to the questions at the end of the day.

Effective ways strategy was implemented:	**Obstacles to implementing the strategy:**
(Consider classroom context & prior knowledge) This is an amazing strategy in cutting back on '6th-grade questions' during class time.	(If things went smoothly, consider what might not work as well in another classroom setting) This works smoothly in Ms. Haley's class. An obstacle might be if students ask inappropriate or rude questions.

Possible Differentiation Strategies

Adaptations/Scaffolding for English Language Learners and/or Special Education Students:	**Enrichment ideas**:
I think this board could be used as a great strategy to differentiate. Low-level learners can write content questions anonymously and the teacher can clarify	Students can write a question specifically about the history content that they want answered

Changes to Strategy's Implementation for Best Future Integration into YOUR Teaching:

I could have this strategy in a high school, just modified. Instead of its purpose being to eliminate irrelevant questions, the board can be used to get clarification, or answer questions the teacher does not know. If students need a clarification on a content issue, they can write the question on the board. If a candidate asks a question that the teacher doesn't know the answer to they can write it on the board for the teacher to research and get back to them.

**Please attach any handouts you might use to help implement this strategy to the end of this document.

REFERENCES

Lemov, D. (2015). *Teach like a champion 2.0.* San Francisco, CA: Jossey-Bass.

Tanner, K. D. (2013). Structure matters: Twenty-one teaching strategies to promote candidate engagement and cultivate classroom equity. *Cell Biology Education, 12*(3), 322–331.

CHAPTER 14

TEACHER CANDIDATES COLLABORATE TO CREATE AN INTERDISCIPLINARY ASSIGNMENT

Lorrei DiCamillo and Nancy M. Bailey

Name: Lorrei DiCamillo and Nancy M. Bailey	Audience: Undergraduate and graduate students
Affiliation: Canisius College	Length: Five to six hours
Course Title: Methods of Teaching Social Studies/Methods of Teaching English	Commonplace featured: Teachers and Teaching
NCSS Teacher Education Standard: Element 2d. Candidates plan learning sequences where learners create disciplinary forms of representation to provide opportunities for meaningful civic learning.	

Teaching Social Studies: A Methods Book for Methods Teachers,
pages 79–83.
Copyright © 2017 by Information Age Publishing

TASK SUMMARY

Teacher candidates in a social studies methods course and an English methods course come together to reflect on the benefits and challenges of working across school subjects by creating an interdisciplinary assignment for their students.

DESCRIPTION OF THE TASK

The Common Core State Standards (CCSS) call for the integration of complex texts, a shift to the teaching of nonfiction texts in literacy classes, and more vocabulary study, analytical reading, and argumentative writing across content areas (Calkins, Ehrenworth, & Lehman, 2012). As a result, the National Council for the Social Studies and the National Council for the Teaching of English are encouraging more interdisciplinary teaching and teacher collaboration to assist students in meeting the CCSS. Yet few current teachers know how to create lessons and teach units collaboratively with colleagues in another discipline (Spalding, 2002). To address this issue we created an assignment for candidates in our respective courses to learn more about interdisciplinary teaching and how to collaborate with a colleague on a common assignment. We believe this opportunity offers candidates the benefit of seeing collaborative, interdisciplinary teaching and learning and the opportunity to strengthen their disciplinary knowledge and improve their abilities to plan units and lessons with future department colleagues.

The Task: Before combining our courses, candidates read and reflect on several articles written by teachers and teacher educators about interdisciplinary teaching in social studies and English courses (e.g., Applebee, Adler, & Flihan, 2007; Turk, Klein, & Dickstein, 2007; Springhorn, 1995). During our first combined class (approximately one and a half hours), candidates form small groups, get acquainted with each other, recount whether they have experienced interdisciplinary teaching and learning, and discuss what they thought about the readings that described the benefits and challenges of interdisciplinary work. We share some of our recent experiences of collaboratively teaching an interdisciplinary class during our sabbaticals (DiCamillo & Bailey, 2016). Nancy then leads a discussion about using new literacies and digital technologies to enhance student engagement and we hand out and explain the assignment. We also show candidates a few examples of high-quality assignments former candidates created, for example, a digital documentary assignment about the Civil Rights Movement paired with Patillo-Beals' *Warriors Don't Cry* (1995).

The candidates then choose a partner or partners (if numbers of candidates are uneven) from the other methods class who are interested in teaching at the same grade level (e.g., 11th-grade American history and 11th grade American literature). We then tell them to imagine they are team teaching a class of 25 students each day in their respective social studies and English courses. Next, candidates choose a familiar topic for their assignments so that they can focus on planning rather than learning new content. Sample topics include the Middle Ages, Elizabethan

England, the Roaring Twenties, World War II, Civil Rights Movements, Cold War, and current national and international conflicts. Then, the candidates collaborate to produce an interdisciplinary assignment for their students. Additionally, the candidates use a wiki that we have created for this assignment to communicate with each other and to learn how useful classroom wikis can be.

We then tell them that the following steps can guide their collaborative process:

1. Choose the literature/historical event at the heart of the unit of study.
2. Create a compelling question for the unit.
3. Devise at least three unit objectives that help students answer the compelling question.
4. Write an interdisciplinary assignment that would be included in the unit (most likely one of several assessments) and write this in a handout that includes a grading rubric.
5. Create a version of the interdisciplinary assignment for students (e.g., a letter written by a historical figure or character, a video diary, a digital documentary, a podcast).

The candidates have about an hour to work collaboratively and then they work for the next week with their partner(s) via the class wiki. We then give them another two hours of class time the following week to finalize their assignments. They turn in the same assignment to their respective methods instructor. We have not always had time to do presentations of the assignments in class, but we have a page on a class wiki, accessible to both methods classes, where the assignments are displayed so that all candidates can see what their peers have created.

Assessing the Task: We assess the assignment with a rubric that includes four required elements. The partners working collaboratively complete the first three elements; each candidate does the last individually. First, they collaboratively devise a compelling question that forms a foundation for their interdisciplinary assignment and three measurable, observable objectives. Second, working together, they describe in a handout the assignment they want their students to complete. The assignment should be appropriate for students' grade level as well as authentic, multimodal, and interdisciplinary. Third, candidates include a version or sketch of the full assignment they want their students to complete. We are more interested in assessing interdisciplinary content than form, at this point. Finally, we ask each candidate to provide thoughtful, well-developed responses to the following reflection questions: a) Do you think it is important to include interdisciplinary curriculum in your lessons? Explain your response. b) What did you learn from the process of working with a colleague from a different subject area? c) What were the benefits and challenges of interdisciplinary work? d) How has your thinking about interdisciplinary teaching changed as a result of this assignment? and e) How could we make this assignment stronger?

CANDIDATES AND THE TASK

When the teacher candidates' work together concludes and we read their individual responses to the project, we find many write about the significant benefits of working collaboratively. For example, June, a pre-service English teacher, said, "my [social studies] colleague definitely came up with some ideas, connections, and texts that I would never have thought of."

Teacher candidates have also disclosed that interdisciplinary collaboration assists them in seeing new connections for their future classrooms. Jennifer, for instance, remarked that her English colleagues helped her remember skills she had learned in school but forgotten: "My colleagues were able to offer me a refresher course that will enable me to use this skill [analyzing a historical event with the help of literature] within my own classroom."

A third common response centers on the benefits of interdisciplinary collaboration in that it helps candidates include different perspectives about the topic they want to teach. For example, Vincent noted that he "found that history teachers and English teachers' think in different ways. Working together is advantageous because the lesson will include different viewpoints and will provide the candidates with different ways of looking at material." Candidates also write that interdisciplinary collaboration is beneficial because they become more excited to teach the topic, feel more confident about lesson planning, and understand more about in-depth lesson planning.

Some groups do experience challenges and personality conflicts that can be expected with group work assignments. We assist them by letting them know that their disputes are reflective of authentic issues that will arise for them with department colleagues or grade-level teams. Overall, though, this assignment provides candidates with a glimpse of what it would be like to plan units and lessons with a teacher or group of teachers outside their discipline, and it helps them reflect on the benefits of creating relevant, meaningful curriculum for their future candidates.

THE TASK IN CONTEXT

Our schedules allow our methods courses to meet on the same day and at the same time, so it was easy for us to combine our classes for the four hours needed for this task. Those who do not have this luxury could have teacher candidates work together online via a wiki or other digital format, but we think the face-to-face element of this assignment is invaluable. This required assignment usually occurs during the fourth or fifth week of our semester-long methods courses.

REFERENCES

Applebee, A. N., Adler, M., & Flihan, S. (2007). Interdisciplinary curricula in middle and high school classrooms: Case studies of approaches to curriculum and instruction. *American Educational Research Journal, 44*(4), 1002–1039.

Calkins, L., Ehrenworth, M., & Lehman, C. (2012). *Pathways to the common core: Accelerating achievement,* Portsmouth, NH: Heinemann.

DiCamillo, L., & Bailey, N. M. (2016). Two teacher educators go to the source: Teaching an interdisciplinary class in an urban charter high school. *The Social Studies, 107*(6), 218–226.

Pattillo-Beals, M. (1995). *Warriors don't cry: A searing memoir of the battle to integrate Little Rock's Central High.* New York: Washington Square/Pocket Books.

Spalding, E. (2002). The hot fudge sundae quiz and other collaborative ventures: Interdisciplinary teaching and learning. *The Educational Forum, 66*(3), 271–282.

Springhorn, D. (1995). A response from a foot soldier in the interdisciplinary trenches. *The English Journal, 84*(7), 75–79.

Turk, D. B., Klein, E., & Dickstein, S. (2007). Mingling 'fact' with 'fiction': Strategies for integrating literature into history and social studies classrooms. *The History Teacher, 40*(3), 397–406.

CHAPTER 15

USING VIDEO STIMULATED RECALL TO REFLECT ON TEACHING AND ADAPT TO CANDIDATE NEEDS

Jason L. Endacott

Name: Jason L. Endacott	Audience: Undergraduate and graduate students
Affiliation: University of Arkansas	Length: Two-three hours
Course Title: Methods of Secondary Social Studies	Commonplace featured: Teachers and Teaching
NCSS Teacher Education Standard: Element 1. Candidates use theory and research to continually improve their social studies knowledge, inquiry skills, and civic dispositions and adapt practice to meet the needs of each learner.	

Teaching Social Studies: A Methods Book for Methods Teachers,
pages 85–90.
Copyright © 2017 by Information Age Publishing

TASK SUMMARY

This assignment utilizes Video Stimulated Recall (VSR), a technologically enhanced mode of observation, to improve teacher candidates' reflection on specific elements of their practice, especially as they relate to content knowledge, inquiry skills, and meeting the needs of individual learners.

DESCRIPTION OF THE TASK

This assignment is designed to improve teacher candidates' classroom instruction through enhanced reflection on their pedagogical decision-making. Candidates plan for instruction in the typical methods course; however, planning for instructional goals does not ensure that those goals will be met. The *Video Stimulated Recall* (VSR) task helps bridge the gap by engaging candidates in technologically enhanced reflection on their teaching. The goals for this assignment are pedagogical content knowledge, promotion of candidate inquiry, and meeting the needs of individual learners. Candidates also identify their strengths, reflect on areas of improvement, and verbalize strategies for improving their instruction and meeting the needs of individual students.

The Task: VSR is a video-based observation protocol in which candidates reflect on their pedagogical reasoning while viewing recorded segments of their classroom instruction (Sturtz & Hessberg, 2012). VSR flips the widely used observational model in which a mentor teacher or university supervisor observes an instructional lesson and uses a pre-determined instrument to guide the conversation that follows. Using VSR, the lesson is video recorded and then reviewed collaboratively by the candidate and the mentor/supervisor. Lessons are typically recorded with a tablet or digital video camera, and the recordings are viewed on the same device or transferred to a laptop or desktop computer. Key is that the candidates control the replaying of the video: They guide the conversation about the lesson, stopping the video whenever they would like to discuss an aspect of their instruction or the reasoning behind their instructional decisions. The mentor/supervisor provides can then provide targeted feedback.

With candidates controlling the video, a guide for the task helps make sure the specific task goals are met. We typically provide an anticipatory set of questions (see Appendix) that offer an overarching purpose to the reflection on any individual recorded lesson. This strategy has been used successfully with state-mandated observation and evaluation protocols to deepen candidates' reflection on their teaching (Endacott, 2016), though it is possible to shape the purpose of each observation to meet specific goals of the teacher/observer. This flexibility makes the use of VSR compatible with multiple stages of candidates' development.

Our methods course utilizes the *College, Career, and Civic Life (C3) Framework for Social Studies State Standards* (National Council for the Social Studies, 2013) to guide candidates' planning for instruction based on the state social studies frameworks, which have also been recently revised to reflect the *C3 Frame-*

work. Candidates plan for instruction by generating compelling and supporting questions, designing inquiries, gathering and evaluating evidence, and creating assessments that require students to communicate conclusions and contemplate ways to take informed action. As they progress through the program, candidates learn how to cede the responsibility for creating the inquiry process to students while providing scaffolded guidance. This approach is why one goal of this assignment is to have candidates reflect on their progress towards becoming facilitators of student inquiry.

Mentors/supervisors provide feedback based on the candidates' reflections, allowing them to guide the conversation, and reserving all non-protocol feedback (e.g., classroom management tips) for the end of the session. Mentors/supervisors should also keep the anticipatory guide at the center of the task, as it is easy for candidates to drift from the main purpose for that particular reflection. This guidance requires a gentle approach, and the mentor/supervisor should redirect candidates to the anticipatory guide to get them back on track rather than taking direct control of the conversation. One strategy that helps candidates and mentors/supervisors maintain this balance involves using the same video segment with multiple anticipatory guides. One might choose to have the candidates focus on general classroom concerns while viewing the video with their classroom mentor and then view the same lesson again with the specific anticipatory guide provided here. This approach promotes the idea that reflection on teaching can move past "how did it go?" to focus on a wide variety of specific and interdependent aspects of quality classroom teaching.

Assessing the Task: The final product is an 800–1000 word written reflection based on the candidates' understanding of their classroom instruction. Candidates must reflect on what they have learned about their teaching in relation to their pedagogical content knowledge base, their ability to promote student inquiry, and their capacity to meet the needs of individual learners. Candidates should also reflect on what they learned about themselves as teachers as a result of the VSR session, their strengths and areas of improvement, and how they plan to improve their efficacy in these areas and overall based on this exercise. In order to make connections between the university classroom and the practicum experience, candidates are also expected to reference specific examples of theories and/or instructional techniques that inform their reflection on these aspects of their teaching.

When evaluating candidate performance, we apply a rubric that is tied to the task criteria as well as the identification of strengths, areas of improvement, and strategies for improvement that draw from theory and/or research covered in the candidates' coursework. The rubric values specificity in the written reflections and focuses in on connections between the candidates' teaching, the C3, and theory. As an additional step in evaluation, we monitor candidates' progress on their identified areas of improvement and incorporate them into future observations.

CANDIDATES AND THE TASK

Assessing the VSR task can be difficult until teacher candidates become accustomed to the protocol and process of reflection. It has been very helpful to use VSR in a more general fashion, such as focusing on general classroom concerns before using it with a goal-specific assignment such as this one. The first viewing is almost universally awkward as candidates see themselves teaching for the first time. Comments such as, "oh wow, I hate the sound of my voice" or candidates talking to themselves—"C'mon Mr. B start class! Geez!"—are not unusual.

However, once they develop a comfort level with VSR, candidates find the process encourages deeper and more specific reflection for improving teaching. Candidates become more mindful of the overall instructional goals they are trying to achieve. For one unit on World War II, a candidate pointed to the screen and remarked, "here I was thinking about how this source on Truman would help them get a better idea of who he was, which would help them answer the compelling question about whether or not he was right to drop the atomic bombs." Later, she referenced the pedagogical content knowledge she possessed but was not ready to reveal to the candidates: "Here I knew that the Soviets were scheduled to enter the war against Japan on August 15th, but I didn't want them to know that just yet." Examples like these would be difficult to cultivate if the candidates were operating purely from memory rather than receiving cues from the video in front of them.

THE TASK IN CONTEXT

This task occurs during the second term of our one-year, Master of Arts in teaching program. Within the methods course, the assignment is completed towards the end of the semester, after the teacher candidates have had significant time teaching in their field placements. Prior to this task, candidates are introduced to the *C3 Framework*, learn multiple instructional techniques in class, and are observed by their mentor teachers in the field. This task and course are followed by a semester-long internship of full-time teaching in a different field placement.

APPENDIX A

Anticipatory Question Guide

As you review the recorded video of your classroom instruction, use these questions to guide your reflection. For all of these questions, you should pay particular attention to how you met the specific needs of your students based upon your knowledge of them as learners.

1.   How did your classroom instruction support the students' understanding of the compelling and/or supporting questions that were generated to guide this inquiry?

- Possible example: Interactions in which you purposefully scaffold-ed or redirected students' thinking back to the compelling/support-ing questions guiding the inquiry.
- Possible example: Instances of instructional decision-making in which you were mentally processing instructional decisions relat-ed to compelling and supporting questions that did not necessarily show up in the video recording.

2. How did your classroom instruction reinforce the disciplinary concepts and tools from Dimension 2 that were used to guide the inquiry?

- Possible example: If your inquiry was framed with *"D2.Civ.12.9–12. Analyze how people use and challenge local, state, national, and international laws to address a variety of public issues"* then you will look for instances in your teaching in which you had this specifically in mind or specifically referenced it when you were interacting with students.
- Possible example: Any interaction or decision that was made based upon content knowledge that you either possessed or lacked during the moment of instruction.

3. How did your classroom instruction promote students' development of claims and critical analysis of the evidence they were using to support their claims?

- Possible example: Interactions in which you queried students about the origin, authority, structure, context, credibility and corrobora-tive value of their sources.
- Possible example: Interactions in which you raised questions or discussed the strengths and weaknesses of students' claims in rela-tion to the evidence that was used to generate them.

4. How did your classroom instruction scaffold students towards commu-nicating their conclusions and contemplating the possibility of taking informed action?

- Possible example: Interactions in which you scaffolded students' thinking towards the construction of arguments or explanations based on evidence and examples.
- Possible example: Interactions in which you encouraged students to provide critiques of other explanations or arguments based upon evidentiary strengths and weaknesses.

5. How do you know that your planning and instruction were effective for this lesson? What formative evidence did you see or collect from your students that provided you with feedback on whether or not students are progressing towards the instructional goals you set forth in your lesson?

- Possible example: Informal interactions with students in which you were able to observe progress towards instructional goals.

- Possible example: Formal formative evidence you collected from the students at the conclusion of this lesson that provided feedback on students' progress towards instructional goals

REFERENCES

Endacott, J. L. (2016). Using video stimulated recall to enhance preservice teacher reflection. *The New Educator, 12*(1), 28–47.

National Council for the Social Studies. (2013). *The college, career, and civic life (C3) framework for social studies state standards: Guidance for enhancing the rigor of K–12 civics, economics, geography, and history.* Silver Spring, MD: Author.

Sturtz, J., & Hessberg, K. (2012). Examining teacher development: The role of teacher thinking, observation, and reflection. In W. B. Russell (Ed.), *Contemporary social studies: An essential reader* (pp. 547–563). Charlotte, NC: Information Age.

CHAPTER 16

FEEDBACK ON THEIR FEEDBACK

Brian Girard and Robert Bain

Name: Brian Girard and Robert Bain	Audience: Undergraduate and graduate students
Affiliation: The College of New Jersey and University of Michigan	Length: 90–120 minutes (although could be shorter)
Course Title: Teaching History and the Social Sciences in Secondary Schools	Commonplace featured: Teachers and Teaching
NCSS Teacher Education Standard: Element 3d: Candidates exhibit data literacy by using assessment data to guide instructional decision-making and reflect on student learning outcomes related to disciplinary knowledge, inquiry, and forms of representation for competence in civic life.	

Teaching Social Studies: A Methods Book for Methods Teachers,
pages 91–96.
Copyright © 2017 by Information Age Publishing
All rights of reproduction in any form reserved.

TASK SUMMARY

Teacher candidates grade and provide feedback on a set of papers that secondary students created in response to an authentic assessment task and then analyze the processes and principles of grading and providing effective feedback to K–12 students.

DESCRIPTION OF THE TASK

Most teachers say that grading and providing feedback are among their least favorite part of the job, yet most recognize it is one of the central tasks of teaching. This common practice—evaluating and offering feedback on student work—demands an understanding of content, students, learning progressions, feedback mechanisms, and evaluative criteria. Typically, teacher candidates learn how to evaluate and comment on student work while on the job, rather than in their professional training.

This assignment requires candidates to work through grading and responding to a small set of student papers. In simulating an authentic task of teaching, our goals are (1) to enable candidates to see the work involved in evaluating students' papers, (2) to provide us the chance to see how the candidates approach and enact this task of teaching, and then (3) to use available scholarship to provide feedback on candidates' feedback. By approximating and decomposing the instructional practice of using assessment and feedback to influence student learning, we seek to influence the candidates' learning.

The Task: To enact this activity, candidates need a set of student-written essays, a copy of the assignment, and the learning outcomes the assignment measures. We typically use papers gathered from our own teaching and research in classrooms. In constructing the set, we include student papers most likely to force candidates to confront issues inherent in grading: (a) judging and affixing a grade to a range of student work, (b) choosing elements in students' papers to comment upon and then crafting an educational response, (c) using objective criteria while individualizing assessments and feedback to specific students, and (d) making time to commit to doing such work. Therefore, we select a few long student papers of varying quality, a few very short papers of varying quality, and papers that are strong on one or two of the criteria but weak on the rest. We also construct short biographies to use after the candidates have graded the papers.

With a set of papers, here are the steps we use:

Step 1: Grading the Papers

As homework, we give each candidate the set of 10–15 essays, a copy of the students' assignment and objectives, and these instructions:

1. Please note the time you begin this task.

2. Read the assignment and the objectives.
3. Create a rubric based on the assessment prompt and the objectives.
4. Try using the rubric with two or three essays and make necessary adjustments in the rubric to make the grading more efficient and effective. Note how long it took you to create the rubric.
5. Use your rubric to evaluate each paper making sure to include either a letter or numerical grade on the paper and provide written comments to each student.
6. Make a note of how much time it takes for you to grade each essay and the entire set.

Step 2: Reflection on Assessment and the Process of Grading

After completing the grading, candidates assess their experience evaluating the papers, using the following prompts:

1. Think and write about assessment and the objectives:
    a. To what extent does the assessment provide opportunities for students to display their understanding?
    b. To what extent does the assessment encourage students to use disciplinary concepts and/or procedures of history?
2. Think and write about the process of grading:
    a. What was difficult? Easy? Did anything help you in this task? Explain.
    b. What knowledge or understandings did you call upon? What knowledge did you need that you did not have?
    c. About what were you most confident? About what were you least confident?
    d. What problems did you face? How did you solve those problems?
3. Finally, candidates read a scholar of practice (e.g., Monte-Sano, 2012) and reflect on how the scholarship supported, extended, or challenged their understanding of the experience.

Step 3: Class Discussion and Analysis of Teacher Candidates' Work.

Assigned to small groups, candidates talk about the experience with their classmates focusing on what they found easy or difficult about this work, what they were most confident and least confident about in evaluating these papers, and how their grade distributions compare.

In whole class discussion, we surface and record candidates' responses and graph their grading profiles. Given the way we designed the samples, we very often end up with a distribution that looks something like this:

	A	B	C	D/F
Student #1	0	5	14	1
Student #2	1	11	8	0
Student #3	18	2	0	0
Student #4	0	2	6	12

We then use the graph as a point of discussion:

1. Justification of grading decisions: Having volunteers explain and justify their grading decisions enables us to raise issues that the candidates generally confront in the activity such as the challenge of designing rubrics, moving from rubrics to letter or number grades, weighting of different variables, and most obviously discrepancies and consistencies among different evaluators.

2. Adding student "biographies" to the discussion: A tension in evaluating student work is the degree to which grades reflect a universal standard, an objective application of the rubric, or a relative standard reflecting a student's growth. Since candidates do not know the students whose papers they graded, we offer a bio of one or two to raise the question of objective or relative grade. For example, Student #4 is repeating the course. He rarely turns in papers, which made the fact that he completed this assignment (the longest he has completed) a rarity. The paper, however, looks more like a set of notes, has an error of fact or two, and the grammar is problematic throughout. With this information, we have the candidates re-read the essay to see if they would change the grade and/or the comments.

3. Developing a concept of effective feedback: Finally, we turn to the written feedback candidates offered. We ask them to identify the features they think constitutes effective and ineffective feedback. Then, drawing on work of scholars of feedback (e.g., Hattie & Timberly, 2007; Sadler, 2010), we direct the candidates to consider the importance of helping their students recognize what quality on the task looks like and how a teacher's feedback might help a student improve (Hattie & Timberly, 2007). Candidates read each other's comments and discuss the potential impact on students by focusing on specificity, tone, and timeliness. The discussion ends with candidates developing a set of key characteristics for effective feedback.

Step 4: Following-up by Building on the Activity

Sometimes we have candidates exchange the set of papers with a peer and then use the newly formed criteria to evaluate the feedback created by their classmates. At other times, we have candidates investigate the incentives teachers use to stimulate their students to use feedback to improve performance, such as mastery learning. We make sure they have access to research on feedback, particularly that of Carol Dweck (1999, 2007).

Assessing the Task: In addition to sharpening candidates' understanding of effective and ineffective feedback, one of the most valuable outcomes of this task is the way it makes visible and explicit a critical component of the work of teaching. Candidates have been on the receiving end of grades and feedback, but few, if any, have ever been responsible for grading papers and giving feedback to students. Therefore, we look for indications that candidates can identify the features of grading and responding to student work that make this task of teaching so important. Typically, we use class discussion and candidates' informal reflections to assess how successful the activity has been in accomplishing this goal. In addition, we are attentive to candidates' subsequent use of the criteria they generated on effective feedback, often to praise or criticize their mentor teachers.

CANDIDATES AND THE TASK

Teacher candidates tend to enjoy this task immensely, likely stemming from the sense that they are doing the real work of teaching. Most begin the activity with strong views on the value of giving grades and feedback; the activity allows them to test and extend their ideas with others, including the scholarly community. Dweck's (1999, 2007) articles, in particular, have helped students both problematize and rethink what they had learned about grading and feedback informally through their long apprenticeship of grading and feedback observations. In end of course evaluations, candidates often identify her pieces as something to which they intend to refer later.

The activity also underscores ideas and practices candidates encounter in our use of backward design. With little experience in planning and enacting instruction, they have little understanding of the problems of practice. This task plunges candidates into one of those problems—grading. In their struggles, candidates recognize the importance of learning goals, assess where they are in relationship to those goals, and then figure out ways to narrow the gap. In doing so, they recognize the value *for teachers,* as well as for students, of having a clear and concise rubric that articulates levels or progressions of quality.

THE TASK IN CONTEXT

We use this task in the latter third of the course, once teacher candidates have had time practicing unit planning with Understanding by Design (including designing assessments as part of that process) and implementing a range of particular instructional strategies. If candidates will be teaching as part of the course, as they do for us, then certainly this happens before they would grade any papers or projects.

REFERENCES

Dweck, C. S. (1999). Caution-Praise can be dangerous. *American Educator, 23*(1), 1–5.

Dweck, C. S. (2007). Perils and promises of praise. *Educational Leadership, 65*, 34–39.

Hattie, J., & Timberly, H. (2007). The power of feedback. *Review of Educational Research, 77*(1), 81–112.

Monte-Sano, C. (2012). What makes a good history essay? Assessing historical aspects of argumentative writing. *Social Education, 76*(6), 294–298.

Sadler, D. R. (2010). Beyond feedback: Developing student capability in complex appraisal. *Assessment & Evaluation in Higher Education, 35*(5), 535–550.

CHAPTER 17

THE OBJECT OF THE EXERCISE

Increasing the Role of Museums in the Social Studies Classroom

Jill M. Gradwell and Kathryn H. Leacock

Name: Jill M. Gradwell and Kathryn H. Leacock	Audience: Undergraduate and graduate students
Affiliation: SUNY Buffalo State and Buffalo Museum of Science	Length: 45 minutes
Course Title: Teaching with Historic Places; Teaching Social Studies; Theory, Research, and Practice in Elementary Social Studies Education	Commonplace featured: Teachers and Teaching
NCSS Teacher Education Standards: Element 1a. Candidates are knowledgeable about the concepts, facts, and tools, in civics, economics, geography, history, and the social/behavioral sciences. Element 2b. Candidates plan learning sequences that engage learners with disciplinary concepts, facts, and tools from the social studies disciplines to facilitate learning for civic life.	

Teaching Social Studies: A Methods Book for Methods Teachers,
pages 97–103.

TASK SUMMARY

The task introduces teacher candidates to the value of using artifacts as a means of illustrating socioeconomic status, historical narratives, cultural associations and personal stories both inside and outside the classroom.

DESCRIPTION OF THE TASK

"Artifacts...three-dimensional additions to the pages of history."

—*Ivor Noel Hume, Archaeologist*

The *Object of the Exercise* task focuses on artifacts as evidence and provides teacher candidates with another tool in their arsenals. The realization that field trip funds are dwindling does not mean that museums and artifacts are eliminated from the curriculum. Instead, candidates can utilize the skills learned in museums and translate them to the classroom. Object-based learning can be engaging and informative and it need not be confined to traditional museum field trips.

Through this task, candidates a) learn to "read" three-dimensional objects as evidence, b) realize that museums, historical agencies, and landmarks have value, and c) develop skills to develop a winning field trip proposal.

The Task: To open up the dialogue and begin to frame the lesson, candidates talk about their favorite museum and why focusing on questions such as were these experiences during their formative or professional years and what the difference is. After describing their perspectives, candidates share if they have used museums in a professional capacity and what motivated them to do so. They typically mention that the purpose of the field trip was to raise student interest, support the curriculum, or for students to see the "real" objects in support of classroom discussion.

The introductory discussion is followed by a modeling activity aimed at discerning the role of the object in the social studies classroom. We distribute different color photographs of an artifact to each candidates or group of candidates depending on the class size.

Once they have had a chance to review their image, we pose the following questions:

- What do you think the artifact is?
- What is its physical description?
- What is its intended use?
- Can you make any inferences about the use, status, or value attributed to the piece?
- What evidence do you have to support your inferences?
- What resources would you utilize to find out more?

After 5–10 minutes of artifact analysis, candidates share their inferences and any challenges they faced during the exercise. We point out that P–12 students face the same types of limitations when they engage with a two-dimensional textbook. We note the added dimension of a tangible object provides the opportunity for making memories alongside content acquisition.

We then bring out the actual artifacts. After the reveal, candidates revisit their initial analyses and discuss the benefits and challenges of having actual artifacts from which to work. If candidates do not mention it, we propose that, if they cannot bring the artifacts into the classroom, perhaps they should bring the classroom to the artifacts.

Thanks to the increased flow of information in the digital age, candidates are often overwhelmed with offerings for classroom enhancement. How do you make the case for museums? Researchers have long known the beneficial impact of field trips and artifact analysis on students' learning (Falk & Dierking, 2013; Paris, 2002; Rosenzweig & Thelen, 2000). This task aims to motivate candidates to see the value in object-based learning and out-of-classroom instruction. The modeling activity stimulates interest and generates the desire to embark on the laborious task of developing a successful proposal based on meaningful objectives.

Framed in a format borrowed from the late-night television host David Letterman, we then share "The Top Ten Teacher Considerations for Planning a Field Trip," a list of ideas to be used to make the case for museum visits. (See Appendix)

As a culminating task, candidates select a museum to visit and determine how it complements a social studies topic they may teach in the P–12 classroom. Based on their visit and a comprehensive review of the museum's offerings and website, they write a detailed 3–5 page museum field trip proposal justifying to the Board of Education the importance of the excursion, requesting permission, and securing funding for the experience. The readings relevant to this task include Kenna and Russell (2015), Marcus (2007), and Noel and Colopy (2006).

The field trip proposal should include:

- field trip destination
- justification
- educational purpose
- alignment to Common Core and/or NYS Social Studies Framework
- learning experiences prior to, during, and after the field trip
- detailed itinerary
- time allotment
- activities
- student selection guidelines
- cost
- potential funding sources.

Assessing the Task: The field trip proposal is assessed based on the rubric below. Beyond the in-class grading and assessment, the overall goal is that candidates submit their proposals to the Board of Education in hopes of their acceptance.

Museum Field Trip Proposal Rubric

Assessment Criteria	Value
Field trip destination with address	1
Justification of the chosen site	1
Educational purpose of the field trip	2
Alignment to Common Core and/or NYS Social Studies Framework	1
Learning experiences prior to field trip	3
Learning experiences during the field trip	3
Learning experiences after the field trip	3
Detailed itinerary	1
Student selection guidelines	1
Cost	1
Potential funding sources	1
Good mechanics: Spelling, grammar and punctuation	2
Total Points	**20**

CANDIDATES AND THE TASK

When teacher candidates view the photographs of the artifacts, some immediately think they know what the artifact is and complete the handout quickly. Others express frustration over being limited to an image rather than the real artifact; they make statements like, "this is unnerving," "I want to know what it is," and "I've never seen anything like this before." With time to analyze the artifacts, the follow-up discussion about the limitations of using two-dimensional representations, issues of scale, static view, and an inability to feel the object is often stimulating and animated.

When candidates are finally able to hold the artifacts, they display a variety of responses. Some find humor around their initial ideas, while others express shock that they miscalculated the artifact altogether. Candidates are often surprised by the size, weight, and material composition of the artifact. Purposely, we photograph the artifacts in ways that obscure their size or physical features. For example, most students' initial analysis of a photograph of a 19th-century wooden doll cradle against a plain black background, suggests they are looking at a human baby cradle. After seeing the actual object, they discover it is much too small to hold a real baby. Another artifact students often have trouble with is a sock darner. In the photograph, it looks like a Mexican maraca. Once they hold the actual artifact and shake it, they discover it is made of solid wood.

Asked about limitations of using actual artifacts, candidates discuss the feasibility (e.g., fragility, expense, and availability) of using artifacts. To combat these limitations, candidates offer ideas that include using artifact reproduction companies, scouring garage sales and flea markets, and borrowing museum artifact kits.

In a separate, on-going course assessment, candidates keep a reflective journal. Excerpts like the following suggest the power of the exercise:

> The activity with the artifacts was also very revealing to me. It made me realize how difficult it is to decipher items without knowing anything about them other than what they look like. It was really cool though to be able to see and hold these items, some of which were made and used long ago or in other places in the world. I think it adds a whole new level of authenticity to history when students can actually hold an item to observe it rather than have to see it in a picture. The picture misled a lot of us into thinking the objects were much different in reality. I always knew that museums were valuable for field trips, but I never really considered the possibility of bringing part of the museum into the classroom.

THE TASK IN CONTEXT

The task may occur at any point in the class when there is a focus on the use of artifacts in the classroom and the potential of field trips enhancing classroom instruction. We sometimes use it to complement an upcoming field trip the class is taking.

APPENDIX

10. Never assume

    Do not assume that the financial resources are unavailable for you to take a field trip. There are many third parties willing to support school visitation and oftentimes these groups are looking for strong school-museum partnerships. Prolonged engagement with a school district is attractive to funders.

9. BFFs

    Make friends. School Boards and administrators are more likely to fund a trip that can meet multiple learning goals and standards. Find ways to market your project within the school to encourage an interdisciplinary approach. When teachers from disparate disciplines come together to propose a field trip, there is strength in numbers.

8. Don't Reinvent the Wheel

    We are all faced with reduced resources and increasing workloads. Rather than develop a unique project, reach out to your local museum or cultural organization and see what materials they have available to strengthen your case. Most museums have already created curriculum for school-age populations. Find out what offerings are already in place and adapt them to your specific needs.

7. What you see is not always what you get

Teachers are often unaware that a museum will, within reason, cater to their needs. It is a misconception that all a museum has to offer is what is on view in the galleries. The opportunities for utilizing a cultural organization are boundless. Go beyond the self-guided tour and consider behind the scenes tours, pathways, workshops, and thematic programming.

6. Bang for your buck

Find out ways for school groups to get the most for their limited budget. District-wide contracts are one solution to responsible fiscal management. Determine what pre and post materials are available that make the experience more than an out of classroom experience for the students.

5. Send in the Marines

Before crafting any field trip proposal, always visit the site first. Museums often allow teachers free entrance visits to meet with the educator and view the facilities. Ask logistical questions about bus parking, lunchroom space, restroom locations, onsite expertise, and exhibition offerings.

4. Scavenger hunts suck!

Students running around the museum trying to "find" things does not work for anyone. Hunt and find does not translate to an engaging experience. The only thing students are engaged with is their paper, their pencil and a race against their classmates to find the answer first. To truly continue the lesson about reading artifacts as evidence, be thoughtful in the deliverables expected from a field trip experience.

3. Virtual Reality

In your planning for your field trip, consider ways you might utilize the museum website to prepare the students for their visit. In recent years, museums have updated their websites to include virtual field trips and other types of online educational activities. While this is no substitute, it is another layer to enhance the goals of the lesson.

2. Take-out counter

The largest expense and obstacle for a school field trip is often bussing. Not only is there an associated cost involved in hiring the bus, but it also limits where you can go if they must return to the school by 1pm in order to start the end of day routine. Many museums have artifacts (and staff) that can travel. While not the same immersive experience, the interaction with the artifact can still occur within the confines of the classroom if all other opportunities have been exhausted.

1. If at first you don't succeed...
   Try, try, again. But for now, let's imagine this is the first time you are trying to plan a field trip for your class. As a culminating task you are going to select a museum to visit that complements a social studies topic you are focusing on in a class and create a field trip proposal.

REFERENCES

Falk, J. F., & Dierking, L. D. (2013). *The museum experience revisited.* Walnut Creek, CA: Left Coast Press.

Kenna, J., & Russell, W. B. (2015). Tripping on the core: Utilizing field trips to enhance the Common Core. *Social Studies Research and Practice, 10*(2), 96–110.

Marcus, A. (2007). Representing the past and reflecting the present: Museums, memorials, and the secondary history classroom. *Social Studies, 98*(3), 105–110.

Noel, A. M., & Colopy, M. A. (2006). Making history field trips meaningful: Teachers' and site educators' perspectives on teaching materials. *Theory and Research in Social Education, 34*(4), 553–568.

Paris, S. (2002). *Multiple perspectives on object-centered learning.* Mahwah, NJ: Lawrence Erlbaum Associates.

Rosenzweig, R., & Thelen, D. (2000). *The presence of the past: Popular uses of history in American life.* New York: Columbia University Press.

CHAPTER 18

CULTIVATING AMBITIOUS PRACTICES

An Interdisciplinary Methods Model

Kevin W. Meuwissen and Jayne C. Lammers

Names: Kevin W. Meuwissen and Jayne C. Lammers	Audience: Graduate students
Affiliation: University of Rochester	Length: Semester long
Course Title: Implementing Innovations in Social Studies and English Language Arts Education	Commonplace Featured: Teachers and Teaching
NCSS Teacher Education Standard: Standard 3. Candidates design and implement instruction and authentic assessments.	

Teaching Social Studies: A Methods Book for Methods Teachers,
pages 105–110.
Copyright © 2017 by Information Age Publishing

TASK SUMMARY

The *Cultivating Ambitious Practices* (CAP) model for interdisciplinary methods courses is less a task than a framework for advancing high-leverage teaching practices via two-week cycles of design, enactment, analysis, and reflection.

DESCRIPTION OF THE TASK

Our conversations about shared aims in teacher education led us to develop an interdisciplinary methods course—the second in a two-course sequence—for teacher candidates in our social studies and ELA teacher education programs. We have two overarching goals: (1) to expand dialogues about learning, teaching, and their inherent dilemmas (Grossman, Wineburg, & Woolworth, 2001); and (2) to help candidates adapt the theoretical and practical foundations from their initial domain-specific methods courses to specific instructional activities in their fields. To select those instructional activities, we drew from the growing base of scholarship on high-leverage teaching practices, which allow novice teachers to better understand how students learn, reveal the complexities of disciplinary thought and activity, are warranted by research, and can be enacted across curricular contexts (Grossman, Hammerness, & McDonald, 2009).

Two questions emerged from our decision to focus on high-leverage teaching practices: what specific practices we would emphasize, and how we would structure our candidates' study and enactment of those practices. For the first question, we delved into our respective literatures on teaching in search of practices that are well represented and are shared across domains. We settled on five focal practices, all characterized as high-leverage by the University of Michigan TeachingWorks Collaborative (2016): (1) facilitating cooperative small-group work; (2) leading classroom discussions; (3) eliciting, interpreting, and identifying patterns in students' thinking; (4) looking together at and evaluating student work; and (5) providing meaningful feedback to students. For the second question, we constructed the CAP Model using five "cycles for collaboratively learning to engage in…ambitious instructional activity" (McDonald, Kazemi, & Kavanagh, 2013, p. 382). Each cycle concentrates on one focal practice and takes two weeks to implement.

The Task: The cycle begins with a reminder of how the model works. The first week consists of two phases—introducing and learning about how to lead discussions via modeling and authentic video representations, then preparing for and rehearsing the practice before trying it in the field. The second week requires a cross-disciplinary pair to present their practices to class for analysis, critique, and reflection. (See Appendix A for the CAP model graphic.)

We initiate phase one by modeling a discussion about discussion, asking students to read and prepare to talk about five articles that elucidate the qualities and challenges of classroom discourse in social studies and ELA. (See Appendix B.) First, we identify several purposes of classroom discussion, drawn from the work of Bridges (1979), Alvermann (2000), and Parker (2003). Next, we facilitate a whole-class, seminar-style discussion addressing five questions: (1) what are common characteristics of good discussions; (2) what conditions tend to endanger good discussions; (3) how might discussions in social studies and ELA classrooms be different and why; (4) what distinguishes seminar-style discussions from deliberative discussions; and (5) how do the qualities of discussion just identified link to the purposes articulated by Bridges, Alvermann, and Parker? From this discussion, we generate a list of discussion components to use throughout this CAP cycle. Afterward, we ask candidates to meta-analyze our conversation—in other words, to use its outcomes to assess the effectiveness of our efforts to facilitate it.

Next, we show two video exemplars of seminar-style and deliberative classroom discussions, asking candidates to identify enactments of the attributes they generated earlier and then assess consequences of those attributes. Using think-pair-share, candidates: (1) observe and consider how the exemplars facilitate or hinder discussions; (2) pair up across subject areas to talk about their observations and implications of the teachers' approaches; and (3) share results of their conversations with the class. This step involves looking at discussion analytically by identifying small-grain, constituent practices that candidates can build into their instruction.

Phase two of week one—preparing for and rehearsing the practice—involves modifying an existing discussion-intensive lesson plan to reflect what candidates learned during the first phase. These changes can take two forms: (1) generating new instructional tools or scaffolds grounded in the characteristics of good discussions and/or (2) revising elements of the lesson plan that are underdeveloped or inconsistent with those characteristics. Past examples of candidates' modifications include clear expectations for discussion preparation, text adaptations to make them more accessible for discussion, and explicit norms for conducting discussion. During this phase, we work flexibly with individuals, pairs, or small groups of candidates to improve their lessons. The class closes with a share-out of progress and an opportunity for week two's facilitators to clarify expectations for the CAP cycle's third and fourth phases and to solicit ideas and resources from instructors and colleagues that might help them implement their lessons.

Although we begin week two of the CAP Model with another reminder of how phases three and four work, its fulfillment largely depends upon the modes and artifacts of enactment the presenting pair chooses to bring in (e.g., videos or transcripts of their teaching) and how the pair structures our analysis of and reflection on those modes and artifacts. We find it incredibly important for course instructors to reinforce purposes and procedures associated with the CAP Model during each two-week cycle, and to demonstrate a complete cycle with candidates at the outset of the course, before relinquishing responsibility for the second week. Past variations among candidates' efforts to enact and analyze the practice of leading discussions include:

- Cora (social studies) and Shaun (ELA) show video clips that focus on pressing students for coherent explanations and mediating disagreements during discussions, with Cora's video recorded before and Shaun's recorded after the CAP cycle's introduction and preparation phases. For analysis, they ask their colleagues to compare and contrast the practices of each teacher using criteria elucidated during the first week, then to propose instructional and classroom-environmental adjustments.
- Angelo (social studies) and Hannah (ELA) bring in several artifacts (e.g., pre-discussion readings and instructions, codes of conduct, video of their teaching) related to deliberative discussions. They organize these artifacts into three stations—"preparing for discussion," "establishing norms for discussion," and "interacting during discussion"—and ask colleagues to analyze how certain kinds of participation are encouraged or discouraged through the artifacts. Afterward, Angelo and Hannah synthesize the station work into a whole-class conversation about how to make discussion more inclusive and equitable.

Assessing the Task: In keeping with the CAP model, the final phase includes collective assessment of the enacted practice qualities and impacts, with all candidates evaluating what they learned and considering how they might strengthen future implementation of the practice. We then step out of the cycle meta-analytically to compare and contrast multiple cycles' benefits and challenges, with an eye toward enhancing the processes of representing, preparing, and rehearsing for, enacting, and reflecting on high-leverage practices in social studies and ELA. Finally, we write qualitative assessments of each pair's performance during week two, providing feedback on three tasks—demonstrating enactment, generating critical analysis, and envisioning future practice—and a summative evaluation of their work's effectiveness in light of the CAP model goals.

CANDIDATES AND THE TASK

At the beginning of the methods course, there tends to be some confusion about the CAP model's implementation trajectory, as teacher candidates are not accustomed to its design. However, via multiple iterations of CAP cycles and regular conversations about the cycles' internal consistencies and intended outcomes, candidates pick up on the model relatively quickly. By the second or third cycle, they generally handle the enactment and analysis phases powerfully and independently.

Course evaluations over several iterations reveal some important candidate response patterns. First, most appreciate the opportunity to work with teachers across subject matter domains, emphasizing the interdisciplinary potential of shared efforts to bolster literacy, writing, and classroom discussion, and common interests in drawing upon students' social and cultural resources for teaching. Second, candidates find the CAP model powerful for parsing out, fine-tuning, and studying the consequences of practices that they initially perceive of as much larger in grain size. For example, the cycle we described above inevitably leads teachers to see facilitating class discussion as containing numerous contingent practices, including asking powerful, open-ended questions, scaffolding larger-group conversations via small-group preparation, and pushing students to connect new ideas to past claims and relevant texts.

THE TASK IN CONTEXT

The CAP model's promise for systematically making social studies and ELA teaching practices visible, dissectible, applicable, and improvable also offers potential to adapt it to various teacher education contexts. Specifically, the model can be modified to focus on different domains, from history to cross-disciplinary science and civic education collaborations; and it can accommodate many high-leverage teaching practices, from building positive and productive interpersonal relationships to assessing students' disciplinary thinking. We use multiple cycles of the model as our interdisciplinary instructional framework because of the synergy it facilitates as teacher candidates from both programs co-construct pedagogical knowledge and practices that they will use throughout their careers.

APPENDIX A

AM1. Graphic representation of the CAP Model, adapted from McDonald, Kazemi, and Kavanagh (2013)

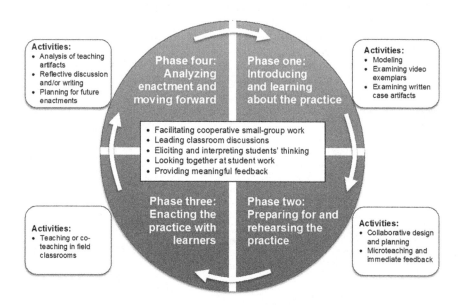

APPENDIX B

Texts about Class Discussions in Social Studies and ELA.

Hess, D. E. (2004). Discussion in social studies: Is it worth the trouble? *Social Education, 68*, 151–157.

Johannessen, L. (2003). Strategies for initiating authentic discussion. *The English Journal, 93*, 73–79.

Lee, C. D. (2004). Literacy in the academic disciplines and the needs of adolescent struggling readers. *Voices in Urban Education, 3*, 14–25.

Parker, W. C. (2001). Classroom discussion: Models for leading seminars and deliberations. *Social Education, 65*, 111–117.

Styslinger, M. E., & Pollock, T. (2010). The chicken and the egg: Inviting response and talk through Socratic circles. *Voices From the Middle, 18*(2), 36–45.

REFERENCES

Alvermann, D. E. (2000). Classroom talk about texts: Is it dear, cheap, or a bargain at any price? In B. M. Taylor, M. F. Graves, & P. van den Broek (Eds.), *Reading and meaning: Fostering reading comprehension in the middle grades* (pp. 136–151). New York: Teachers College Press.

Bridges, D. (1979). *Education, democracy, and discussion.* Windsor, UK: National Foundation for Educational Research.

Grossman, P., Hammerness, K., & McDonald, M. (2009). Redefining teaching, re-imagining teacher education. *Teachers and Teaching: Theory and Practice, 15*, 273–289.

Grossman, P., Wineburg, S., & Woolworth, S. (2001). Toward a theory of teacher community. *Teachers College Record, 103*, 942–1012.

McDonald, M., Kazemi, E., & Kavanagh, S. S. (2013). Core practices and pedagogies of teacher education a call for a common language and collective activity. *Journal of Teacher Education, 64*, 378–386.

Parker, W. C. (2003). *Teaching democracy: Unity and diversity in public life.* New York: Teachers College Press.

University of Michigan TeachingWorks Collaborative (2016). *High-leverage practices.* Ann Arbor, MI: TeachingWorks. Retrieved from http://www.teachingworks.org/work-of-teaching/high-leverage-practices.

CHAPTER 19

CONSTRUCTING RATIONALES TO TEACH CONTROVERSIAL ISSUES

Thomas Misco

Name: Thomas Misco	Audience: Undergraduate students
Affiliation: Miami University	Length: Paper
Course Title: Secondary Social Studies Methods I	Commonplace featured: Teachers and Teaching
NCSS Teacher Education Standard: Element 4c. Candidates engage learners in ethical reasoning to deliberate social, political, and economic issues, communicate conclusions, and take informed action toward achieving a more inclusive and equitable society.	

Teaching Social Studies: A Methods Book for Methods Teachers,
pages 111–114.

TASK SUMMARY

The *Constructing Rationales* paper assignment asks teacher candidates to explicate, analyze, and discuss a range of scholarly work in order to develop a one-page rationale for teaching controversial issues that can be easily disseminated.

DESCRIPTION OF THE TASK

The work of developing tolerant, reflective, and engaged democratic citizens hinges upon the full release and discussion of controversial issues in the classroom (Misco & De Groof, 2014). A teacher candidate fortified with a strong philosophical rationale for teaching about controversial issues and armed with appropriate instructional strategies and curriculum within a supportive context is positioned to develop understandings of nuanced normative issues and confront prejudices. Every free society struggles with this most critical and foundational educative enterprise. Moreover, controversial issues evolve. They often come into being as taboo, develop into topics for discussion inside and outside of classrooms, and ultimately become settled (Hess, 2009). Stakeholders in different contexts may view the current controversial state of an issue differently and it is incumbent upon candidates to apply judgment in their gatekeeping decisions about controversial issue inclusion. Yet, even with a provocative curriculum, eager students, and well-prepared candidates poised to confront controversy, the milieus can act as obstacles to opening and discussing closed areas (Misco, 2012).

Schwab (1973) referred to "the milieus" as the school, classroom, and relations of students to each other. The relations of students to subgroups, students to structures of authority, teachers to educational leaders, as well as student to student, teacher to student, and teacher to teacher all help shape not only what is taught, but how it is taught. Other relevant milieus include the "family, community, the particular groupings of religious, class or ethnic genus" (p. 367) and the aspirations of these groups. Milieus also include the relations of groups and individuals within town, city, country, and locale as "represented in miniature" by the students of each genus (p. 367). Many of these milieus are preferred idea purveyors, desirous of students developing views similar to their own, ultimately undermining a marketplace of ideas as a barrier to the discussion of controversy.

The Task: In response to the imperative of teaching controversial issues and the potential barriers within milieus, I assign readings within a paradigm of curricular instructional gatekeeping. It is the teacher as a "curricular-instructional gatekeeper" who makes the "day-to-day decisions concerning both the subject matter and the experiences to which students have access" (Thornton, 1991, p. 237) and determines which criteria are used to make those decisions. Of particular note is that the explication, analysis, and discussion process is predicated on candidates recognizing the value in broaching controversies as a part of citizenship education. Ultimately, how candidates frame issues, context, and interpretation of events, ideologies, and power relations (Camicia, 2008) helps to inform the degree to which an issue can be considered not only controversial but also worthy of attention in a particular classroom, at a particular time and place.

The *Constructing Rationales* task asks candidates to prepare a succinct rationale (one page, single-spaced) that they can hand to students, parents, administrators, or other stakeholders who might question the exploration of controversial topics and issues in their future classrooms. Candidates read empirical studies on controversial issue instruction and provide an explication, analysis, and discussion. I also encourage candidates to employ additional justifications (e.g., connection of topics to the U.S. constitution) and other course readings to aid in their rationale papers. Finally, candidates practice verbally articulating why they have chosen to address controversial issues in their classroom through role-playing events within the methods classroom. My hope is that this particular assignment leads to more controversial issue discussions in their future classrooms, not only from fortification and clarification of rationale, but also as a prophylactic defensive mechanism prepared in advance for any individuals from the milieu who question such curriculum and instruction.

Suggested readings that I provide for candidates include:

Byford, J., Lennon, S., & Russell, W. (2009). Teaching controversial issues in the social studies: A research study of high school teachers. *The Clearing House, 82*(4), 165–170.

Camicia, S. P. (2008). Deciding what is a controversial issue: A case study of social studies curriculum controversy. *Theory & Research in Social Education, 36*(4), 298–316.

Hahn, C. L., & Tocci, C. M. (1990). Classroom climate and controversial issues discussion: A five nation study. *Theory and Research in Social Education, 18*(4), 344–362.

Hess, D. E. (2002). Discussing controversial public issues in secondary social studies classrooms: Learning from skilled teachers. *Theory & Research in Social Education, 30*(1), 10–41.

Hess, D., & Posselt, J. (2002). How high school students experience and learn from the discussion of controversial public issues. *Journal of Curriculum and Supervision, 17*(4), 283–314.

Journell, W. (2011). Teachers' controversial issue decisions related to race, gender, and religion during the 2008 presidential election. *Theory & Research in Social Education, 39*(3), 348–392.

Kelly, T. E. (1986). Discussing controversial issues: Four perspectives on the teacher's role. *Theory & Research in Social Education, 14*(2), 113–138.

Misco, T. (2012). The importance of context for teaching controversial issues in international settings. *International Education, 42*(1), 69–84.

Misco, T., & Patterson, N. C. (2007). A study of pre-service teachers' conceptualizations of academic freedom and controversial issues. *Theory & Research in Social Education, 35*(4), 520–550.

Washington, E., & Humphries, E. (2011). A social studies teacher's sense making of controversial issues discussions of race in a predominantly white, rural high school classroom. *Theory & Research in Social Education, 39*(1), 92–114.

Assessing the Task: I assess the rationale papers on the breadth of sources employed and the clarity of explication, analysis, and discussion. Each paper should offer compelling and coherent justifications for teaching controversial issues.

CANDIDATES AND THE TASK

On occasion, teacher candidates suggest that social studies education *should be* social science education, or even history education, with a focus primarily on disciplinary knowledge rather than engaging social injustice and contested normative issues. In these cases, there may be some resistance to the assignment, but these candidates are also those who resist the foundational axioms upon which the field rests.

THE TASK IN CONTEXT

This assignment occurs at the end of the first of two semesters of secondary social studies methods. At this point in the course, most teacher candidates have already developed substantive rationales for democratic citizenship education.

REFERENCES

Camicia, S. P. (2008). Deciding what is a controversial issue: A case study of social studies curriculum controversy. *Theory and Research in Social Education, 36*(4), 298–316.

Hess, D. (2009). *Controversy in the classroom: The democratic power of discussion.* New York: Routledge.

Misco, T. (2012). The importance of context for teaching controversial issues in international settings. *International Education, 42*(1), 69–84.

Misco, T., & De Groof, J. (2014). *Cross-cultural case studies of teaching controversial issues: Pathways and challenges to democratic citizenship education.* Oisterwijk, The Netherlands: Wolf Legal Publishers.

Schwab, J. J. (1973). The practical: Translation into curriculum. In I. Westbury & N. J. Wilkof (Eds.), *Science, curriculum, and liberal education.* Chicago, IL: University of Chicago Press.

Thornton, S. J. (1991). Teacher as curricular-instructional gatekeeper in social studies. In J. P. Shaver (Ed.), *Handbook of research on social studies teaching and learning* (pp. 237–248). New York: Macmillan.

CHAPTER 20

ANTICIPATING SOCIAL STUDIES CONTENT

Kari Muente, Timothy Lintner, and Darren Minarik

Name: Kari Muente, Timothy Lintner, and Darren Minarik	Audience: Undergraduate and Graduate Students
Affiliation: University of Missouri University of South Carolina Aiken Radford University	Length: Semester-long
Course Title: Teaching Social Studies in the Middle/Secondary School	Commonplace featured: Teachers and Teaching
NCSS Teacher Education Standard: Element 3b. Candidates design coherent and relevant learning experiences that engage learners in disciplinary knowledge, inquiry, and forms of representation for competence in civic life and demonstrate alignment with state-required content standards.	

Teaching Social Studies: A Methods Book for Methods Teachers,
pages 115–119.
Copyright © 2017 by Information Age Publishing
All rights of reproduction in any form reserved.

TASK SUMMARY

Teacher candidates learn how to create a Framing Routine, an anticipation guide that serve as both a prereading strategy and a way to activate prior knowledge and focus students on the new content to be learned (Kozen, Murray, & Windell, 2006).

DESCRIPTION OF THE TASK

With increasing numbers of students with diverse learning needs accessing content in general education classrooms (U.S. Department of Education, 2013), it is imperative that teacher candidates have the knowledge, skills, and dispositions to teach social studies to all students. Yet many students enter social studies classrooms with deficits in organizational efficiency and the often concomitant inability to engage with text in substantive, meaningful ways (Bulgren, Deshler, & Lenz, 2007).

To assist teacher candidates in designing instruction to meet the learning needs of all students, the University of Kansas Center for Research on Learning developed Content Enhancement Routines (CERs). CERs encourage flexibility in the way candidates plan, teach, and assess core content knowledge, including social studies. CERs support three main instructional objectives:

- They ensure that the adequate prior knowledge needed in the content area is already present, or they provide the scaffolding to help students acquire the critical facts, concepts, vocabulary, principles, procedures, and propositions that represent foundational knowledge.
- They facilitate the transformation or manipulation of two or more pieces of information through categorizing, comparing and contrasting, exploring causation, inquiring into critical questions, evaluating options and claims, or making decisions.
- They provide mechanisms for knowledge generalization, which involves predicting, inferring, problem-solving, or synthesizing information into a main idea that can be used in a variety of situations (Bulgren, Deshler, & Lenz, 2007, p. 123).

CERs serve as excellent tools for developing structured and creative anticipation guides to support and enhance both organizational and literacy skills. One particularly effective CER preservice teachers can use to support the learning needs of diverse learners is the Framing Routine (see Appendix). The Framing Routine is an evidence-based graphic organizer developed by Ellis (1998) to provide organization and structure to content and to visually demonstrate relationships between pieces of information.

The Task: When developing a Frame as an anticipation guide, the candidate identifies a key topic and one or more main ideas based on the content to be addressed. Then content is placed on the Frame that is "a mixture of true, false, essential, and nonessential details pertaining to each of the main ideas" (Ellis, 1998, p. 36). Students might first work individually to examine the statements and determine and indicate if the statement is a true essential piece of information (TE), a true, but trivial or non-essential piece of information (TT), or false information (F) (Ellis, 1998). The candidate then pairs up students to share their individual responses and discuss why they may have coded certain statements differently. This Think, Pair, Share model of cooperative learning creates a more accessible and inclusive environment for students who struggle with the content due to their reading and comprehension challenges. A well-structured model of cooperative learning creates a supportive environment that reduces the risk of struggling readers being stigmatized by their peers.

The Frame anticipation guide is introduced to candidates during their social studies methods course and follows a three-step process, moving from introduction to Frame construction and ending in classroom application.

Introduction: To introduce preservice educators to the Frame anticipation guide, we initially model the step-by-step process of constructing a completed guide. Candidates need to see how each part of the anticipation guide serves a unique purpose yet is also inter-dependently designed to produce specific outcomes (organizational efficiency, critical analysis, and enhanced literacy skills).

Construction: With our assistance/feedback, candidates choose a topic and construct their own completed anticipation guide. The topics should be based on the curriculum candidates anticipate teaching in a K–12 social studies classroom.

Application: Using their constructed Frame, candidates incorporate a completed guide into their social studies instruction.

Assessing the Task: Candidates are assessed in two ways: (1) their ability to construct a Frame anticipation guide: and (2) their ability to incorporate—and ultimately teach with—an anticipation guide in a K–12 social studies classroom.

In the construction phase, the objective is to assure the fidelity of both the process and the product of the Frame. The structural design of the Frame is linear. This linearity moves learners through different phases of understanding (e.g. topic construction, main ideas, synthesizing statement). Each phase builds up and complements the other. It is important that candidates understand this conceptual hierarchical design before they select the curriculum to teach.

With a Frame in hand, candidates need to embed it into their instruction. We observe the embedded lesson and provide targeted feedback as to how well the guide enhanced students' organizational efficiency, critical analysis, and literacy skills. Upon lesson completion, candidates provide a reflective analysis focusing on their pedagogical ability (How well did I use the anticipation guide?) and student outcome (How well, and in what measurable ways, did my students respond to it?)

CANDIDATES AND THE TASK

Teacher candidates find the Frame theoretically easy to understand in terms of its overall purpose and function. Challenges come with Frame construction. Some struggle with how to scaffold the Frame to ensure student understanding. Part of this struggle comes with identifying the key concepts to include in the Frame. Candidates have a difficult time creating four to six statements that challenge preconceived ideas or false understandings relevant to the content being addressed. Yet once these challenges are mitigated, candidates find that embedding a Frame within social studies instruction leads to an increase in student understanding, note-taking, and study skills.

The ability of candidates to successfully instruct with the Frame hinges on exposure. Candidates need to be placed in classrooms in which the Frame is routinely used and where they have many opportunities to use the Frame within their own instruction. Candidates who were introduced to the Frame in their methods course and consistently use it during their field-based instruction report being far more comfortable and confident in their ability to design engaging, relevant, and targeted social studies instruction.

Though the Frame is a relatively simple tool to enhance the social studies understanding of all students, it should not be seen as the only tool in which to do so. Candidates need multiple instructional strategies at their disposal that are specifically designed with diverse learners in mind (Minarik & Lintner, 2016). The Frame is but one such strategy. By constructing—and ultimately instructing with—the Frame anticipation guide, candidates may be better positioned to meet the learning needs of all students in the social studies classroom.

THE TASK IN CONTEXT

During the typical semester-long social studies methods course, both Frame introduction and construction are covered in the same 2–3-hour block of time, often early in the term (within the first three weeks). Frame application typically takes place later in the terms (by the 10th week or so). This schedule allows teacher candidates several weeks to observe and assist students they will ultimately teach. Candidates are required to teach at least one social studies lesson using their designed Frame.

Key Topic

Major Civil Rights Movements in American Society

is about ...

The impact a non-violent demonstration, like the *March on Washington*, had in advancing the Civil Rights Movement's goals towards social and legislative changes on equality and desegregation.

Main idea

The March on Washington

Main idea

Dr. King's "I have a dream" Speech

- Referred to as the *"March on Washington for Jobs and Freedom,"* this event's aim was to call national attention to the injustice and inequalities African Americans faced.

- The *March on Washington* is the largest Civil Rights demonstration in the history of the U.S.

- Civil Rights activist Malcolm X was a vocal supporter of this event.

- *The March on Washington's* peaceful demonstration paved the way for both the ratification of the 24th Amendment to the U.S. Constitution and the Civil Rights Act of 1964.

- Dr. King's speech was influenced by Lincoln's *Gettysburg Address.*

- Dr. King uses the phrase "promises of democracy" as not being fulfilled due to segregation laws, and inequality amongst individuals based on sex, color, religion or creed.

- Dr. King's speech reinforced his commitment to nonviolent protests.

- In his speech, Dr. King makes specific reference to the signing of the *Declaration of Independence.*

So what? What is important to understand about this?

When society comes together to fight injustice, nonviolent demonstrations can inspire social and legislative changes.

FIGURE 20.1. Example of a Frame Anticipation Guide

REFERENCES

Bulgren, J., Deshler, D. D., & Lenz, K. B. (2007). Engaging adolescents with LD in higher order thinking about history concepts using integrated content enhancement routines. *Journal of Learning Disabilities, 40*(2), 121–133.

Ellis, E. S. (1998). *The content enhancement series: The framing routine.* Lawrence, KS: Edge Enterprises.

Kozen, A. A., Murray, R. K., & Windell, I. (2006). Increasing all students' chance to achieve using and adapting anticipation guides with middle school learners. *Intervention in School and Clinic, 41*(4), 195–200.

Minarik, D., & Lintner, T. (2016). *Social studies and exceptional learners.* NCSS Bulletin 115. Silver Springs, MD: National Council for the Social Studies.

United States Department of Education. (2013). *35th annual report to Congress on the implementation of the Individuals with Disabilities Education Act.* Retrieved from http://www2.ed.gov/about/reports/annual/osep/2013/parts-b-c/35th-idea-arc.pdf

PART 3

SUBJECT MATTER

CHAPTER 21

LEARNING TO CROSSWALK

Horizon Content Knowledge in Economics

Cheryl A. Ayers

Name: Cheryl A. Ayers	Audience: Undergraduate and graduate students
Affiliation: University of Virginia and Virginia Tech	Length: Two class periods
Course Title: Economics for Educators	Commonplace Featured: Subject Matter
NCSS Teacher Education Standard: Element 4e. Candidates facilitate collaborative, interdisciplinary learning environments in which learners use disciplinary facts, concepts, and tools, engage in disciplinary inquiry, and create disciplinary forms of representation	

.

Teaching Social Studies: A Methods Book for Methods Teachers,
pages 123–130.
Copyright © 2017 by Information Age Publishing

TASK SUMMARY

The *Horizon Content Knowledge in Economics (HCK-E) Crosswalk* assignment provides an opportunity for teacher candidates to critically think about the interdisciplinary nature of social studies learning standards in preparation for effective economic instruction.

DESCRIPTION OF THE TASK

A component of pedagogical content knowledge (PCK), horizon content knowledge is a teacher's understanding of how the knowledge and skills of a particular discipline relate to other subjects and grades across the K–12 curriculum (Ball, Thames, & Phelps, 2008). The Horizon Content Knowledge in Economics (HCK-E) Crosswalk assignment is designed to develop teacher candidates' HCK-E as a prerequisite to meeting the objectives of the *College, Career, and Civic Life (C3) Framework* (National Council for the Social Studies, 2013). High school graduates who develop the interdisciplinary knowledge, skills, and perspectives needed for an increasingly complex world and economy will be better-prepared change agents as democratic citizens and problem-solvers in 21st-century careers.

Secondary social studies teachers are often ill-equipped to promote such cross-curricular, higher-order thinking in students because methods courses often limit coverage of interdisciplinary instructional practices in general and economic instructional practices in particular (Joshi & Marri, 2006). Subsequently, the integration of economic concepts into other social studies subjects is often inaccurate and incomplete (Miller & VanFossen, 2008). Researchers suggest that interdisciplinary economic instruction is most effective when teachers thoughtfully and explicitly incorporate economic concepts into other social studies subjects rather than mention economics as an afterthought or side note (Schug & Niederjohn, 2008). It was these findings that inspired the creation of the HCK-E Crosswalk assignment, an adaptable learning activity that easily and efficiently integrates into regular social studies methods courses.

The Task: The HCK-E Crosswalk serves as the preliminary planning phase for writing and delivering thoughtful and effective interdisciplinary economic lessons. The additional components (i.e., intradisciplinary economic concepts and skills, real-world student relevance, and economic misconceptions) are also important aspects of PCK in economics and should be included in the assignment. (See the Appendix for an example of an HCK-E Crosswalk.)

The first and second columns of the HCK-E Crosswalk state the economic concept or skill under exploration and the corresponding learning standards from the required Virginia *Economics and Personal Finance* course (instructors in other states may want to use their state standards or the *Voluntary National Content Standards in Economics*). The third column features state standards from at least two other social studies subjects in Grades 6–12 that highlight an interdisciplinary connection to the economic content in the first two columns. Since many candidates are likely unfamiliar with the standards in their state, they should use the search function within the history, geography, and civics/government standards documents to find where the economic concept or skill is integrated. If no interdisciplinary connections are found, candidates should choose a different economic concept or skill and conduct another shared terminology word search or challenge themselves to identify a place in the standards where economic content integration might occur. To assure a legitimate understanding of the connection between the economics and the other social studies standards, candidates should consult the details of the curriculum frameworks. This extra step requires them to review social studies content that they learned in previous coursework.

The next step is helping candidates brainstorm how their newfound curriculum connections might form the basis of an interdisciplinary lesson. The lesson description should encompass key ideas from all of the standards listed and is a way for candidates to assess disciplinary knowledge and skills as well as interdisciplinary curriculum connections. Pedagogical strategies are less important at this stage.

The Intradisciplinary Economic Concepts and Skills column provides a space for candidates to list more complex economic concepts and skills that build on the basic economic concepts, skills, and standards described in the first two columns. This exercise has multiple benefits. First, candidates become familiar with the inherently interdependent nature of economic content. Second, understanding the interdependence of economic concepts and skills helps candidates activate students' prior knowledge and to ground their conceptual understandings in real-world economic experiences. Third, intradisciplinary economic instruction helps prevent the teaching of economic concepts and skills in isolation (Ayers, under review). To identify intradisciplinary economic content, candidates should conduct keyword searches using basic economic concepts (e.g., resources) within state or national learning standards and curriculum frameworks in economics in the same way they found interdisciplinary connections.

The last two columns of the HCK-E Crosswalk promote an aspect of PCK that Ball et al. (2008) call Knowledge of Content and Candidates—that is, how disciplinary knowledge intersects with knowledge of student learning and development. The Real-World Candidate Relevance column reflects excerpts from the Student Relevance Journal. Completed throughout the semester, this journal lists economic concepts and skills on the left side of a T-chart and corresponding connections to current events, students' daily lives, and future citizenship responsibilities on the right side. These examples are interspersed throughout the descriptions and benchmarks from the *Voluntary National Content Standards in Economics* and serve as an introduction to culturally relevant teaching practices (Ladson-Billings, 1995) in economic education.

The Economic Misconceptions column anticipates ways in which students struggle to learn new economic content by identifying potential stumbling blocks of inaccurate and incomplete prior knowledge in economics. After my interdisciplinary economic lesson demonstrations, candidates read two practitioner-friendly articles that explicate common economic misconceptions of secondary students and remedial instructional practices (Baumann, 1996–1997; Schug & Baumann, 1991) and create an Economic Misconceptions Tip Sheet that informs the last column of the HCK-E Crosswalk. The descriptions and benchmarks of the *Voluntary National Content Standards in Economics* are also helpful in identifying common economic misconceptions.

I pair candidates from different disciplinary backgrounds and levels of teaching experience to expedite the learning curve in completing the HCK-E Crosswalk, to facilitate a more holistic conceptualization of the various disciplines in social studies education, and to encourage interdisciplinary lesson planning. Candidate pairs exchange the HCK-E Crosswalk for peer review, then revise accordingly before it is submitted for a grade and shared on Google Docs for all candidates to add to their Economic Instructional Resources binders.

CANDIDATES AND THE TASK

In a self-study on the Economics for Educators course, I found that most teacher candidates initially struggled to make interdisciplinary connections between economics and other social studies subjects (Ayers, 2016). As one candidate described, "picking a subject that was not economics in order to teach economics was a hard concept for me. At first I did not see how this was possible" (p. 81). The ease of making interdisciplinary connections often depended on the candidates' level of content knowledge in the various social studies subjects. Asked about the challenges of integrating economics and geography standards, another candidate claimed, "[it] was harder than I thought it would be, granted geography is not one of my specialties, something I should work on" (p. 81). By the end of the semester, candidates had discovered a vast array of interdisciplinary connections because of the highly versatile and life-applicable nature of economics content. In reference to her interdisciplinary lesson that combined economics and history concepts, a third candidate succinctly captured the overarching goal of the HCK-E project: "I felt that it really brought together what could've been considered two separate lessons on economics and history into an easily understandable activity that really encompassed and presented concepts for both disciplines" (p. 82).

TASK IN CONTEXT

The HCK-E Crosswalk assignment occurs midway through the course after the teacher candidates' basic understanding of HCK-E is scaffolded by my modeling of HCK-E in action and the candidates' written critiques of interdisciplinary economic lessons. Candidates also read the chapter (Ellington, 2011) to spark interest in the interdisciplinary nature of economics as it pertains to major historical events. Following the HCK-E Crosswalk assignment, candidates collaboratively write and deliver interdisciplinary economic lessons that are videotaped and analyzed by classmates and myself as well as a guided self-reflection exercise.

APPENDIX: HORIZON CONTENT KNOWLEDGE IN ECONOMICS (HCK-E) CROSSWALK

Economic Concepts and Skills	Economics and Personal Finance Standards	History, Geography, and Civics/Government Standards	Intradisciplinary Economic Concepts and Skills	Real-world Candidate Relevance	Economic Misconceptions
Capital Investments	(Standard 2) The candidate will demonstrate knowledge of the role of producers and consumers in a market economy by (g) examining how investment in human capital, capital goods, and technology can improve productivity; and (f) describing how increased productivity affects costs of production and standard of living.	**World History I** (Standard 6) The candidate will demonstrate knowledge of ancient Rome from about 700 B.C. (B.C.E.) to 500 A.D. (C.E.) in terms of its impact on Western civilization by (j) listing contributions in art and architecture, technology and science, medicine, literature and history, language, religious institutions, and law. **World History II** (Standard 6) The candidate will demonstrate knowledge of scientific, political, economic, and religious changes during the sixteenth, seventeenth, and eighteenth centuries by (f) describing the expansion of the arts, philosophy, literature, and new technology. **World Geography** (Standard 2) The candidate will analyze how selected physical and ecological processes shape the Earth's surface by (c) explaining how technology affects one's ability to modify the environment and adapt to it. **Virginia and United States History** (Standard 8) The candidate will demonstrate knowledge of how the nation grew and changed from the end of Reconstruction through the early twentieth century by (b) describing the transformation of the American economy from a primarily agrarian to a modern industrial economy and identifying major inventions that improved life in the United States.	circular flow of economic activity, price, supply determinants, income, incentives, entrepreneurship, economic growth, gross domestic product (GDP)	Candidates who invest in human capital after high school (e.g., attend college or a trade school) are often more productive and earn higher incomes. Higher incomes afford increased economic freedom and choices. Certain occupations in the future will experience an increase in job openings while other occupations will experience a decline in job openings due to advances in technology.	Capital goods are man-made resources used over and over in production. In economics, capital goods do not include money or intermediate goods used in the production process (e.g., nails, flour). The price of labor, a person's salary is often set by the supply and demand for his or her human capital. There is no such thing as a "free lunch" because resources have alternative uses.

(continues)

Economic Concepts and Skills	Economics and Personal Finance Standards	History, Geography, and Civics/Government Standards	Intradisciplinary Economic Concepts and Skills	Real-world Candidate Relevance	Economic Misconceptions
		Virginia and United States Government (Standard 14) The candidate will demonstrate knowledge of economic systems by (e) examining productivity and the standard of living as measured by key economic indicators.			

Curriculum Connections: An interdisciplinary economic lesson on capital investments might…start by showing pictures of technological advances from ancient Rome and around the world during the 16th – 20th centuries and discussing the impact (i.e., costs and benefits) on productivity and daily life. A similar analysis of modern-day investments in technological advances might follow.

Economic Concepts and Skills	Economics and Personal Finance Standards	History, Geography, and Civics/Government Standards	Intradisciplinary Economic Concepts and Skills	Real-world Candidate Relevance	Economic Misconceptions
Cost-Benefit Analysis	(Standard 1) The candidate will demonstrate knowledge of basic economic concepts and structures by (c) describing how effective decision making requires comparing the additional costs (marginal costs) and additional benefits (marginal benefits).	**United States History II** (Standard 1) **Virginia and United States History** (Standard 1) The candidate will demonstrate skills for historical and geographical analysis and responsible citizenship, including the ability to (i) identify the costs and benefits of specific choices made, including the consequences, both intended and unintended, of the decisions and how people and nations responded to positive and negative incentives. **Civics and Economics** (Standard 1) **Virginia and United States Government** (Standard 1) The candidate will develop [then "demonstrate mastery of" in Government] the social studies skills responsible citizenship requires, including the ability to (f) identify a problem, weigh the expected costs and benefits and possible consequences of proposed solutions, and recommend solutions, using a decision-making model.	scarcity, resources, decision-making models, alternatives, criteria, opportunity cost, trade-offs, incentives, economic systems (command, market, and traditional), voluntary exchange, intended and unintended consequences	Candidates need to weigh costs and benefits when making decisions about cars, computers, cell phones, careers, higher education, insurance, housing, savings, health care, retirement, politicians, economic policy proposals, controversial issues, etc.	Economic systems influence individual and collective incentives and decisions. Intended and unintended consequences of decisions lie in the future. Opportunity cost is the second best alternative not chosen when making a decision.

Curriculum Connections: An interdisciplinary economic lesson on cost-benefit analysis might…provide candidates the opportunity to gain a deeper understanding of history and citizenship responsibilities by identifying and evaluating the costs and benefits of events and decisions made in the past (e.g., Westward Expansion, American Revolution, Civil War, WWI & II, Amendments to the Constitution) and present (e.g., globalization, trade, foreign aid, election process, political candidates, conservative and liberal public policy proposals on immigration), including an assessment of who benefits and who bears the costs.

REFERENCES

Ayers, C. A. (under review). A first step toward a practice-based theory of pedagogical content knowledge in secondary economics. *Journal of Social Studies Research.*

Ayers, C. A. (2016). Developing preservice and inservice teachers' pedagogical content in economics. *Social Studies Research and Practice, 11*(1), 73–92.

Ball, D. L., Thames, M. H., & Phelps, G. (2008). Content knowledge for teaching: What makes it special? *Journal of Teacher Education, 59*(5), 389–407.

Baumann, E. K. (1996–1997). High school candidates' misrepresentations of basic economic concepts. *International Journal of Social Education, 11*(2), 91–104.

Ellington, L. (2011). Economics and history: What every high school candidate and teacher needs to know. In M. C. Schug & W. C. Wood (Eds.), *Teaching economics in troubled times: Theory and practice for secondary social studies* (pp. 200–212). New York, NY: Routledge.

Joshi, P., & Marri, A. R. (2006). An economics methods course? Challenges of teaching an economics education methods course for secondary social studies candidate. *The Social Studies, 97*(5), 197–202.

Ladson-Billings, G. (1995). Toward a theory of culturally relevant pedagogy. *American Educational Research Journal, 32*(3), 465–491.

Miller, S. L., & VanFossen, P. J. (2008). Recent research on the teaching and learning of pre-collegiate economics. In L. S. Levstik & C. A. Tyson (Eds.), *Handbook of research in social studies education* (pp. 284–304). New York, NY: Routledge.

National Council for the Social Studies. (2013). *The college, career, and civic life (C3) framework for social studies state standards: Guidance for enhancing the rigor of K–12 civics, economics, geography, and history.* Silver Spring, MD: Author.

Schug, M., & Baumann, E. (1991). Strategies to correct high school candidates' misunderstanding of economics. *The Social Studies, 82*(2), 62–66.

Schug, M., & Niederjohn, M. (2008). Can candidates learn economics in U. S. history? *The Journal of Private Enterprise, 23*(2), 167–176.

CHAPTER 22

MAPS AND APPS FOR RESPONSIBLE CONSUMER LITERACY

Jason Harshman

Name: Jason Harshman	Audience: Undergraduate students
Affiliation: University of Iowa	Length: Two class sessions
Course Title: Middle/Secondary Social Studies Methods	Commonplace featured: Subject Matter
NCSS Teacher Education Standard: Elements 1a-c. Candidates demonstrate knowledge of social studies disciplines. Candidates are knowledgeable of disciplinary facts, concepts, and tools; structures of inquiry; and forms of representation.	

Teaching Social Studies: A Methods Book for Methods Teachers,
pages 131–136.

TASK SUMMARY

This consumer and spatial literacy activity incorporates mobile technology and place-based learning for teacher candidates to examine issues of ethics, access, and privilege related to consumerism in a global economy.

DESCRIPTION OF THE TASK

The question driving this activity is: How does the intersection of civics, place, and economics affect your agency as a citizen, consumer, and educator? By moving away from abstract activities related to budgeting and opportunity costs that assume access and food security, teacher candidates ask critical questions about capitalism and geography and their roles as citizen educators responsible for reducing and teaching about food insecurity and consumer literacy.

The Task: My course is framed by the question: How will you teach about social (in)justice for informed active citizenship in the social studies? Candidates answer the question multiple times throughout the course using readings and strategy discussions on topics such as civil rights, global education, human rights, gender, indigenous perspectives, and labor and socio-economic status. They read Kumashiro's (2009) *Against Common Sense* and work with the Freedom Schools curriculum to interrogate issues of power, culture, and injustice in society and schools (Radical Teacher, 1964/1990). Candidates compare the Freedom Schools curriculum with the Iowa social studies curriculum to identify spaces where more diverse perspectives can be included to promote critical thinking and action in alignment with Dimensions 3 and 4 of the C3 Inquiry Arc (National Council for the Social Studies, 2013).

Candidates complete a scavenger hunt based on food products they consider to be the staples of their diet in advance of the scheduled class discussions during the last third of the course. For each of the twelve items they select, teachers use the Good Guide, Ethical Barcode, and Human Rights Education (HRE) Buy4Equality apps to scan the barcode of the food items to learn more about the companies that manufacture the products. They record the information in a table available through Google docs.

The classroom discussion begins with candidates' experiences of place and capitalism in relationship to teaching about social (in)justice. They work with Dimension 2 of the C3 content standards to make connections between the activity and the concepts they would teach around geography and economics. Candidates then divide into groups to participate in a station activity that focuses on issues of race, class, gender, mobility, access, transportation, global connections, and other topics that emerge from their analyses.

One station asks candidates to use Google maps to plot local food access and evaluate issues related affordability, transportation, and equity. They identify four places where one can purchase food (excluding restaurants) in the immediate area and plot them on a Google map. Candidates examine housing data to learn about redlining, property values, and discuss why food access and security is higher in some parts of the city than in others. Using the C3 standards and the Iowa standards for geography and economics, candidates compile a list of vocabulary terms and concepts related to the station. Collectively, the class generates a standards-based list that can be used with their future students.

Another station is organized around the question "would you like a piece of chocolate?" Here, candidates debate free trade and fair trade, as well as human rights issues related to the production of chocolate. Thinking of the candy bars provided at the station as texts—one is labeled free trade, one is labeled fair trade, one is labeled "Rain Forest Alliance Certified" and one is labeled as having less sugar—prompts further investigation of these texts. This activity models how to develop questions for inquiry (Dimension 1 of the C3 Inquiry Arc) while providing space to discuss the pros and cons of free and fair trade policies. This station incorporates a global perspective as candidates investigate how free and fair trade impact labor and human rights in countries where cocoa is harvested. This station also places candidates in a decision-making scenario regarding how they can incorporate what they learn about trade, human rights, and consumerism into their own purchasing and consumption of chocolate, coffee, tea, and clothing.

At a third station, candidates work with maps and state data related to hunger, poverty, and free and reduced lunches to learn about food access and food insecurity. Organized around the idea of reducing food insecurity, in this station candidates create proposals to reduce hunger as a way to model how their students might fulfill the civic action element of Dimension 4 of the C3 Inquiry Arc.

The second-class session dedicated to debriefing the consumer activity focuses on the products the candidates created during the first session and how the materials they created through the stations fulfill the C3 and Iowa social studies standards. Candidates also discuss the technology components used outside and inside the classroom and their ideas for engaging students in Dimensions 3 and 4 of the C3 Inquiry Arc and taking action toward reducing food insecurity in the state. Their analysis of the Inquiry Arc serves the purpose of modeling the creativity and sequencing of learning activities they create on a topic of their own choosing by the conclusion of the course.

Assessing the Task: I assess candidates on the following artifacts: 1) responses to the reflection questions posed during the scavenger hunt; 2) connections between the concepts and skills utilized during the station activities to the C3 and Iowa standards for economics, geography, and civics; and 3) connections between the concepts and experiences investigated locally and through supplemental texts to teaching for social justice in the social studies in their own lesson sequence projects for the course.

CANDIDATES AND THE TASK

In addition to being apprehensive about teaching economics, many teacher candidates subsist on a fixed budget that requires them to consider affordability and perhaps health value, rather than the ethics and the labor rights of others. As one candidate shared, "I try to eat as healthy as possible, but often I cannot afford to buy healthier food. But now, I realize that my wanting to be healthy may also have a negative effect on someone because I am supporting a company that does not make the well-being of employees, but only profit, a priority."

This lesson activity offers candidates an opportunity to learn about concepts, vocabulary, and topics related to economics education while working with the standards to inform what they design as part of the stations activity. This activity also provides opportunities for candidates to incorporate local connections to their students' lives so that social justice education is not marginalized in an economics course. As a candidate reflected on the stations activities, "we do economics, capitalism, every day, but teaching it seems so hard. I feel like I spent two days talking about economic issues that students also do, but do not consider to be economics. I think we can make economics more interesting and meaningful."

Candidates see potential to incorporate these reflective exercises within their own classrooms and recognize how they can play a role in holding corporations accountable through their decisions as citizens and consumers. This activity provides them with opportunities to address all four dimensions of the C3 Inquiry Arc, make connections to local and global issues, and engage in creative tasks that can be applied across multiple content areas within social studies education.

THE TASK IN CONTEXT

Recognizing that capitalism permeates many aspects of their lives outside of the classroom, teacher candidates must go beyond a financial literacy curriculum that promotes consumerism without critical thinking (Sandlin, 2005). The consumer spatial literacy activity involves time out of the classroom to collect information on one's current consumer practices and then two class sessions to investigate and debrief the relationship between the activity and the C3 Inquiry Arc, Common Core State Standards, and social justice education in the social studies (Harshman, 2015).

APPENDIX

Reflection Questions:

1. How did time and place factor into your decision-making?
2. How did financial (in)security factor into your decision-making?
3. How did information gathered through use of the mobile apps factor into your decision-making?

4. How would you work with students to take informed and sustainable action for change related to one aspect (production, distribution, access, labor rights, civil rights, etc.) of the activity you completed?

TABLE 22.1.   Sample of the Station Activities Used

Station Topic	Discussion Questions and Key Vocabulary/Concepts	Relevant CCSS and C3 Content Standards
Mapping Local Food Access & Equity	• Based on your knowledge of the city and what you learned from the Equity & Economics apps, label 4 places on the map that you can go to purchase groceries. • Discuss your decision-making regarding health, affordability, and sustainability with regard to purchasing habits and preferences. • Discuss the relevant vocabulary terms and the social conditions related to the places identified on the map. • Vocabulary and Concepts used: access, capitalism, disposable income, divided, globalization, health conscious, inequity, inequality, interconnected, living wage, mobility, opportunity costs, poverty, privilege, responsibility, scarcity, segregation, sustainability, transportation, unjust, value/values.	**C3** D2.Geo.2.9-12. Use maps, satellite images, photographs, and other representations to explain relationships between the locations of places and regions and their political, cultural, and economic dynamics. **CCSS** CCSS.ELA-Literacy.RH.9-10.4 Determine the meaning of words and phrases as they are used in a text, including vocabulary describing political, social, or economic aspects of history/social science. CCSS.ELA-Literacy.RH.9-10.7 Integrate quantitative or technical analysis (e.g., charts, research data) with qualitative analysis in print or digital text.
Would you like a piece of chocolate?	• Choose either one square from a free or fair trade candy bar or two candy bars from the bag of Hershey's. Which one did you choose and why? • Thinking of the candy bars as texts, what questions would you investigate to learn more about the candy bars? *(For example, what does it mean to be Rainforest Alliance Certified?).* • Candidates design and record the questions they would ask to learn more about the texts (i.e. candy bars). No group can repeat an already recorded question.	**C3** D2.Eco.14.9-12. Analyze the role of comparative advantage in international trade of goods and services. **CCSS** CCSS.ELA-Literacy.RH.9-10.1 Cite specific textual evidence to support analysis of primary and secondary sources, attending to such features as the date and origin of the information

REFERENCES

Harshman, J. (2015). Developing a critical consumer literacy in social studies teacher education. *Oregon Journal for the Social Studies, 3*(2), 58–71.

Kumashiro, K. (2009). *Against common sense: Teaching and learning toward social justice.* London: Routledge.

Mississippi Freedom School Curriculum-1964. (1991). *The Radical Teacher, 40*, 6–34.

National Council for the Social Studies (NCSS). (2013). *The college, career, and civic life (C3)framework for social studies state standards: Guidance for enhancing the rigor of K–12 civics, economics, geography, and history.* Silver Spring, MD: Author.

Sandlin, J. (2005). Culture, consumption, and adult education: Refashioning consumer education for adults as a political site for using a cultural studies framework. *Adult Education Quarterly, 55*(3), 165–181.

CHAPTER 23

HISTORY AS LIVED AND LOCAL

Jennifer Hauver

Name: Jennifer Hauver	Audience: Undergraduate and graduate students
Affiliation: University of Georgia	Length: Six weeks
Course Title: Teaching History	Commonplace featured: Subject Matter
NCSS Teacher Education Standard: Element 1a. Candidates are knowledgeable about the concepts, facts, and tools in civics, economics, geography, history, and the social/behavioral sciences	

Teaching Social Studies: A Methods Book for Methods Teachers,
pages 137–141.
Copyright © 2017 by Information Age Publishing
All rights of reproduction in any form reserved.

TASK SUMMARY

Teacher candidates interview family or community members about their experiences of an historical event/period as a way of thinking about history as lived and local.

DESCRIPTION OF THE TASK

The purpose of the *Oral History Assignment* is three-fold: (1) to help teacher candidates understand that individuals make sense of history in unique ways that are reflective of their experiences, (2) to deepen candidates' understanding of the historical moments they select, and (3) to grow candidates' appreciation of local and personal history as a means of making history relevant and meaningful to their students.

The Task: When I introduce the assignment, I explain that candidates should identify someone outside of class to interview about an event in U.S. history. The person interviewed should have a particular interest in/experience with the historical topic/event chosen. Thus, typically the event is either local and/or has occurred within the last 75 years. Occasionally, candidates interview someone about an event that happened earlier and thus reply on family history or oral history as it was passed down over time. I ask candidates to identify someone who is likely to have had different experiences or hold different understandings of the event chosen than they have.

Candidates are expected to choose an event that is part of what is considered to be the grand narrative of U.S. history. They should seek out an alternative point of view (or at least a personal point of view) on an event that is typically taught as part of the canon of U.S. history in our nation's schools. In this way, we can begin to see the complexity of history and reflect on the role of local and personal history in formal history education.

I ask candidates to read two chapters from Levstik and Barton's (2015) *Doing History* about personal and family history. These chapters offer concrete examples of how to help students think deeply about how the past shapes our understandings of the present and how to make larger historical narratives relevant and meaningful to students. We also read excerpts from Paul Thompson's (1978) book, *The Voice of the Past: Oral History*, paying particular attention to the appendix in which he includes a sample interview protocol. In class, we talk about the goals of our interviews and work together to generate a list of possible questions candidates might ask. Using Thompson's work as a guide, we discuss the importance of open-ended questions, following the interviewee's lead, and listening carefully so that we can ask helpful follow-up questions.

Candidates then prepare a proposal in which they explain why they chose the topic, what they know about it already, who they plan to interview, and how they expect their own knowledge of the subject to deepen as a result. They bring this proposal to class along with a draft list of questions, which they review with a small group of their peers. Candidates take notes on their proposals regarding peer feedback and the revisions they intend to make before submitting the proposal for grading.

After candidates have conducted their interviews, they submit a 5-7-page paper that includes:

1. a copy of the interview protocol (list of questions asked)
2. an introduction to the person interviewed, the topic, and the interview setting
3. a written synthesis (not complete summary) of what was shared by the interviewee
4. an analysis of the perspective shared as it compares to the candidates' perspectives and other perspectives they have encountered on this aspect of history
5. a reflection on what candidates have learned and how it may inform their teaching in the future

Assessing the Task: In order to assess candidates' progress, I rely primarily on their participation in the peer-review process, their proposals, and their final papers. In listening to and reading the feedback candidates offer one another, I get a sense of how well they understand the purpose of the assignment and how to develop open-ended questions. Reading candidates' proposals gives me an idea of their understanding of the topics they have chosen and what they hope to learn from their interviews. I spend a good amount of time reading candidates' final papers. It is here that I have an opportunity to assess their understanding of the particularistic nature of historical knowing, their willingness and ability to grow their understanding of the topic in light of what their interviewees shared, and the degree to which they see local and personal history as useful to history education broadly.

In grading, I look for evidence that candidates' papers:

- Include all required pieces
- Are well-written, free of grammatical errors, and coherent
- Demonstrate a willingness to learn from the experience and to consider alternate perspectives on the past
- Demonstrate an understanding of how our retellings of history may be shaped by our experience (past and present)
- Demonstrate a willingness to consider the practice and purpose of oral history for making history education relevant and meaningful
- Are thoughtful and reflective of one's experience of conducting history.

CANDIDATES AND THE TASK

I have taught this course many times. Each semester, teacher candidates point to this assignment as being the most powerful for shifting their thinking about history. Engaging in analysis and comparison of these local, lived retellings, candidates begin to ask critical questions about how we come to know history, what counts as official history and why, what role memory plays in history, and how we make sense of competing accounts about the past. I include here a few excerpts from Andrea's final paper as an example. Andrea interviewed her grandmother about her experience living through WWII. In this first excerpt, Andrea describes what her interview taught her about popular narratives of women's lives during this era:

> Her experiences as a woman during this time period differ from the popular narrative. Most treatment of the topic focuses on middle-class white women and their experiences as homemakers, specifically their deep dissatisfaction with "homemaker" being the only available role to them. Textbooks briefly describe the journey from Rosie the Riveters during WWII, to women being pushed back into the home, to those disgruntled women starting the women's movement to address their oppression, influenced by other social movements. If my grandmother were reading that synopsis, she wouldn't find herself in those lines....

Andrea goes on to explain why her grandmother's story stands in such contrast to the textbook:

> Her socio-economic context also explained her disconnect with feminists at the time. Not only were they wealthier, but they had also gone to college. "Nobody I knew was rich enough to go to college," she remarked. And so, my grandmother never had the intellectual space to explore subjects such as politics, philosophy, and even history that could have oriented her perspective to recognizing gender roles and female discrimination as a problem in society. In the end, it's not surprising that my grandmother could not relate to the feminist movement because her life was so fundamentally different from those women who participated.

Later, Andrea reflects on what she learned about history through doing this project, and how it will affect her teaching in the future:

> No matter how open-minded I considered myself, I was still not prepared for the contradictions in her account. History, as it is generally experienced in classrooms, has little use for complex, personal experiences of events and periods. But I found this project to be so rewarding and meaningful to my understanding of womanhood, feminism, and the history of women in this country in a way that I could not have found elsewhere.

> This assignment also undoubtedly affected the way I will teach this topic and others in history....At the very least, this project cemented the idea that it is necessary for students to study different perspectives, especially in a critical, hands-on way.

Otherwise, students are left with a naïve realist version of events, an idea that seems much more dangerous after attempting to fit my grandma's account into "the" history of the period.

THE TASK IN CONTEXT

I include this assignment in the first half of the semester as we are exploring the nature of history and how we come to know it. Leading up to and while candidates are engaged in this assignment, we read from texts written by Wineburg (2001), VanSledright (2008, 2011), Epstein (2009), and Barton and Levstik (2004). We also explore competing narratives about historical topics as mini-lessons that serve as context for thinking about authorship, perspective, and context as they relate to historical knowing.

REFERENCES

Barton, K., & Levstik, L. (2004). *Teaching history for the common good.* Mahwah, NJ: Taylor & Francis.

Epstein, T. (2009) *Interpreting national history: Race, identity, and pedagogy in classrooms and communities.* New York, NY: Routledge.

Levstik, L., & Barton, K. (2015). *Doing history: Investigating with children in elementary and middle schools* (5th edition). New York, NY: Routledge.

Thompson, P. (1978). *The voice of the past: Oral History.* Oxford, UK: Oxford University Press.

VanSledright, B. A. (2008). Narratives of nation-state, historical knowledge, and school history education. *Review of Research in Education, 32*(1), 109–146.

VanSledright, B. A. (2011). *The challenge of rethinking history education: On practices, theories and policy.* New York, NY: Routledge.

Wineburg, S. (2001). *Historical thinking and other unnatural acts: Charting the future of teaching the past.* Philadelphia, PA: Temple University Press.

CHAPTER 24

DOCUMENTING DEMOCRACY

The Digital Short Project

Todd S. Hawley

Name: Todd S. Hawley	Audience: Undergraduate Students
Affiliation: Kent State University	Length: Semester-long project
Course Title: Issues and Trends in Social Studies	Commonplace featured: Subject Matter
NCSS Teacher Education Standard: Element 2e. Candidates use theory and research to plan learning sequences that integrate social studies content, disciplinary sources, digital learning, and contemporary technologies to foster inquiry and civic competence.	

Teaching Social Studies: A Methods Book for Methods Teachers,
pages 143–146.
Copyright © 2017 by Information Age Publishing
All rights of reproduction in any form reserved.

TASK SUMMARY

The Digital Short Film Project positions teacher candidates to (re)consider their conceptions of democracy and democratic living by creating a digital short focused on answering the question, "what is democracy?"

DESCRIPTION OF THE TASK

The Digital Short Film project is designed to give teacher candidates, as democratic citizens and future social studies teachers, the opportunity to reflect on the meaning of democracy. The project challenges them to connect their definitions of democracy, their developing purposes for teaching social studies, and their thinking about what counts as subject matter in social studies. Given that the majority of our candidates enter this course with limited experience connecting social studies content with democratic living, the goal is to push them to make their new thinking visible in their digital shorts.

The Task: The Digital Short Film assignment is a semester-long project. Candidates work in groups of 2 or 3 to produce films that synthesize their learning in the course by returning to big ideas in the course readings, conducting interviews, by watching the news and paying attention to civic engagement in their local and university communities, and finding engaging and creative examples that they consider to be democracy in action. Candidates create 8 to 10 minute digital short films in a group; individually, they submit a two to three-page Director's Statement. In the Director's Statement, candidates discuss the following prompts: What did I learn about democracy? What did I learn about social studies content? How has working collaboratively helped and hindered this learning? and What did I take away from the experience that can help me develop into a powerful social studies teacher?

The course is framed around two books, Levinson's (2012) *No Citizen Left Behind* and Parker's (2003) *Teaching Democracy: Unity and Diversity in Public Life.* Throughout the semester students also read the Introduction and first chapter of Barr, Barth, and Shermis's (1977) *Defining the Social Studies,* Stanley's (2005), *Social Studies and the Social Order,* Westheimer and Kahn's (2004), *What Kind of Citizen?: The Politics of Educating for Democracy,* and Wheeler-Bell's (2014) *Educating the Spirit of Activism: A "Critical" Civic Education.* These readings push candidates to make connections between their definitions of democracy, their developing sense of purpose as a social studies teacher, and their developing sense of the relationship between social studies content and educating democratic citizens.

Groups are formed at our fourth class meeting. Candidates exchange contact information, review the project guidelines, and develop an initial plan of action. Groups review course readings and their discussion notes to reflect on their current thinking about connections between social studies content and education for democratic citizenship. Candidate groups have time during the 8th and 12th class meetings to work on the project. I encourage groups to develop a plan of action, and to use class time to enact their plan. I also encourage groups to network with other groups in class as a way to develop their thinking about social studies content and education for democratic citizenship. During the 12th week of class, the focus is on filming, editing, and finalizing the films.

At the end of the semester, we open up our classroom to the faculty, staff and students and have a Digital Shorts Film Festival. Many of the Digital Shorts feature on-campus interviews with students around campus and some students also interview their parents and siblings. In general, these interviews focus on how people define democracy. In addition, Digital Shorts have focused on protests held by student groups or faculty on campus. Finally, many of the digital shorts bring in current events that candidates feel reflect the status of American democracy. Doing so gives candidates an opportunity to present their work and to answer questions from their peers as well as other faculty in the Integrated Social Studies Teacher Education Program.

Assessing the Task: I assess the Digital Shorts project on the candidates' Director's Statements and on their presentations during the Film Festival using a rubric I co-design with the candidates. In the syllabus, I highlight the importance of candidates' ability to work collaboratively and to integrate their learning from the course readings, interviews, and experience watching the news and exploring the local community into their videos. These elements typically find their way into the assessment rubric along with a focus on the technical aspects of the project. This process gives candidates an opportunity to co-design a rubric and to learn how to assess collaboration and the various ways groups demonstrate their conceptions of democracy in action.

In addition to the rubric, candidates receive feedback from their peers on notecards following their Film Festival presentations. Feedback is encouraged, as are questions and suggestions for improvement. The cards are given to each group at the end of the Film Festival and candidates have time to discuss the comments on their cards and to discuss what they learned from the Digital Shorts project.

CANDIDATES AND THE TASK

As might be expected, initial responses about the Digital Short project range from uncertainty to excitement. That range typically reflects teacher candidates' experience creating digital films and their comfort with alternative forms of assessment. Jeremy (all names are pseudonyms) explained that he was excited because "I had experience making films and videos so I was excited when I saw the assignment." The majority of candidates, however, are not as excited and initially express some worry about the openness of the Digital Short Project. Sarah worried that she "wasn't very comfortable with the idea of doing something other than a paper." Despite varying levels of comfort with the idea of the project, most candidates enter the class with an unstructured definition of social studies and an even more uncertain about connections between social studies and education for democratic citizenship.

Through course discussion and engagement with the readings, candidates begin to refine their thinking about social studies and education for democratic citizenship. Most had never thought about social studies as something other than content and, as Amanda said, had "not spent a great deal of time trying to define democracy. That was new for me." To develop their Digital Shorts, candidates spent time reading, discussing, disagreeing, and collaborating with peers. For many, doing so meant thinking outside of their comfort zones. Robinson noted that he "never really talked to any of my family members about democracy or citizenship or anything really." Chris experienced significant stress while "attending the student protest about the Black Lives Matter Movement student protest." While interviewing protesters for his groups' digital short, Chris saw firsthand the protestors' passion and commitment for justice. Discussing these uncomfortable experiences made a little more sense when candidates presented their videos. As Sarah explained, "the Film Festival was great because we got to see how creative and funny everyone is." Although not all candidates found the experience to be engaging, the majority came away from the project with a deeper sense of the connections between social studies and education for democratic citizenship.

THE TASK IN CONTEXT

The Digital Short project is the culminating project in a course is for Integrated Social Studies majors who have not yet been admitted to Advanced Study. The majority of the candidates are sophomores who are also taking their required core coursework along with their required content-area courses. Given that most have a limited conception of the connections between teaching social studies and developing democratic citizens, the project is designed to make these connections more concrete.

REFERENCES

Barr, R. D., Barth, J. L., & Shermis, S. (1977). *Defining the social studies*. Washington, DC: The National Council for the Social Studies.

Levinson, M. (2012). *No citizen left behind*. Cambridge, MA: Harvard University Press.

Parker, W. C. (2003). *Teaching democracy: Unity and diversity in public life*. New York: Teachers College Press.

Stanley, W. B. (2005). Social studies and the social order: Transmission or transformation? *Social Education, 69*(5), 282–286.

Westheimer, J., & Kahn, J. (2004). What kind of citizen?: The politics of educating for democracy. *American Educational Research Journal, 41*(2), 237–269.

Wheeler-Bell, Q. (2014). Educating the spirit of activism: A "critical" civic education. *Educational Policy, 28*(3), 463–486.

CHAPTER 25

WHAT IS SIGNIFICANT?

Grappling with Pre-service Teacher Perceptions of Historical Significance and Subject Content Knowledge

Aaron Johnson, David Hicks, and Stephanie van Hover

Name: Aaron Johnson, David Hicks, Stephanie van Hover	Audience: Graduate students
Affiliation: University of Nebraska-Lincoln, Virginia Tech, University of Virginia	Length: One class period
Course Title: History and Social Science Methods	Commonplace featured: Subject Matter
NCSS Teacher Education Standard: Standard 1. Candidates demonstrate knowledge of social studies disciplines. Candidates are knowledgeable of disciplinary concepts, facts, and tools; structures of inquiry; and forms of representation.	

Teaching Social Studies: A Methods Book for Methods Teachers,
pages 147–151.
Copyright © 2017 by Information Age Publishing

TASK SUMMARY

The *Perceptions of Significance* activity challenges teacher candidates to identify and unpack "significant" topics/events/individuals and to begin to problematize positionalities and/or stations of privilege.

DESCRIPTION OF THE TASK

The *Perceptions of Significance* activity is grounded in the notion that teachers operate as primary "gatekeepers" over the day-to-day instructional choices and activities for candidates (Thornton, 1991). Extending the gatekeeper analogy to include teacher candidates, the activity captures curriculum decision making in situ through the specific exploration of the second-order concept historical significance. Historical significance, broadly, assigns value to what should be researched and written about by historians and by corollary what history should be learned in schools (Seixas & Morton, 2012). Further to the point, Seixas (1997) adds, "questions of curriculum selection, textbook construction, historical interpretation—the meaning of history itself—all hinge on the question of significance" (p. 27). Perceptions of historical significance, then, bear particular impact on the preparation of social studies teachers.

The primary goals for the activity are to:

- Recognize factors that influence teacher perceptions of historical significance including standards-based instruction within schools
- Assess the impact perceptions of historical significance may have on underrepresented populations within schools
- Consider avenues for developing diverse notions of historical significance that enhance classroom practice and candidate learning/development.

The Task: With these foci in mind, candidates list the top 10 individuals and the top 40 historical events they feel should be taught in United States history, world history, and government courses. Building from the work of Frisch (1989) and Wineburg and Monte-Sano (2008), we shift the conversation to include candidates for the purposes of probing their understanding of the concept of historical significance and its reach within standards-based settings. Prior to the start of the methods course, candidates receive the following email and supporting power-point based significance cards (see Appendix) that they are to complete and bring to class:

As a soon-to-be social studies teacher, this is a once-in-lifetime opportunity! *You* decide what should be taught! Think about teaching the following courses: United States history, world history, and government. For each course, please generate a list of the top 40 events/concepts/essential knowledge that you consider as vital for students to learn after they have taken these courses from you. In addition, please provide a brief rationale for each choice. Just brainstorm from the gut. Also, for each course, please identify a minimum of 10 key individuals who you think must be taught. Again, provide a rationale for their inclusion. In your rationales for each choice, explain not just why you think it should be included, but where and how you learned about the event or person. So give some provenance/contextual origins to your choices. Again do this quickly—just free-flowing thought and brainstorm away....Please bring your power-point historical significance cards (one slide/card for each event and/or person) to class. You will have a total of 50 cards for each of the three courses.

In class, candidates first display their top 40 events and top 10 individuals. They then compare and contrast their conceptions of essential content for each course and the provenance for their decisions across the cohort. Classroom space, essential for this activity, becomes a gallery-viewing environment where candidates can read and reflect on their colleagues' compilations. To enhance the experience and to encourage classroom dialogue, candidates consider the following questions:

- Where did your ideas come from?
- What overarching themes do you see connecting your events and individuals?
- Do you have sub-themes and how do these ideas connect?
- What do your lists tell us about the nature of history and government?

In the next step of the activity, candidates consider their choices and rationales within the context of Virginia's Standards for Learning (SOLs). Candidates receive the standards documents for middle and high school and compare the individuals and events they selected with those cited in the SOLs. Doing so, candidates begin to see how their views of historical significance reflect today's standardized educational climate through the extensive overlap of their perceptions of significance with that evident within the standards.

This realization sparks larger conversations regarding the impact of standards-based instruction on teaching and learning, but it also introduces an awareness of the final layer of the activity—recognition of whose history we value and see as significant and whose histories are too often omitted. Therefore, we then ask candidates to consider who or what is missing from their lists. It soon becomes evident that their lists typically reflect a white male, western-centric orientation, one that ignores the richness and diversity of current thinking in social studies and history education. To invite further introspection, we offer the words of Adrienne Rich (1986), who speaks directly to the casualties of selective/segregated representations of the past: "When someone with the authority of a teacher...describes the world and you are not in it, there is a moment of psychic disequilibrium, as if you looked into a mirror and saw nothing" (p. 199). We ask candidates, "what are the implications for classroom candidates who are not represented on your lists?" and "how can we design inquiry-based learning experiences that offer more nuanced and diverse understanding of the concept of historical significance in secondary level social studies classrooms?"

Assessing the Task: The *Perceptions of Significance* activity serves as an informal assessment in the sense that a numeric grade is not assigned the activity. The significance cards are, however, highly formative in nature and can serve as pre-assessment data that provide us with a unique glimpse into the instructional design thought processes of candidates at a formative period in their training. Revisiting the activity at selected points later within the semester invites continued dialogue and provides further support for a critical vision for historical significance—one that is inclusive in nature and represents the diversity within today's classrooms.

CANDIDATES AND THE TASK

Despite changing demographics, colleges and schools of education continue to be dominated by European-American teacher candidates whose lived experiences and cultural understandings do not reflect the diversity of the classrooms in which they teach (Patterson-Dilworth, 2004; Tyson, 2002). The *Perceptions of Significance* activity represents an entry point to begin conversations with teacher candidates about historical significance and whose history we value. To this end, one candidate noted:

> It is my personal goal to make sure my future students receive a multicultural education in which they learn and grow. I know this will be one of my biggest challenges as a teacher and I realize that I need to take self-check steps to ensure that I am including information from all cultures and not just my own. This activity showed me that I have the natural inclination to include "important" historical events as those that I relate with or that I have been taught. When asked to identify the top ten important figures and top forty important events in United States history I found that I only included one woman, no minorities, and most of the events were from the colonial era. And while I do not completely understand how my subconscious brain functions, I can attempt to explain this because my favorite aspect of history is the colonial era and within this time period, as well as many historical eras, the success of white men is stressed in school. I am by no means discounting the founding fathers and other iconic figures from back in the day, but I did not realize that if I taught what I thought of as "important" history that many of my students would not be able to relate. Knowing this now, I can recognize and improve.

THE TASK IN CONTEXT

The *Perceptions of Significance* activity is scheduled during the first methods class meeting in fall semester and revisited later as teacher candidates accrue further classroom experience in their practicum and student teaching placements. The iterative nature of the activity encourages continued development and refinement of candidates' professional dispositions toward and their critical introspection around curriculum and practice prior to their transition into the role of classroom teacher.

APPENDIX: EXAMPLE OF CANDIDATE SIGNIFICANCE CARDS

Top 10 US figures

Rationale for inclusion:

He was the first President of the United States. His choice to step down after 8 years began a long history of peaceful succession. In early US history courses in school, we are bombarded with stories of his heroism.

- **George Washington**
- **Date(s): 1732-1799**

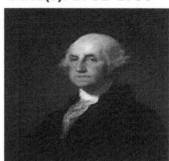

REFERENCES

Frisch, M. (1989). American history and the structures of collective memory: A modest exercise in empirical iconography. *Journal of American History, 75*(4), 1130–1155.

Patterson-Dilworth, P. (2004). Multicultural citizenship education: Case studies from social studies classrooms. *Theory & Research in Social Education, 32*(2), 153–186.

Rich, A. (1986). Invisibility in academe. In *Blood, bread and poetry: Selected prose 1979–1985* (p. 199). New York: Norton.

Seixas, P. (1997). Mapping the terrain of historical significance. *Social Education, 61*(1), 22–27.

Seixas, P., & Morton, T. (2012) *The big six historical thinking concepts.* Scarborough, Ontario: Nelson Education.

Thornton, S. J. (1991). Teacher as curricular-instructional gatekeeper in social studies. In J. P. Shaver (Ed.), *Handbook of research on social studies teaching and learning.* New York: MacMillan.

Tyson, C. A. (2002). "Get up offa that thing": African-American middle school students respond to literature to develop a framework for understanding social action. *Theory & Research in Social Education, 30*(1), 42–65.

Wineburg, S., & Monte Sano, C. (2008). "Famous Americans": The changing pantheon of American heroes. *The Journal of American History, 95*(1), 1186–1202

CHAPTER 26

DOING LOCAL HISTORY

An Exercise Using the *C3 Framework* for Social Studies Methods Courses

Michael P. Marino and Margaret Smith Crocco

Name: Michael P. Marino and Margaret Smith Crocco	Audience: Undergraduate or graduate candidates
Affiliation: The College of New Jersey Michigan State University	Length: One class session
Course Title: Teaching Secondary School Social Studies	Commonplace featured: Subject Matter
NCSS Teacher Education Standard: Standard 3. Candidates design and implement instruction and authentic assessments for social studies that promote learning and competence in civic life	

Teaching Social Studies: A Methods Book for Methods Teachers,
pages 153–157.

TASK SUMMARY

Doing local history helps promote understanding of inquiry learning (as outlined in the *C3 Framework*) by using teacher candidates' knowledge of their own communities as a way to engage with historical themes and concepts.

DESCRIPTION OF THE TASK

Local history is a powerful way to develop teacher candidates' understanding of inquiry-oriented teaching in history and geography. Multiple reasons explain its utility in promoting an approach consonant with the *C3 Framework* (National Council for the Social Studies, 2013) and higher-order thinking skills in the classroom.

Selwyn (2010) notes that much of history remains "hidden" and that local history helps candidates uncover the history around them in an engaging fashion. Local sites reveal in uniquely accessible ways how history and geography have shaped all communities. Local history can show candidates "how the town or city in which their school is situated was touched or affected by the course of the nation's defining moments" (Danker, 2003, p. 112). Thus, local history can enhance the teaching of traditional historical topics by providing a sense of place and context for studying far-away places and times through nearby places, monuments, and historical figures.

Stevens (2001) goes so far as to assert that doing local history offers a way of personalizing the curriculum, giving candidates observable, material linkages between abstract historical events and their own lives, family histories, and experiences. Rooting inquiry in the ecologies of candidates' own stories, she asserts, motivates interest in history while providing a powerful tool for understanding how complex and multi-layered the process of uncovering the past can be (Levstik & Barton, 2010).

In this exercise, we share an approach used successfully many times in a college-level methods course. In marrying local history with an inquiry-oriented approach aligned with the *C3 Framework*, we have witnessed local history's ability to induce pre-service candidates into the teaching of history as inquiry. They gain the tools and understandings that allow them to transfer an inquiry-oriented approach into their secondary classrooms, and they find that the teaching of local history in schools has similar engaging and motivating effects.

The Task: The idea behind this activity is to demonstrate how local history topics can connect to broad, national themes associated with the panorama of American history. This connection helps candidates see how local history can augment the "big" picture by studying its effects on some aspect of local history (to be sure, sometimes causality works in the other direction, e.g., Bunker Hill, but this is less common). Using local history in a methods class also prepares candidates' for placements in lower grades (often 3rd or 4th grade) where state history is a required part of the social studies curriculum.

For this activity, candidates are placed into groups of four or five and instructed to write down the names of their hometowns. The groups select one of these places as the focus for their investigation. After each group deliberates, class discussion focuses on how they made their selections, what they know about the town's history, and what they currently understand about the place's geographic and historical significance. If necessary, we may overrule a group's choice in the interest of promoting geographic, historical, and demographic diversity of choices within the class.

We then introduce an overarching question: How does the history of Trenton (for example) illustrate some of the larger themes of 20th-century urban history? We distribute a set of 25 index cards containing various themes important to American history (e.g., suburbanization, deindustrialization, transportation) to the class. Each group chooses five index cards randomly and then discards one, leaving four themes that they know best and are most interested in investigating.

Using resources that we provide (or they find on their own), candidates research how each of their four topics is manifested in the history and geography of the town selected. For example, the construction of a road or highway might have shaped the town's boundaries as illustrated through maps over time. A theme that comes up regularly in the context of New Jersey history is that industrialization brought widespread demographic change to its cities, for example, immigration's impact on Paterson in the 19th century or the Great Migration of southern African Americans to Newark in the first half of the 20th century. Readily accessible online census records tell these stories clearly and emphatically. Other examples of New Jersey's impact on national history might be the ascendancy of Woodrow Wilson to the presidency from his role as governor of New Jersey or the place of Atlantic City in the national story of women's suffrage.

The groups then use large poster paper to make a semantic map of the results of their investigations, including the town's or city's name, the themes used for the inquiry, and descriptions of the relationship between the themes and the specific history and geography of the place. The graphic can take the form of a spoke-and-wheel design, a flow chart, or any other graphical representation that conveys the relationship between the history of the place and larger themes of U.S. history. In the discussion that follows this activity, two pedagogical ideas are reviewed with the candidates: a) the utility of local history to engage students, and b) the importance of this approach in accessing students' prior knowledge, using this knowledge as an entry point to an instructional task, and presenting an experience in which students generate historical understandings.

Assessing the Task: Candidates are assessed by gauging their ability to create compelling connections between local places and the narrative of American history more generally. They are also assessed on the quality of information and appearance of the posters they create. Finally, they are evaluated on their ability to define inquiry learning and the extent to which they are able to connect their experiences during the activity to the principles embedded in inquiry learning.

CANDIDATES AND THE TASK

Teacher candidates generally respond positively to the task. Typically, they enjoy discovering the connections between places they know and the larger American history narrative, and they appreciate bringing their local contexts into their learning experiences. Most of the candidates come from New Jersey, a state that suffers from negative stereotypes. Seeing how their home state is historically significant generates positive energy. The biggest challenge is that the task is used as way to access inquiry learning concepts with which candidates may be unfamiliar based on their own "apprenticeship of observation" (Lortie, 1975). As a result, they can find it challenging to see the connection between historical content and the pedagogical premise that underlies this content.

THE TASK IN CONTEXT

This activity occurs about halfway through the semester, during a session devoted exclusively to inquiry learning. The task is predicated on the idea that inquiry learning needs to be experienced, modeled, and defined by the students themselves, as it would be counterproductive to use a teacher-centered approach to introduce a topic that stresses the importance of students' ideas and experiences. In many ways, the challenges are like those associated with teaching with and for discussion (Parker & Hess, 2001), where the experiential contribution of the learning process is a critical component.

The activity discussed here is designed in this way because it a) allows candidates to see the significance of local history by connecting it to wider themes and concepts in U.S. history; b) illustrates how local history can be engaging and motivating; c) utilizes historical and geographic inquiry to illuminate connections between local places and American history; and d) provides an opportunity for enhancing interpersonal skills through group work and visual-spatial and conceptual skills in developing the graphic representations. Perhaps most significantly, this approach advances an understanding of and facility with historical inquiry as embodied in the *C3 Framework*.

REFERENCES

Danker, A. C. (2003). Multicultural social studies: The local history connection. *The Social Studies, 94*(3), 111–117.

Levstik, L., & Barton, K. (2010). *Doing history: Investigating with children in elementary and middle Schools* (4th ed.). New York: Routledge.

Lortie, D. (1975). *Schoolteacher*. Chicago, IL: University of Chicago Press.

National Council for the Social Studies. (2013). *The college, career, and civic life (C3) framework for social studies state standards: Guidance for enhancing the rigor of K–12 civics, economics, geography, and history.* Silver Spring, MD: Author.

Parker, W., & Hess, D. (2001). Teaching with and for discussion. *Teaching and Teacher Education 17,* 273–289.

Selwyn, D. (2010). *Following the threads: Bringing inquiry research into the classroom.* New York: Peter Lang.

Stevens, R. L. (2001). *Homespun: Teaching local history in grades 6–12.* Portsmouth, NH: Heinemann.

CHAPTER 27

POSTING PERSPECTIVES

Evaluating Sources on Controversial Issues

Paul B. McHenry

Name: Paul B. McHenry	Audience: Graduate students
Affiliation: University of California, Riverside	Length: Approximately 1 hour
Course Title: Curriculum Theory and Instructional Processes: Secondary Social Studies	Commonplace featured: Subject Matter
NCSS Teacher Education Standard: Element 3b. Candidates design coherent and relevant learning experiences and engage learners in disciplinary knowledge, inquiry, and forms of representation for competence in civic life and demonstrate alignment with state-required content standards.	

Teaching Social Studies: A Methods Book for Methods Teachers,
pages 159–162.
Copyright © 2017 by Information Age Publishing
All rights of reproduction in any form reserved.

TASK SUMMARY

For this task, teacher candidates examine and evaluate a number of sources surrounding a controversial issue by placing them on a continuum relative to their degree of alignment with perspectives on the issue.

DESCRIPTION OF THE TASK

The goals of this task are threefold. The first is to help prepare teacher candidates to use sources other than the textbook to build instruction in their history-social studies classrooms. The task offers a practical example of how one uses a variety of sources while giving candidates a classroom-ready activity they can use with their students.

The second goal of this task is to offer candidates a relatively safe way to approach the discussion of controversial issues in their classrooms. Candidates in past methods classes reported discomfort around discussions of controversial issues, in large part, because of their vulnerable status as pre-service teachers and, to a lesser degree, because they feared indoctrinating their students with a particular point of view. By positioning the sources in dialogue with one another, this activity facilitates an analysis of sources based on the circumstances of a historical event rather than a present-day interpretation of the event.

The third goal is to provide candidates with a vehicle for promoting disciplinary literacy in their classrooms. Rather than simply reading a document, candidates use disciplinary skills such as attending to "context, perspectives, analysis, and interpretation" (Monte-Sano, De La Paz, & Felton, 2014, p. 3). This type of close reading of documents supports skills called for in standards documents such as the Common Core State Standards (California Department of Education, 2010) and the *C3 Framework* (National Council for the Social Studies, 2013).

The Task: This task is inspired by a Ritchhart, Church, and Morrison (2011) activity in which candidates create "tugs" that pull them to one side or another of an issue and by a professional development workshop offered by Densoho (www. densho.org). Here, rather than having candidates generate tugs from their own perspectives, the tugs are drawn from source materials relating to a historical event.

This activity relies on a variety of primary and secondary sources related to a historical event or issue, e.g., the bombing of Hiroshima and Nagasaki. Documents include a textbook account of the bombings, letters and memoranda related to the decision to drop the bomb, Truman's account of the event, an eyewitness account, and photos. Documents are chosen for their ability to raise questions and problematize issues, as well as their variety of perspectives.

Candidates are placed in home groups, each of which has one or more primary sources to examine. For this example, using eight sources in a class of 16 candidates, four groups of four candidates examine two sources each. Each source is accompanied by 3–4 blank Post-it notes, with each of the sources designated by a different color Post-it. On one of the Post-its for each source, candidates write a one to two sentence summary of the perspective of the source creator on the issue at hand. On the other Post-its, candidates write questions that they may have about the sources. Home group members must agree on both the descriptions and the questions, so that each member enters the next phase of the task with the same things.

With their summaries and questions, candidates participate in constructing several continua (created with masking tape on various classroom surfaces) where one member from each home group presents her or his document, summary, and questions. The candidates' presentations conclude with them placing their Post-it notes along the continuum in a location that represents where they believe their issues fall. The sources candidates use for this activity include, among others, photographs by Dorothea Lange and Ansel Adams, contemporary newspaper accounts, and Executive Order 9066. In the case of this example, the spectrum ranges from "the bombing of Hiroshima and Nagasaki was not justified," to "the bombing of Hiroshima and Nagasaki was justified." Positions may not overlap, so each candidate must choose a position to the left or right of other Post-it notes. In the event of a disagreement, the group is invited to discuss the proper placement of a note and reach consensus.

Once candidates have completed their continua, we re-group as a class and examine the results. The color-coding of the notes makes it immediately obvious how each group has structured their rankings, and it is inevitable that there is at least one source whose placement is not consistent. This discovery sparks further analysis of that source. We also discuss ways in which candidates might use the activity as a foundation for a structured discussion and a possible writing activity for students in the courses they teach.

Assessing the Task: This task is formative in nature and is designed to provide additional foundation for candidates to draw from as they complete the unit plan and analytical paper that are required for the course. Rather than a formal assessment, we pause at various points during the activity to reflect on the purpose and rationale for each of the activities in the task. Candidates then complete a reflection at the end of class that addresses what they have learned and how they might put this or a similar activity into practice in their classrooms.

CANDIDATES AND THE TASK

Prior to this task, teacher candidates often report difficulty conceiving of how to plan lessons that involve controversial issues and they are particularly fearful of backlash from school administrators and parents if they do so. Candidates also express worry about deviating from the so-called official story in the textbook. In written reflections and course evaluations, candidates credit this activity and others with a means of framing issues as a debate among historical figures rather than as a debate among students.

Candidates also face difficulty understanding the concept of disciplinary literacy, and often confuse it with any task involving reading and/or writing. This confusion surfaces in candidate selections of literacy activities in lesson plan drafts that privilege decoding skills, vocabulary acquisition, and reading comprehension. Too often the tasks that candidates require ask students to restate facts they have acquired from one or more sources, but not to go beyond that. As we complete this lesson in class, a candidate who told me all of his history classes had been "bubble tests" remarked how the ideas we discussed were now beginning to make sense. In this instance, he had not previously had context to understand what this type of lesson might look like. For this candidate, the idea of why he might introduce documents in a secondary classroom had become clearer.

THE TASK IN CONTEXT

This task is presented as part of instruction on tackling controversial issues in the classroom, and is a continuation of our study of the use of resources other than the textbook. I introduce this activity in the second half of the quarter, before our study of disciplinary literacy in social studies.

REFERENCES

California Department of Education. (2010). *California's Common Core state standards for English language arts & literacy in history/social studies, science, and technical subjects.* Sacramento, CA: California Department of Education.

Monte-Sano, C., De La Paz, S., & Felton, M. (2014). *Thinking, reading, and writing about history: Teaching argument writing to diverse learners in the Common Core classroom, grades 6–12.* New York: Teachers College Press.

National Council for the Social Studies. (2013). *The college, career, and civic life (C3) framework for social studies state standards: Guidance for enhancing the rigor of K–12 civics, economics, geography, and history.* Silver Spring, MD: Author.

Ritchhart, R., Church, M., & Morrison, K. (2011). *Making thinking visible: How to promote engagement, understanding, and independence for all learners.* San Francisco, CA: Jossey-Bass.

CHAPTER 28

WHAT SHOULD I TEACH?

Conceptualizing Subject Matter

Rebecca Mueller, Lauren Colley, and Emma Thacker

Name: Rebecca Mueller, Lauren Colley, and Emma Thacker	Audience: Undergraduate students
Affiliation: University of South Carolina Upstate University of Alabama James Madison University	Length: Five hours
Course Title: Teaching Middle and Secondary Social Studies	Commonplace featured: Subject Matter
NCSS Teacher Education Standard: Element 1a. Candidates are knowledgeable about the *concepts, facts, and tools* in civics, economics, geography, history, and the social/behavioral sciences.	

Teaching Social Studies: A Methods Book for Methods Teachers,
pages 163–167.
Copyright © 2017 by Information Age Publishing
163

TASK SUMMARY

In *What Should I Teach*, teacher candidates examine and deepen their content knowledge about an assigned topic by completing a series of scaffolded exercises to help them make well-informed and purposeful choices about content selection.

DESCRIPTION OF THE TASK

The goal of *What Should I Teach* is to help teacher candidates make intentional and appropriate choices about what content to include—and exclude—as they design curriculum.

The Task: Candidates can struggle to make intentional choices about subject matter. In evaluating our candidates' unit plans, we notice weaknesses in their abilities to make thoughtful, logical decisions about what to teach, often because they think too little about why the content is valuable. In response, we developed a "training exercise," through which they linger over this important piece of curriculum design.

The task is designed to help candidates navigate two major challenges regarding content selection: 1) gaining additional knowledge about an unfamiliar topic, and 2) paring down and packaging content in a way that is logical and compelling for secondary students. Working collaboratively, candidates engage in *research*, *reflection*, and *selection* exercises:

> **Research:** The task begins with the *research* phase, in which we randomly assign candidates to pre-determined topics corresponding with social studies standards in our states and representing content with which candidates frequently struggle (e.g., Ancient Islamic Civilizations, U.S. Women in the Early 1900s). Groups begin by brainstorming what they know (or don't know) about the assigned topic. They examine a series of instructor-provided resources representing a variety of mediums and perspectives (e.g., Simon de Bolivar's 1819 Message to Congress, political cartoons depicting the New Deal). These resources are designed to complicate candidates' understandings of the topic. Instead of narrowing the scope for them, we want candidates to struggle with the challenge of harnessing vast swaths of content. In addition to reviewing the provided resources, candidates find and select supplemental resources to share with their groups.

> With additional sources in-hand, group members discuss all of the resources and add to their original brainstorms. Should these discussions prompt new questions, we encourage candidates to consult additional resources to develop fuller understandings of the assigned topics. To conclude the *research* phase, candidates consult state and national social studies standards documents and make necessary additions to their brainstorm. Groups use a different color at each step of this phase to demonstrate their growing knowledge.

> We emphasize throughout this phase that candidates will never have a complete understanding of these topics. The process of research itself is limiting. The resources candidates consult, the lenses through which they read the resources, the quality

of their group discussions, and other forces inevitably narrow and shape their understanding. Certain information is inherently left out, so candidates must consider the implications of these factors on their content knowledge and curricular choices.

Reflection: The temptation to jump straight from listing content to choosing instructional strategies typically results in disjointed, activity-driven units. For this reason, the *reflection* phase of the task matters because it creates a space for candidates to consider why this content matters.

As candidates review their ballooning brainstorm, they realize that it is neither possible nor wise to address all of the content. Groups begin this winnowing process by discussing ideas that most resonate with them, big ideas that pervade the list, and overarching questions that arise. Groups return to their brainstorms and sort individual items into categories that capture these larger themes. We draw upon Loewen's (2010) analogy of forests, trees, and twigs to help candidates better understand different dimensions of content. Ultimately, they need to determine what really matters and why. Using the sentence starter "Students absolutely need to know _____ because _____," groups craft three to five statements that reflect what they believe students most need to encounter about this topic. Groups share their statements and receive feedback through class discussion or a graffiti exercise.

Selection: Simply put, teachers cannot teach all that they know; during the *selection* phase, candidates make important content choices. Previously, candidates learned about designing instruction around big ideas and questions (e.g., Caron, 2005; Grant & Gradwell, 2010) and applying the Inquiry Arc of the *C3 Framework* (National Council for the Social Studies, 2013), specifically using compelling and supporting questions. Candidates then use these concepts to revise their brainstorms and "students absolutely need to know" statements. In the final step, groups determine the compelling questions that will center their units and craft student learning objectives appropriate for a five to seven-day unit. Groups submit this information through a graphic organizer on which groups articulate how each learning objective supports the compelling question and identify the content that will be addressed. Groups also submit three to four paragraph rationales for their curricular choices. The rationales address what the group chose to include (e.g., compelling question and learning objectives) and what they chose to exclude, encouraging them to consider the implications of their explicit narrowing of content.

Assessing the Task: Throughout the task, candidates engage in informal and formal assessments. The goal of the informal assessments is to capture and maximize the development of students' content knowledge. These assessments consist of the various brainstorming lists (i.e., initial brainstorming, additional brainstorming, sorting of content). They allow us to identify candidates' content knowledge and any possible gaps. It is only after candidates adequately increase their content knowledge that they move toward formally considering why these content topics matter.

The goal of the formal assessments is to measure the degree to which candidates are able to justify their instructional content choices. The formal assessments include candidates' written statements on what their students should know and their final objectives and paragraph explanations on what to teach. Candidates' written statements are assessed on their clarity and connection to the content, as well as the soundness of their reasoning. Learning objectives should include what students will be able to do and the criteria upon which these students will be assessed. Moreover, these learning objectives should resemble candidates' previous written statements and encompass the breadth and depth of content covered in their instructional units. Last, we assess candidates' written paragraphs on their ability to explain the instructional implications of their content choices and to justify why particular content was excluded. Paragraphs should be clearly written and provide specific evidence and reasoning to support candidates' instructional decisions.

Ideally, a final formal assessment occurs through candidates' development of an instructional unit plan featuring 5–7 lessons that revolve around their compelling question in fluid, dynamic, and powerful ways. Lesson plans should reflect not only the connection to the compelling question, but also the thoughtful and purposeful selection of content for instruction.

CANDIDATES AND THE TASK

What Should I Teach is often preceded by an examination of state and national standards, which frequently leaves teacher candidates feeling overwhelmed by content expectations, particularly if they are tied to high-stakes testing. They typically exit that examination wondering "how can I cover that much information clearly in that much time?" The *research* phase of this task can contribute to that fear, as one candidate noted, "the more I research the New Deal, the more it becomes clear I don't know very much about it." Through the collaborative *reflection* and *selection* exercises, however, that same candidate could identify big ideas that more effectively structure a unit: "Every time I think about the New Deal, it keeps coming back to how the New Deal still affects society today." The impact of the collective assignments was clear, as the resulting learning objectives were far more cohesive than the initial brainstorm suggested.

THE TASK IN CONTEXT

What Should I Teach does not eliminate subject matter challenges. Teacher candidates enter our programs with varying degrees of disciplinary knowledge, and teacher educators are not in a position to fill all the gaps. Candidates are products of textbook-driven curriculum and schools in which the pressures of high-stakes testing are profound, and teacher educators can struggle to override the influence of these apprenticeships of observation (Slekar, 1998). Nonetheless, *What Should I Teach* emphasizes teacher agency and equips candidates with tools and strategies for approaching content selection in ways that are meaningful to them and, more importantly, to their future students. These exercises can be executed consecutively or spaced throughout the course

REFERENCES

Caron, E. G. (2005). What leads to the fall of a great empire? Using central questions to design issues-based history units. *The Social Studies, 96*(2), 51–60.

Grant, S. G., & Gradwell, J. M. (2010). *Teaching history with big ideas: Cases of ambitious teachers*. Lanham, MD: Rowman & Littlefield.

Loewen, J. W. (2010). *Teaching what really happened: How to avoid the tyranny of textbooks and get kids excited about doing history*. New York: Teachers College Press.

National Council for the Social Studies (2013). *The college, career, and civic life (C3) framework for social studies state standards: Guidance for enhancing the rigor of K–12 civics, economics, geography, and history.* Silver Spring, MD: Author.

Slekar, T. D. (1998). Epistemological entanglements: Preservice elementary school teachers' "apprenticeship of observation" and the teaching of history. *Theory and Research in Social Education, 26*(4), 485–507.

CHAPTER 29

METHODS OF INTEGRATING CURRENT EVENTS INTO SOCIAL STUDIES LESSONS

Jeff Passe

Name: Jeff Passe	Audience: Undergraduate and graduate students
Affiliation: The College of New Jersey	Length: Single lesson plus assignment
Course Title: Teaching Social Studies in the Middle School	Commonplace featured: Subject Matter
NCSS Teacher Education Standard: Element 2d. Candidates plan learning sequences where learners create disciplinary forms of representation to provide opportunities for meaningful civic learning	

Teaching Social Studies: A Methods Book for Methods Teachers,
pages 169–174.
Copyright © 2017 by Information Age Publishing

TASK SUMMARY

Whether it begins with specific social studies content or the current event itself, integrating current events into social studies lessons offers important opportunities to examine social studies concepts and themes.

DESCRIPTION OF THE TASK

The assignment begins as teacher candidates review criticisms of the school curriculum with a particular focus on social studies (e.g., Gibson, 2012; Goodlad, 1984) and summarize the prime contributors to disinterest among students. Although the issue of relevance typically surfaces quickly, the question is how to address the issue. When candidates suggest teaching current events as a promising solution, I ask them to analyze their own educational experiences to determine why current events were not taught more often. The most common offered is that textbook instruction dominated their social studies classes. Further discussion yields the observation that textbooks cannot possibly be current due to the lengthy publication process and use of the same textbook edition for many years.

The Task: I build upon that initial discussion by presenting two strategies for integrating current events into the social studies curriculum:

Strategy #1: Beginning with Social Studies Themes

Every social studies lesson taps into important themes and concepts. These themes and concepts may be provided by state curricular guides, recommended by textbook authors and editors, or identified by social studies teachers themselves. Themes and concepts are general in nature and, therefore, should be applicable to a variety of social studies disciplines and grade levels.

Candidates who integrate current events should examine their lessons for a key theme or concept. In the example below, the right-hand column identifies key themes that correspond to specific content in the left-hand column. I encourage candidates to study the examples in the chart below:

Examples of Social Studies Content:	Examples of Significant Themes:
Abolition of slavery	Tensions between governmental levels
Disputes over state boundary lines	Conflict over scarce resources
The 1970s oil shortage	Interdependence
European settlement	Cultural conflict
The advent of naval warships	Technological change
Child labor laws	The power of coalitions

To apply the social studies content to current events, candidates look for examples from the present day at the local, state, national, or global level. These topics can be the basis of a current events lesson. I show candidates the chart below and then we discuss the connections in class:

Examples of Significant Themes:	Current Events Applications:
Tensions between governmental levels	The Affordable Care Act
Conflict over scarce resources	Access to Colorado River water
Interdependence	Refugee policies
Cultural conflict	Immigrations issues
Technological change	Job loss due to robots
The power of coalitions	Neighborhoods uniting to stop a pipeline

Some candidates may argue that it is difficult to predict what will be a current event because one can never be sure what issues will be in the news when a lesson is scheduled to be taught. Fortunately for teachers, and unfortunately for society, certain issues never go away. There will always be military conflicts somewhere, injustice is a perennial news topic, and some group somewhere will be complaining about another group. Teaching toward important themes and concepts (Larson, 1999) ensures that social studies content is relevant and interesting to students.

For maximum relevance, I go local. Local or regional events are often more interesting to candidates because they are likely to be familiar with the location and the issue being studied. School-related current events can serve as particularly powerful reminders that social studies content is not just in books or newspapers. The chart below shows the same key themes and concepts applied to a school. (Note: The current events are fictional because each school has its own specific, but similar, examples.) Candidates examine these examples and then offer their own local applications. I do this in a large-group setting to ensure that the examples are pertinent and to help clarify the nature of the fictional school events:

Examples of Significant Themes:	School Current Event Applications:
Tensions between governmental levels	The Schood Board overruling a principal
Conflict over scarce resources	Allocation of PTA funds
Interdependence	Parking lot safety
Cultural conflict	Tensions between various cliques
Technological change	Social media policies
The power of coalitions	Teach associations joining forces with social service agencies.

Strategy #2: Beginning with a Current Event

Although many candidates use a textbook or curriculum guide in their initial planning steps, others prefer to begin with an actual current event. Doing so is the basis of an issues-centered approach to social studies as compared to a content-centered approach. Despite the differences in title, both approaches can address current events.

Candidates may also choose to use the issues-centered approach when a current event is so immediate and compelling that it becomes the first segment of a social studies lesson. Examples of extraordinary moments include major elections, natural or human disaster, or local crises.

In this case, the planning process is simply reversed. Thus, the examples cited in Strategy 1 could start with highlighting a current event (e.g., a major accident in the school parking lot when the drivers and pedestrians did not cooperate) and then connecting it to a key theme (in this case, interdependence), which would connect to the social studies content (depending on the grade level and unit, possibly refugee policies or settlement of the American West or NATO). After doing two examples in a large group, I ask candidates to come up with their own examples. Once they have completed that task, we create a big chart for the whole class.

Using recent events at the time this chapter is being written, a planning chart may look like this:

Current Event	Significant Theme or Concept
Police killing of unarmed African Americans	Unequal justice
Presidential debates	Political philosophies
Negotiating cease-fire in Syria	Conflict resolution
Hacked emails	Impact of technology
Prescription drug prices	Marketplace regulation

Once a candidate has a significant theme established, students can be led into applying that theme to whatever content the class is studying. If the significant theme or concept is truly universal, there should be some sort of application at any level. The chart below shows a variety of examples. Candidates study the chart and add their own applications:

Significant Theme or Concept	Content Applications
Unequal justic	Slavery, Nazi persecution, Watergate
Political philosophies	War on poverty, Tories, anti-communism
Conflict resolution	Treaty of Paris, Camp David Accord, Roe v. Wade
Impact of technology	A-bomb testing, assembly-lines, TVA
Marketplace regulation	Trust building, New Deal, bank bailouts

As a follow-up activity, I engage the entire class in an activity that has them read a middle or high school social studies textbook passage. As a large group, we identify and discuss key themes or concepts. For each important theme or content, candidates brainstorm possible current events applications. If they do not include local current events, I encourage them to do so. In essence, candidates are adding to the charts presented for Strategy #1. I also do another whole-class activity where I identify a major current event and have candidates follow Strategy #2.

After candidates demonstrate mastery as a whole-class, I form small groups. I present half of the groups with social studies content (Strategy #1) while the other half receives a list of recent current events (Strategy #2.) I ask the small groups to add content, important themes/concepts, and current events applications using the charts presented earlier.

Assessing the Task: To assess candidate mastery of the two strategies for integrating current events, I assign individual candidates to work on units or lessons that they developed earlier in the course. I have them complete the charts for Strategies #1 and 2, based on the grade-level content with which they have been working. A note of warning: It is possible that their earlier lessons lack important themes or concepts because the textbook passage or curriculum standard was focused on trivia (e.g., simple definitions of geographic terms). I direct those candidates to find deeper content elsewhere in the book or curriculum. Once students are comfortable planning for the integration of current events, they are ready to prepare actual lessons on the topic.

CANDIDATES AND THE TASK

Research on the teaching of current events identifies a variety of constraints that cause teacher candidates to shy away from dealing with them in class. These constraints include the need to cover a vast array of important content goals, the desire to avoid controversy, and the need to prepare for standardized tests (Lipscomb& Doppen, 2013). A significant factor for elementary teachers, which can probably be extrapolated to secondary teachers, is their knowledge of current events. Deeper news awareness is correlated with a greater likelihood of teaching current events (Passe, 1988).

All of these concerns can be addressed by establishing a mission for social studies that emphasizes preparation for active citizenship. In addition, it should be pointed out that students have a strong interest in controversial issues (Hess & McAvoy, 2014). Demonstration and analysis of effective current events lessons would help students develop the confidence to manage classroom controversy, an area that has been well addressed by scholars in social studies education (e.g., Hess & McAvoy, 2014; Merryfield & Wilson, 2005; Passe, 1988).

THE TASK IN CONTEXT

This task is best presented after the teacher candidates have been introduced to the process of unit planning, which includes the identification of significant concepts and themes. Having focused on the importance of selecting relevant curricular goals, the issue of teaching current events should resonate at that time. Preparation of lesson and unit plans that include study of current events immediately follow this lesson.

REFERENCES

Gibson, S. (2012). "Why do we learn this stuff?" Students' views on the purpose of social studies. *Canadian Social Studies, 45*(1), 43–58.

Goodlad, J. (1984) *A place called school*. New York: McGraw-Hill.

Hess, D., & McAvoy, P. (2014). *The political classroom: Evidence and ethics in democratic education*. New York: Routledge.

Larson, B. (1999) Current events and the Internet: Connecting headline news to perennial issues. *Social Studies and the Young Learner, 12,* 25–28.

Lipscomb, G., & Doppen, F. (2103) Finding one's place in the world. Current events in the K–12 social studies classroom. In J. Passe & P. Fitchett (Eds.), *The status of social studies: Views from the field* (pp. 247–256). Charlotte, NC: Information Age Publishing.

Passe, J. (1988) The role of internal factors in the teaching of current events. *Theory and Research in Social Education, 16*, 83–89.

CHAPTER 30

PROBLEMATIZING THE SOCIAL STUDIES

Mark Pearcy

Name: Mark Pearcy	Audience: Undergraduate and graduate students
Affiliation: Rider University	Length: 20–25 minutes each activity/occurrence
Course Title: Teaching Social Studies in Secondary Schools	Commonplace featured: Subject Matter
NCSS Teacher Education Standard: Element 3b. Candidates design coherent and relevant learning experiences and engage learners in disciplinary knowledge, inquiry, and forms of representation for competence in civic life and demonstrate alignment with state-required content standards.	

Teaching Social Studies: A Methods Book for Methods Teachers,
pages 175–180.
Copyright © 2017 by Information Age Publishing

TASK SUMMARY

In a *Problematizing* task, teacher candidates utilize a three-level framework to determine the scope and sequence of social studies content, the value of such knowledge towards the development of civic literacy, and the appropriate pedagogical strategies to best present that content.

THE TASK

Social studies methods classes often focus on strategies, resources, and teaching tools. Equipping our teacher candidates with ready-made tools and tactics is important, but so is helping them acquire a disciplinary mindset that enables them to shape social studies content into effective lessons.

Effective social studies education is grounded in what the National Council for the Social Studies (2013) *College, Career, and Civic Life (C3) Framework for Social Studies Standards* describes as "the development of questions and the planning of inquiries" (p. 17). Doing so means candidates must reconceptualize their views of social studies knowledge *towards* inquiry and *away* from the acquisition of content. Developing their ability to select and manipulate content is the chief goal of problematizing activities.

Problematizing means creating "open-ended problem to solve, a task to complete, a judgment to reach, a decision to make, or a list to create—something that begs for closure" (Center for Innovative Teaching and Learning, 2015). Veteran teachers recognize that this process is at the center of developing meaningful, engaging social studies lessons. Like any skill, the ability to problematize can be acquired and made habitual when given opportunities to practice it.

At the beginning of the course, candidates are presented with a three-level framework as the foundation for problematizing exercises:

- What am I teaching?
- Why am I teaching it?
- How do I teach it?

The first question requires candidates to conceptualize the disciplinary skills or knowledge they are trying to teach and commit to instructional goals for their students. For instance, when pushed to describe a discipline-specific topic, such as the Civil War, in the form of a desired outcome or objective, my candidates come up with statements like—"The Civil War was a product of an ongoing national debate over state sovereignty, particularly with regard to slavery." Doing so, suggests that candidates are beginning to infer the pedagogical choices they will have to make in their planning.

The second question—"why am I teaching it?"—compels candidates to prioritize knowledge. With limited time available, candidates must learn to ask the question that every veteran teacher asks—"is this worth the investment of time, resources, and effort for my candidates?" In addition, there is a value-based component to this analysis; candidates must determine if a given topic of study represents a topic of sufficient moral, ethical, or intellectual weight to merit its inclusion.

After determining the scope and value of the content to be taught, candidates learn to ask the question, "how do I teach this?" It is important to note that, in answering this question, a teacher's choices are informed by the decisions made at the first two levels of the problematizing framework. In determining the nature of the disciplinary skills and knowledge to be featured, candidates delimit pedagogical choices to those most effective and most appropriate to the desired ends. In determining the value of the prioritized topic, they determine which aspects of that topic to weight most heavily in order for the lesson to be effective.

At this stage, candidates engage a challenge—how to make the content engaging, critical, and inviting to inquiry. In problematizing the curriculum, I encourage them to focus on two essential elements of problematizing—developing supporting content and creating critical questions.

Like any skill, problematizing requires regular practice. For instance, in each class meeting, I present candidates with a "teachable moment" activity in which they must take a specific example of disciplinary content and address it with the problematizing framework. Candidates must apply the first two questions—what am I teaching? what is the value of this knowledge?—and produce an applicable problematized question, which forms the basis for addressing the third question, how do I teach this?

One exercise in particular represents the skills emphasized in this framework. Candidates enter the room to see several short case studies printed and affixed to large poster boards. These case studies describe a range of content-based topics, events, or biographies. Candidates work in small groups to read each case study and accomplish two tasks:

1. List as many topics, ideas, or concepts that may connect to the case study.
2. Create a problematized question, one which creates controversy, includes multiple perspectives, and would form the basis of a compelling critical inquiry.

One of these case studies details the story of Claudette Colvin, an African-American teenager from Montgomery, Alabama. Colvin boarded a city bus on March 2, 1955, to go home from high school. A white passenger was left without a seat, and the driver demanded that Colvin surrender hers. Colvin refused and, after the driver alerted nearby police officers, was arrested. The incident drew the attention of African-American activists, who first thought to use it as a platform from which to challenge the bus law's constitutionality; after considering Colvin's age and background (i.e., her parents were working class and Claudette allegedly used obscenities during her arrest), they decided against it. Nine months later, Rosa Parks' refusal to give up her own seat on a city bus made her a national icon of civil rights.

In this activity, candidates collaboratively generate a list of linked topics by activating prior knowledge about the events themselves or related ones. These often include themes like civil rights, civil disobedience, memorialization, African-American icons, and women in U.S. history or specific historical events such as the Montgomery bus boycotts, Supreme Court cases that expanded or redefined citizen rights, and contemporary events (e.g., the 2014 riots in Ferguson, Missouri).

Next, the candidates create problematized questions, drawn from this case-study and the connected themes. Examples include:

- Was the case of Claudette Colvin more noteworthy than that of Rosa Parks?
- Could Colvin's age and background have been a positive factor, if her demonstration had become a national symbol?
- Should African-American youths be emphasized as a greater factor in the civil rights movement?
- Is it okay to break an unjust law?
- Is America conditioned to support a sympathetic figure?

These questions infer a variety of positions and conclusions, and allow for different and defensible perspectives. More to the point, they infer a set of pedagogical choices. For example, in considering the possibility that Americans might be drawn to more sympathetic historical figures, candidates might ask a class to compare the historical legacies of Thomas Jefferson and Sally Hemmings, Fred Korematsu and Earl Warren, or John Kennedy and James Meredith. In deciding on the scope and value of selected social studies knowledge—and by problematizing that knowledge—candidates can make effective pedagogical choices.

Assessing the Task: There are multiple occurrences of problematizing-based activities throughout the course. The case-study approach described above includes the following topics:

- The trial of Standing Bear, a Ponca Sioux chief who was put on trial in 1878 for trying to return to his tribal land in order to bury his son.
- The case of Mary Mallon, better known as "Typhoid Mary," who was interned against her will on an island in Manhattan Bay for 33 years
- The internment of Quakers during the American Revolution, whose adherence to nonviolence made them suspect to patriot leaders. (See Appendix for case notes.)

In problematizing these case-studies, candidates have created a variety of controversial, multifaceted questions which can form the basis of engaging social studies lessons such as—Was it in the public interest to intern Mary Mallon, in defiance of her personal wishes? Did Standing Bear have a right of ownership to the land that his tribe had surrendered to the federal government? Is an adherence to nonviolence a sufficient cause to have interned Quakers during the Revolution?

How can we reconcile religious freedom with national security, or the cause of independence? Candidate-generated problematized questions serve as objectives for collaboratively designed lessons.

Candidates are assessed in these tasks by evaluating the degree to which the questions they develop can be expanded into effective classroom activities. In particular, the problematized questions become central to follow-up assignments, in which candidates must create lessons for classroom use. These lessons and activities are shared via a class discussion board and subjected to peer review.

CANDIDATES AND THE TASK

Given their experiences in content-transmission classrooms, teacher candidates often find problematizing to be highly disorienting (Pearcy & Duplass, 2011). Candidates are challenged to develop a habit that is ingrained in veteran teachers—making social studies lessons engaging, centered on complex inquiries, and worth the investment of time and resources.

THE TASK IN CONTEXT

Versions of this task are situated in the secondary social studies methods class typically taken by teacher candidates in their senior year. Candidates engage in problematizing activities in all class meetings over the course of the semester, to learn to create meaningful, class-specific lines of inquiry, as well as to promote the autonomy that is instrumental to teachers' curricular decision-making (Thornton, 1991).

APPENDIX: SAMPLE CASE STUDIES USED TO PROMOTE PROBLEMATIZING SKILLS

The Trial of Standing Bear, 1878
Standing Bear was the chief of the Ponca Indian tribe in 1878, located in present-day Nebraska. The Ponca relinquished all their land to the U.S. government except for a small reserve along the Niobrara River and tried to convert from a nomadic hunting lifestyle to agriculture. In the Treaty of 1868, the government mistakenly assigned the Ponca's land to the Sioux, who began raiding Standing Bear's tribe. In 1876, the Ponca were told to move to Indian Territory, in present-day Oklahoma. After seeing it, the Ponca refused to move; they were forced to travel on foot by the U.S. Army. By 1878, more than a third of the tribe had died from starvation, malaria, and other causes (including Standing Bear's son). Standing Bear had promised to bury his son in the Ponca's homeland, so he and a number of followers tried to return home to the on the Niobrara. They were arrested by U.S. troops and taken to Omaha. At this point, sympathetic lawyers helped Standing Bear file a lawsuit against the U.S. government, claiming the Ponca had the right to stay on their land.

Mary Mallon
Mary Mallon, now known as "Typhoid Mary," was an Irish-born cook in the early 1900s who carried the bacteria for typhoid fever, a form of salmonella that can cause fever, diarrhea, and death. But Mallon herself was immune to the disease. In 1907, health inspectors accosted and detained her, since she had been determined to be the first "healthy carrier" of typhoid fever in the United States. Mallon did not comprehend this, since she had never had typhoid and exhibited no symptoms. When authorities discovered that her employment as a cook had been the primary cause for the city's typhoid outbreak, they sentenced her, against her will, to a three-year quarantine on North Brother Island, in the East River. Mallon promised to give up her profession as a cook, though she did not keep her word; when it was discovered that she was working as a cook again in 1915, she was sent back into quarantine. She spent the rest of her life on North Brother Island, 23 years, until her death in 1938.

Internment of Quakers During the American Revolution
Before the American Revolution, Pennsylvania had a large population of the Society of Friends, generally known as Quakers. While Quakers at first supported patriotic resistance to the British, they soon grew uncomfortable with the radical nature of the movement. Quakers felt that Patriots' interest in reconciliation with the British was waning, and their fears of imminent warfare proved well founded by the outbreak of fighting at Lexington and Concord.
Many patriots didn't trust Quakers, in part because of their adherence to Peace Testimony. Dating back to the English Civil War, the Testimony committed Friends members to nonviolence. In August 1777, the British Army was advancing on Philadelphia, and local patriots feared that Quakers might give them aid. Congress asked the Pennsylvania Supreme Executive Council to take Quaker leaders into custody, and the Council complied. Forty-one Quakers were arrested, and 20 were ordered into exile in Virginia After considerable hardship and expense, the exiles were allowed to return to Philadelphia in April 1778, just two months before the British army took the city.

REFERENCES

Center for Innovative Teaching and Learning. (2015). *Discussion: Basic strategies*. Indiana University. Retrieved from http://citl.indiana.edu/resources_files/teaching-resources1/teaching-handbook-items/discussion.php

National Council for the Social Studies. (2013). *The college, career, and civic life (C3) framework for social studies state standards: Guidance for enhancing the rigor of K–12 civics, economics, geography, and history*. Silver Spring, MD: Author.

Pearcy, M., & Duplass, J.A. (2011). Teaching history: Strategies for dealing with breadth and depth in the standards and accountability age. *The Social Studies, 102*, 110–116.

Thornton, S. (1991). Teacher as curricular-instructional gatekeeper in social studies. In J. Shaver (Ed.), *Handbook of research on social studies teaching and learning* (pp. 237–248). New York: Macmillan.

CHAPTER 31

"COMMITMENT TO SOCIAL JUSTICE IS NOT ENOUGH; LOVE IS NOT ENOUGH"

Helping New Social Studies Teachers Develop Content Knowledge for Teaching

Dave Powell

Name: Dave Powell	Audience: Undergraduate students
Affiliation: Gettysburg College	Length: Semester-long
Course Title: Teaching Social Studies	Commonplace featured: Subject Matter
NCSS Teacher Education Standard: Standard 1. Candidates demonstrate knowledge of social studies disciplines. Candidates are knowledgeable of disciplinary concepts, facts, and tools; structures of inquiry; and forms of representation.	

Teaching Social Studies: A Methods Book for Methods Teachers,
pages 181–185.
Copyright © 2017 by Information Age Publishing

TASK SUMMARY

This project is designed to stimulate the development of "content knowledge for teaching" (CKT) by encouraging teacher candidates to explore subject matter specifically for the purpose of adapting it to teaching.

DESCRIPTION OF THE TASK

Most of the first half of my methods course focuses on the development of strong and defensible rationales for teaching social studies—rationales centered on deep understanding of the nature of democracy and on the rights and responsibilities of citizenship. The course focuses on cultivating a pragmatic view of democracy, one in which thoughtful engaged deliberation about social problems and discussion of potential solutions is the centerpiece of social studies education.

Teacher candidates' rationales and sense of purpose are built on and draw from a strong base of knowledge. As Lee Shulman (2005) notes, simply wanting to accomplish high-minded goals will not bring them to fruition: "Commitment to social justice is not enough," he warned, "love is not enough" (p. xx). I want to encourage candidates to connect the aims and purposes they have chosen to subject matter content that helps advance their goals. We try to accomplish that through the content analysis project.

The Task: The project is designed to help candidates reframe their understanding of what it means to have content knowledge by transforming it into "content knowledge for teaching." This phrase, borrowed from Ball, Thames, and Phelps (2008), refers to the specialized knowledge teachers need to have in order to make the subject matter they teach accessible to students. Here's how I explain the concept to candidates:

> Content Knowledge for Teaching is a term that should help you differentiate your *disciplinary* content knowledge from the knowledge you'll use in teaching. Why the difference? Well, for starters, what you study here in college in your major and across the curriculum is not exactly what you'll be teaching in secondary schools. That paper you wrote on the history of the Guyanese working people from 1881 to 1905 is probably not going to immediately translate to the work you do with your students. To be sure, it matters: You can glean valuable insights from the research you've done and connect it to themes that touch other topics you may teach. But it's unlikely that a detailed exploration of labor history in Guyana is going to show up in the high school or middle school curriculum anytime soon. To make that particular store of knowledge relevant to your students you'll need to think about *transforming* it, or at least refocusing it in a way that connects to the secondary school curriculum and to the needs and interests of your students. You'll need to think carefully about how to connect what you know to the goals and purposes you have established for teaching, and you'll also have to consider how to align it with curricular goals, standards, and other expectations.

Learning subject matter for the purpose of preparing to teach it is not something candidates are typically asked to do. Instead, the assumption seems to be that, if they have completed a certain number of classes and done well enough in them, then they must *know* what they need to know in order to teach effectively. This project requires candidates to establish a fuller and deeper understanding of subject matter by asking them to keep a range of issues and ideas in mind—How would I present this to others? How can I organize what I know in a way that will be accessible to students? How might students from different backgrounds respond to this information?

The project has two parts. The first is a *content analysis questionnaire*, which requires candidates to identify a topic of interest and articulate why it is important for students to learn and how it might fit into the larger curriculum. On the questionnaire, candidates describe the ideal citizen and explain how the topic can be related to citizenship education in school; identify resources (including a central text) used in the project; detail any conflicts or controversies associated with the topic; and write both a topic question—one designed to stimulate student inquiry into the topic—and a brief response to it. These exercises are designed to encourage candidates to apply their nascent curriculum development skills to the task of considering what they want to teach and how they might teach it. They are not writing lesson plans. They are learning subject matter so they can effectively plan instruction later.

The second part of the project consists of a series of activities designed to make the candidates' thinking and knowledge visible:

- *Overview essay.* The overview essay is a succinct piece of writing (750–1,000 words) that provides readers with the crucial information they need to know about the topic, a kind of encyclopedia entry on the topic. The goal here is to help the candidates whittle what they have learned down to its most essential parts in an effort to bring more clarity to their presentation of it to students.
- *List of key terms.* Identifying the substantive knowledge associated with the topic serves as an extension of the overview essay, and draws upon the distinction Schwab (1964, 1978) drew between substantive and syntactic knowledge as the foundation of academic disciplines. Here, candidates make a list of key terms or ideas associated with the topic that their students should know after it has been taught.
- *Perspective essay.* To address the syntactic knowledge associated with the topic, candidates write a second short essay (750–1,000 words) that provides a perspective on the topic. Syntactic knowledge includes an understanding of the methods used within a given discipline to generate new knowledge and awareness of the major interpretations of the knowledge. To write this essay well, candidates must analyze and synthesize what they have learned and written about it in a clear and compelling way.

- *Document-based question.* Finally, candidates create an assignment that might be given to students in their classrooms modeled after the Document-Based Questions (DBQ) commonly given on Advanced Placement exams. Candidates select a key portion of text, broadly conceived (e.g., text, film or audio clip), and write a task that encourages analysis of it. The DBQ should also address the key questions contained in the questionnaire: What does this topic have to do with citizenship in a democratic society? How does this topic enable students to deal with conflict and controversy and find solutions to social problems?

Assessing the Task: My assessment of these projects focuses on the four pieces assembled in Part 2; the questionnaire given in Part 1 is not assessed beyond any suggestions that are made for strengthening the project in the preparation phase. Generally speaking, the best projects are those that clearly and definitively provide a window into the emerging skills of the candidates who authored them. They are focused, insightful, comprehensive, and compelling. I provide a score using a rubric and offer detailed written feedback.

CANDIDATES AND THE TASK

In the end, the content analysis project is part unit plan and part research project, but less of the former and more of the latter. I encourage teacher candidates to choose topics they may know something about, but would not be comfortable teaching yet. I push them to consider their topics from the perspective of a person preparing to *teach* it to others. The turn from candidate to teacher is accomplished almost imperceptibly as candidates complete the project, weaving their way through the topics they have chosen with an eye fixed explicitly on preparing to share what they have learned with others so they can learn it too.

Candidates typically respond to the task with the excitement one would expect from beginning teachers hungry to develop their teaching skills. Many are surprised by how difficult it is to do the project well—especially with regard to narrowing a topic and writing about it with precision and clarity. Most attack the project with genuine verve; nearly all emerge with a much stronger sense of the difference between their college major knowledge and the broader, yet more focused, knowledge they need to have to teach well. The project also helps candidates develop the analytic research skills they need to interpret new subject matter effectively and quickly, by encouraging them to filter and focus their knowledge in ways that will make it accessible to students.

Maybe the most powerful impact of the project is the license it gives candidates to explore topics of interest to them. Candidates have authored fascinating projects on the Stonewall Riots, the Iran-Contra Affair, John Brown, Jack the Ripper, the House Un-American Activities Committee, wealth inequality, school shootings, and other topics not often featured in the secondary school curriculum. The rich array of topics candidates choose speaks eloquently of the power of this project to shape the way they eventually teach—and that alone makes it well worth doing.

THE TASK IN CONTEXT

The content analysis project is completed in the second third of the methods course, after we have spent a substantial amount of time defining social studies and citizenship education, and before a culminating project focused on developing curricular plans for teaching. The project functions as a natural bridge between the other two sections of the course—it serves to help teacher candidates see the practical implications of articulating their goals for teaching while also pushing them toward a more traditional unit plan that is more explicitly connected to the curriculum taught in the local schools where they will student teach.

REFERENCES

Ball, D. L., Thames, M. H., & Phelps, G. (2008). Content knowledge for teaching: What makes it special? *Journal of Teacher Education, 59*(5), 389–407.

Schwab, J. J. (1964). Structure of the disciplines: Meanings and significances. In G. W. Ford & L. Pugno (Eds.), *The structure of knowledge and the curriculum* (pp. 6–30). Chicago, IL: Rand McNally.

Schwab, J. J. (1978). Education and the structure of the disciplines. In *Science, curriculum, andliberal education: Selected essays* (pp. 229–272). Chicago, IL: University of Chicago Press.

Shulman, L. (2005). Teacher education does not exist. *The Stanford educator.* Palo Alto, CA: Stanford University School of Education.

CHAPTER 32

CONNECTING CONTENT TO THE WORLD

Mardi Schmeichel

Name: Mardi Schmeichel	Audience: Undergraduate and graduate Students
Affiliation: University of Georgia	Length: 90–120 minutes
Course Title: Social Studies Senior Practicum Seminar	Commonplace featured: Subject Matter
NCSS Teacher Education Standard: Element 2b. Candidates plan learning sequences that engage learners with disciplinary concepts, facts, and tools from the social studies disciplines to facilitate learning for civic life.	

Teaching Social Studies: A Methods Book for Methods Teachers,
pages 187–191.
Copyright © 2017 by Information Age Publishing

TASK SUMMARY

In the *Connecting Content to the World* activity, teacher candidates working in practicums participate in collaborative planning tasks to improve their capacity to design lessons that connect the curriculum and standards to students' lives and the real world.

DESCRIPTION OF THE TASK

Just learning to create one 60- or 90-minute lesson plan for a classroom of adolescents poses a daunting challenge to most teacher candidates. Teacher education programs provide some structure to help them make sense of the theoretical components underpinning the design of curriculum frameworks and introduce the preparation of courses and units, but the alchemy involved in turning a single standard into a meaningful and purposeful class period for middle or high school students is often lost. This disconnect is troubling, as this is the context in which most candidates find themselves within clinical placements: They are dropped into placements mid-stream and asked to begin lesson planning without any of the conversations about curriculum frameworks and course planning that occur in college classrooms.

This activity acknowledges the reality that, instead of planning for long-range goals or working with the mentor teacher to shape the themes of a course, most candidates find themselves having just a couple of days to prepare for a lesson on a particular standard. Although they may have neither the agency nor capacity to set the instructional goals for their classrooms, we urge them to see their daily lesson plans as a space to push beyond the prescribed content. In particular, we challenge them to draw from their knowledge of the students in the classroom, the subject matter, and current events to connect the content to something that has meaning for their students.

This activity is completed during one class meeting after candidates have completed several rounds of lesson planning in the practicum. The goals of this activity are:

- Surface the critical importance of finding ways to make the curriculum relevant to students
- Provide opportunities to practice and evaluate the quality of these efforts in applied contexts
- Strengthen collaboration skills and further refine the ability to self-assess strengths and weaknesses in curriculum planning

The Task: Prior to the activity, candidates read King, Newmann, and Carmichael's (2009) *Authentic Intellectual Work: Common Standards for Teaching Social Studies* as an introduction to AIW and the concept that curriculum should have value beyond school. Candidates also read the work conducted by the Social Studies Inquiry Research Collaborative (Saye et al., 2013) with attention to the conclusion that "measures of connections to the real world and students' lives were consistently lower for all quartiles than scores for other five AIW standards in the rubrics" (p. 102). Finally, candidates review the article titled "Science Shows Making Lesson Relevant Really Matter" (Bernard, 2010). This author cites scientific studies connecting personal relevance and memory storage and asserts that students fail to learn information presented in irrelevant fashion.

In their practicum lesson planning, candidates must connect their lessons to students' lives and to the real world and document these efforts in their weekly lesson plans. They receive feedback each week from their field supervisors. In week 4 of the practicum, I draw from all of the lesson plans to create a bank of standards, lesson topics, and accompanying descriptions of connections to the world. To do this, I create a table that lists the standard to be taught and every description of the connections to the world that appear in the candidates' lesson plans. The following image depicts one entry into the table. It represents a 7th-grade standard and the way that three different teacher candidates described their efforts to make the content relevant beyond school:

SS7CG6 The student will compare and contract various forms of government. Describe the ways government systems distribute power: unitary, confederation, and federal.
Explain how goverments determine citizen participation: autocratic, oligarchic, and democratic.

- The systems of government we were covering are found throughout the world. I connected democracy and federal systems of government to the United States, illuminating how their own government is divided into federal, state, and local authoiries.
- We showed some pictures from an Instagram account of a *National Geographic* photographer who takes picture of everyday life in North Korea. The photos showed monuments that people have in the homes of Kim Jonh-un and his predecessors and also of some national building and monuments in North Korea that have huge images of these leaders on the side. We asked the students to think about how an autocratic government might lead to this kind of society and whether this would happen in a democracy.
- Governments shape the lives of citizens all over the world; the fact that America is both a federal system and a democracy is something that impact the lives of our students every day.

I use this bank to create Part I of the activity, in which candidates assigned to the same grade levels review the connections to the world pieces designed by their peers.

The activity begins with small groups of candidates using the previously assigned texts as a basis to devise a short list of characteristics that signal the kinds of real-world connections promoted by the authors. Each list is shared with the class via an electronic document and I facilitate a discussion that helps the class to come to consensus on what should appear on the final list.

Using this list as a kind of rubric, I pair candidates placed in the same grade level and subject area, though I manipulate assignment of the lessons to ensure that group members are not evaluating each other's work. I take these actions to help candidates feel comfortable giving a wide range of feedback to their peers. Each group reviews the standards and accompanying connections taught by their peers and discusses the merits and weaknesses of each. They also generate written feedback via an electronic document made accessible to the entire class.

In Part 2 of the assignment, I re-group candidates in multi-grade and multi-subject practicum groups. I provide the upcoming content and standards in their various placements and ask them to brainstorm options for making connections to the world in the future weeks. I collect evidence from the brainstorming sessions specific to grade and subject and make it available to the class.

In the final step of this lesson, I gave candidates five minutes to respond in writing to the following prompt: "Assess your progress in connecting content to the world in your lesson planning."

Assessing the Task: Although the candidates' capacity to design and facilitate connections to the world in their practicum lessons is assessed throughout the semester, I evaluate the activities described above in markedly different ways. In this task, assessment first focuses on the candidates' ability to identify the strengths and weaknesses of connections in a given lesson and then to self-assess their own capacity to build this into their own lessons.

Throughout this activity, I circulate among the groups to observe candidates' conversations and evaluations of the lessons, taking notes of the statements and contributions of particular candidates and probing knowledge and understanding when opportunities are presented. Further, I assess the written evaluations of each small group on the candidates' ability to apply the characteristics identified by the group as indicating powerful and productive connections to actual examples of such efforts.

Finally, I evaluate individual candidates on their ability to recognize their own progress toward this goal. The final writing prompt asks candidates to apply what they learned in this activity about connecting content and make it relevant to an evaluation of their own efforts. In particular, I look for the degree to which candidates recognize the qualities and areas of improvement in their own practices.

CANDIDATES AND THE TASK

The collaborative tasks in these activities generate rich conversations about the difficult work of turning sterile standards into dynamic and relevant curriculum content for students. Discussions about this goal held in our pre-practicum class meetings often result in "well, duh" moments indicating that many teacher candidates feel the importance of making the content relevant to students is too commonsensical to warrant attention. This activity, however, creates the space for candidates to name and identify their struggles in trying to make these connections on a regular basis.

By examining the work of their peers, candidates discover two things: they see that others struggle and they find powerful examples of what connecting the content to the world can look like. Further, they know that these strong connections have been designed by their peers rather than by curriculum designers or veteran teachers. This peer-to-peer comparison, evaluation, and analysis create a far more productive feedback loop than one resulting from feedback by me or field instructors.

Finally, these conversations enable productive brainstorming spaces. Offering candidates the chance to build upon each other's ideas, draw on each other's content knowledge, and see how strong connections between the curriculum and the real world can be forged, generates positive future lesson planning by all candidates. The activity validates those candidates who already demonstrate a strong capacity for this skill; those who struggle to see these connections receive a significant hand up from their peers. I reached this conclusion based on the fact that the connections to the world described in lesson plans submitted after this activity are much stronger and more clearly articulated than those submitted prior.

THE TASK IN CONTEXT

This task occurs four weeks into the teacher candidates' first practicum rotation. It requires that candidates compile several weeks of lesson plans and document their specific efforts to connect their content to the world. Topics addressed prior to this activity included curriculum design and the basic components of lesson planning (we use *Understanding by Design* as the curriculum design model). After this activity, topics include assessment and the use of questioning to further student understanding.

REFERENCES

Bernard, S. (December, 2010). *Science shows making lessons relevant really matters.* Retrieved from http://www.edutopia.org/neuroscience-brain-based-learning-relevance-improves-engagement.

King, M. B., Newmann, F., & Carmichael, D. (2009). Authentic intellectual work: Common standards for teaching social studies. *Social Education, 73*(1), 43–49.

Saye, J., & Social Studies Inquiry Research Collaborative (SSIRC). (2013). Authentic pedagogy: Its presence in social studies classrooms and relationship to student performance on state-mandated tests. *Theory & Research in Social Education, 41*(1), 89–132.

CHAPTER 33

TEACHERS AS DECISION MAKERS

Using a Document-Based Activity Structure (DBAS) to Create Social Studies Curriculum

Corey R. Sell and Philip E. Bernhardt

Name: Corey R. Sell and Philip E. Bernhardt	Audience: Undergraduate and graduate students
Affiliation: Metropolitan State University of Denver	Length: Semester-long
Course Title: Social Studies Methods	Commonplace featured: Subject Matter
NCSS Teacher Education Standard: Element 2a. Candidates plan learning sequences that demonstrate alignment with the C3 Framework and state- required content standards. Element 2c. Candidates plan learning sequences that engage learners in disciplinary inquiry to develop literacies for civic life	

Teaching Social Studies: A Methods Book for Methods Teachers,
pages 193–198.
Copyright © 2017 by Information Age Publishing
All rights of reproduction in any form reserved.

TASK SUMMARY

Using a Document-Based Activity Structure (DBAS), teacher candidates create a disciplinary inquiry learning experience that highlights the integrative nature of the social studies in two ways: (a) across the disciplines and (b) with literacy.

DESCRIPTION OF THE TASK

K–12 social studies teachers face curricular challenges that can thwart their efforts to engage students in historical inquiry and disciplinary thinking. Those challenges include the struggle between literacy and subject matter priorities, the press for content coverage over interpretation, and the scarcity of good classroom resources.

The Task: Given such challenges, we developed a task that structures teacher candidates' knowledge development of historical inquiry and disciplinary thinking. Reisman's (2012a, 2012b) activity structure for the teaching of historical inquiries focuses on discipline-specific literacy instruction—the document-based lesson. We adapted Reisman's work to create a Document-Based Activity Structure (DBAS) to guide candidates' thinking and curricular decision-making. The DBAS delineates core practices for historical inquiry (Fogo, 2014) within three sequential lesson segments: (a) framing the inquiry and building background knowledge, (b) employing sources, and (c) determining and communicating results. Using such a structure allows the complex teaching practices within each segment to be decomposed, examined, and practiced independently of the larger framework. The DBAS, then, provides a practical tool for candidates to make sense of the complexities in social studies teaching and learning and scaffolds their future social studies curriculum work.

The objective of the DBAS assignment is for candidates to create a disciplinary inquiry learning experience for students that highlights the integrative nature of social studies. To achieve this goal, candidates must:

1. Use a disciplinary question to frame a series of lesson plans for teaching social studies.
2. Explain and connect disciplinary content utilizing strategies for literacy strategies for activating and/or building background knowledge.
3. Employ sources by determining literacy access approaches (e.g., read aloud, shared reading, buddy reading) and the meaning-making processes that promote student understanding (e.g. general reading strategies and historical literacy skills).
4. Develop and utilize techniques for determining results of an inquiry and facilitating deliberations of such results including attention to the development of communication skills.
5. Write a rationale statement that justifies their curricular choices with regards to powerful and purposeful social studies teaching and learning:

(a) active, (c) meaningful, (c) values-based, (d) challenging, and (e) integrative.

The Task in Context: We use an inductive approach to introduce the DBAS during the second week of class. First, candidates complete an on-line historical inquiry on Japanese internment during WWII that was adapted from a similar unit developed by the Stanford History Education Group and placed on Blackboard Learn. Second, candidates engage in a class discussion in which they reflect on the cognitive demands of the activity, the teaching format (i.e., historical inquiry), and the relationship between the two. The conversation elicits elements of the DBAS, which are explicitly presented to candidates by the end of class (see Appendix).

During the next eight weeks of class, we introduce candidates to three other disciplinary inquiries we designed using the DBAS. The first, a historical inquiry, asks, "did George Washington want to be the Commander-in-Chief of the Continental Army?" The second, a historical and geographical inquiry, uses the question, "what did John Smith value?" The third inquiry emphases civic-mindedness along with the historical inquiry process through the question, "how did Harriet Tubman and Susan B. Anthony work to change our society?" Through in-class modeling, we draw candidates' attention to the instructional techniques used within each DBAS component: (a) presenting and/or forming the inquiry question, (b) building background knowledge, (c) providing ways for students to access the sources, (d) providing explicit instruction in meaning-making processes for students to comprehend the sources, (e) determining the results of the inquiry, and (f) communicating the results.

Following the introduction to the DBAS and the three models, candidates create a DBAS-based disciplinary inquiry beginning around week 10. This shift to planning focuses candidates' attention on curricular decisions with the DBAS components organized into three lesson-planning segments. In week 10, candidates learn to frame inquiries using questions as well as methods for activating and/or building students' background knowledge. Practical tools such as anticipation guides and KWLs are modeled for the candidates.

In week 11, candidates learn explicit methods for providing students with access to a variety of primary and secondary sources. Such explicit teaching provides a space for candidates to discuss issues of selection, organization, and adaptation of primary sources as well as issues of accessibility for struggling readers. This class also focuses on general and discipline-specific methods to help students make meaning of the sources. The general methods include teaching tools for making connections, questioning, inferring, determining importance, summarizing, and synthesizing. The discipline-specific methods taught include sourcing, contextualizing, close reading, and corroborating.

In week 12, we emphasize methods for determining results of an inquiry and communicating these results to others. Such decisions emphasize key components of the Common Core State Standards (i.e., the collaboration involved in form-ing knowledge and the presentation of knowledge) and Dimension 4 of the *C3 Framework* (National Council for the Social Studies, 2013), that is, determining and communicating results.

Assessing the Task: As described above, weeks 10–12 are devoted to teach-ing each of the lesson-planning segments. Therefore, candidates complete a draft of the lesson-planning segment and submit it for feedback before the start of next week's class. Doing so gives candidates opportunities to gradually design the DBAS and receive immediate instructor feedback. At the end of these three weeks, candidates compile a draft of all three segments and bring a copy to class during week 13. Within groups of four, candidates adopt a commonplace lens through which to examine their peers' work and provide formative feedback. This activity, which reflects the curriculum-making process described by Schwab (1973), engages candidates in curriculum making that requires attention to the other curriculum commonplaces.

After week 13, candidates finalize their DBAS and write a rationale statement that justifies their curricular choices within a frame of powerful and purposeful social studies teaching and learning: (a) active, (c) meaningful, (c) values-based, (d) challenging, and (e) integrative. Doing so pushes them to elaborate on why a practice was chosen. Such emphasis highlights the conditional knowledge of their curricular decisions—a type of knowledge often absent in methods courses in comparison to declarative and procedural knowledge.

CANDIDATES AND THE TASK

Entering social studies methods, many teacher candidates are unfamiliar with strategies for facilitating meaningful learning experiences situated around dis-ciplinary inquiry. It is also common, especially at the secondary level, for candi-dates to ignore the integration of literacy instruction into daily lesson plans and activities. DBAS provides an instructional framework for engaging candidates in an authentic meaning-making process that achieves these goals. DBAS incor-porates three distinct instructional advantages that social studies candidates can integrate into their classrooms.

First, DBAS positions candidates as curriculum makers. For many, this is an important experience as they typically participate in field observations where the curriculum, lessons, and activities are prescribed. Candidates often find the DBAS design to be transferable and adaptable to their contexts. The DBAS struc-ture creates intentional conversations about subject matter, teaching, and student learning. The focus on literacy helps to emphasize that this component of instruc-tional planning and implementation needs to be more present. This realization has proven powerful, especially for secondary candidates, who often perceive literacy instruction as separate from teaching content and not an element of their work.

Second, the DBAS structure directly supports the use of all four *C3 Frame-work* dimensions, a framework utilized in social studies methods coursework.

Candidates value the time they spend examining questions that spark inquiry, employing sources, and examining methods for evidence-based interpretation. This work results in candidates developing more nuanced understandings of what rigorous content looks and feels like, and provides access to a national conversation occurring within the field around curriculum development. They appreciate how the C3 dimensions enhance the rigor of the units and lessons they develop and teach as part of methods courses. Once candidates get to student teaching, DBAS provides a tool for encouraging participatory skills as well as facilitating critical thinking and interdisciplinary connections, which are all central to the *C3 Framework*.

Finally, DBAS supports the approach to historical inquiry advocated within the Reading Like a Historian curriculum. Candidates gain experience in designing instructional activities that emphasize and prioritize important historical questions. These questions drive the selection of primary and secondary sources and the literacy modifications for groups of students with varied reading skills and capabilities. One example of a specific skill candidates are able to practice is evaluating the trustworthiness of claims related to historical issues. There is an intentionality here that candidates appreciate because it provides an activity structure that does more than focus on the teaching of content. DBAS privileges inquiry experiences over memorization as well as integration over isolation.

APPENDIX

Pose Inquiry Question		
Activate or Build Background Knowledge		
Elicit a Hypothesis		
Source 1	Source 2	Source 3
Literacy Access Approach	Literacy Access Approach	Literacy Access Approach
Meaning-Making Process	Meaning-Making Process	Meaning-Making Process
Determine & Communicate results *refute or support hypothesis This is a Document-Based Activity Structure separated into three lesson segments for planning inquires within the social studnets disciplines that has bee3n adapted from the work of Reisman (2012a, 2012b)		

REFERENCES

National Council for the Social Studies (NCSS). (2013). *The college, career, and civic life (C3) framework for social studies state standards: Guidance for enhancing the rigor of K–12 civics, economics, geography, and history*. Silver Spring, MD: National Council for the Social Studies.

Fogo, B. (2014). Core practices for teaching history: The results of a Delphi panel survey. *Theory & Research in Social Education, 42*(2), 151–96.

Reisman, A. (2012a). The "document-based lesson": Bringing disciplinary inquiry into high school history classrooms with adolescent struggling readers. *Journal of Curriculum Studies 44*(2), 233–264.

Reisman, A. (2012b). Reading like a historian: A document-based history curriculum intervention in urban high schools. *Cognition and Instruction, 30*(1), 86–112.

Schwab, J. J. (1973). The practical 3: Translation into curriculum. *The School Review, 81*(4), 501–522.

CHAPTER 34

DISCUSSING STANDARDS

A Dialogic Analysis of the NYS Social Studies Framework

Dennis Urban and Elina Lampert-Shepel

Name: Dennis Urban and Elina Lampert-Shepel	Audience: Graduate students
Affiliation: Touro College	Length: Two-three online sessions over 10 days
Course Title: Teaching Social Studies and the Arts in General Education and Special Education, Grades 1–6	Commonplace featured: Subject Matter
NCSS Teacher Education Standard: Element 1c. Candidates are knowledgeable about disciplinary forms of representation in civics, economics, geography, history, and the social/behavioral sciences.	

Teaching Social Studies: A Methods Book for Methods Teachers,
pages 199–205.

TASK SUMMARY

Teacher candidates analyze the *New York State K–8 Social Studies Framework* (New York State Education Department, 2015), reflect upon their experiences of learning and teaching social studies, and participate in mediated online discussions to process, examine, question, extend, and critique the NYS Framework.

DESCRIPTION OF THE TASK

The NYS Framework Analysis assignment enables teacher candidates to understand and critique current social studies standards in a blended-learning environment. Online education promotes high levels of cognitive engagement, adapts to learners' individual needs, balances student autonomy with teacher guidance, and promotes generative and measurable dialogue among participants (Smith & Brame, n.d.). In this context, the assignment supports four main learning objectives. First, students understand the NYS social studies standards and practices. Second, they critically analyze the NYS Framework's themes and practices relative to Common Core Learning Standards (CCLS). Third, they reflect upon their experiences with social studies education in relation to the NYS Framework standards. Finally, throughout the assignment, candidates engage in an instructor-mediated online dialogue with their peers regarding the assignment's analytical and reflective processes.

   The Task: The Framework analysis requires candidates to engage with various texts through close reading (and re-reading) and to build arguments supported by evidence. In addition to the NYS Framework, candidates read about the social studies standards (New York State Education Department, n.d.), CCLS for literacy (Bullmaster-Day, 2013), and lesson design principles (Wiggins & McTighe, 2011). As they read, students post responses to our guiding questions and pose their own questions on the Discussion Board (DB), making the Framework Analysis a recursive process. The guiding questions include:

1. Explain your understanding of the "Social Studies Practices: Vertical Articulation K–4 and 5–8."
2. What connections can you make between the NYS framework and concept-based teaching and learning?
3. Select one of the 10 Themes and a related Key Idea and Conceptual Understanding. What ideas do you have—what strategies might you use—to help your students understand this selected Key Idea/Conceptual Understanding?
4. Which of the Common Core Anchor Standards for Reading and Writing are incorporated in your current grade-level Social Studies Curriculum or Project-Based Learning Units? How are they incorporated? [This question assumes they are in-service teachers.]

5.   Which of the Social Studies Practices do your students use in your current grade-level Social Studies curriculum or Project-Based Learning Units? How do they use these practices? [This question assumes they are in-service teachers.]

6.   What experience did you have as a K–12 student with any of the Learning Standards for Social Studies? How did you learn about these areas?

7.   What questions do you have about the NYS Framework? Explain your thinking.

Candidates submit their responses to the DB and engage in asynchronous dialogues with their classmates.

The Discussion Board allows candidates to process, examine, question, and extend their knowledge of elementary social studies in relation to the NYS Framework. Grounded in theories of Dialogic Pedagogy (Bakhtin, 1986; Matusov, 2009), the DB requirement rests on the premise that the human "mind" resides among people, not just within the heads of individuals, and that distributed cognition is the result of socially-mediated learning. Not every human interaction, however, promotes development and growth. Therefore, we have been intentional about creating a group dialogue as a mediated activity (Vygotsky, 1986) through discussion threads, weekly Teaching Memos, and a detailed DB rubric.

We organize the initial discussion by posing questions related to the session's assigned texts. Candidates participate by posting *initials posts* and *responses* to other candidates. Initial posts include answers to the session's DB questions and require candidates to ask additional questions that emerged from the assigned texts. Responses include discussions of questions posted by other candidates. For the Framework Analysis project, we pose the following questions:

1.   According to the text, in what ways does the NYS Framework incorporate concept-based teaching?

2.   In what ways does the NYS Framework align with what we know about attention, memory, and learning?

3.   According to the text, how can concept-based social studies instruction help students meet the CCLS?

We then facilitate group interaction with additional content and questions, which promote analysis, synthesis, and evaluation of ideas rather than description and rote memorization of facts. Candidates participate in discussions via one initial post and a minimum of three substantive responses to others' posts during each session. They must participate in the discussion forums on five different days within the specified DB segment; submit two initial posts (one for each session) that respond to the guiding questions; cite at least four specific points from the text(s) in each initial post; pose three original and insightful questions based on the texts and discussion content; post eight or more responses to other candidates, supported by evidence from course texts; offer at least one additional relevant text or website; and make connections to self as a teacher/student/learner in at least four posts.

In addition to participating in DB threads, we share a Teaching Memo with the whole class at the end of every DB session. Doing so allows us to offer a mini-lecture on the session's content, answer candidates' questions, highlight their insights, address their misconceptions or biases, and share additional resources.

Assessing the Task: There are two principal assessment components of the Framework Analysis project. First, throughout the task, we assess candidates' participation according to the DB rubric (see Appendix). Second, as a summative assessment, we evaluate the candidates' final NYS Framework analysis responses based on their thoughtfulness about and reflection on their learning and teaching of social studies, their demonstrated knowledge of the NYS Framework, and their incorporation of information gleaned from DB participation.

CANDIDATES AND THE TASK

The Framework Analysis assignment allows teacher candidates to relate a potentially abstract set of state standards to their prior knowledge about social studies. Shawn, a current first-grade teacher, wrote, "since the social studies framework highlights key ideas and concepts instead of content, this prevents teachers from teaching solely content and memorization." Abigail, another elementary school teacher, posed questions and began a dialogue about implementing the NYS Framework:

> **Abigail**: Do you see in your classroom the interdisciplinary standards that are used in the framework? Do you think the framework is set up to be easily implemented in every classroom?

> **Chris**: To answer your first question, I do see the interdisciplinary standards that are used in the framework in my classroom. The framework promotes civic competence and the acquisition of understanding key concepts....I see instances where they have incorporated a few social studies concepts; for instance, students were learning about the Wampanoag and the Pilgrims' migration patterns and about their culture in general.

> **Brianna**: I do think that the framework was made to be easily implemented in every classroom. This is primarily because of the freedom that educators have when it comes to the social studies curriculum....I wonder if the framework was created to be implemented in every classroom in order to entice educators to include social studies within the school day. What do you think?

By encouraging the discussion of new ideas, this type of dialogue deepens candidates' understandings of social studies education. A major concern of the candidates was how the NYS Framework might look in practice. Through online discussion, they were able to tease out components of the NYS Framework and share standards-based approaches to teaching elementary social studies.

THE TASK IN CONTEXT

The Framework Analysis assignment takes place early in the course, around the second or third week. By this point, teacher candidates have read and discussed texts about concept-based learning (Hilburn & Wall, 2011) and cognition (Bull-master-Day, 2011). The Framework Analysis assignment serves as source material for catalyzing social studies curriculum, lessons, and activities (Schwab, 1973). Ultimately, it helps prepare candidates for the final project, a concept-based Learning Segment modeled after edTPA guidelines, which requires candidates to choose a social studies theme from the NYS Framework and to develop lessons that teach social studies content and address CCLS.

APPENDIX: GRADING RUBRIC: DISCUSSION GROUP CONTRIBUTIONS

Criteria	Advanced (3)	Proficient (2)	Novice (1)	Points
Discussion Participation and Timeliness	Over the course of the 2 sessions, candidate participates in the discussion on *at least 3* different days. All required posts are posted before the end of the second session.	Over the course of the 2 sessions, candidate participates in the discussion on *at least 2* different days. All required posts are posted before the end of the second session.	Over the course of the 2 sessions, candidate participates in the discussion on *at least 1* different day. All required posts are posted before the end of the second session.	
Initial Post Timeliness	Initial Post is posted within the first 1–2 days from the session start.	Initial post is posted on DB within the first 3 days from the session start.	Initial Post is posted on DB within the first 4 days from the session start.	
Initial Post Quality	**Candidate submits 2 initial posts (one for each session) in which:** 1) Candidate responds to the guiding questions/ discussion prompts by synthesizing information from course texts; 2) Candidate cites *at least 3 specific points from the text(s).*	**Candidate submits 2 initial posts** (one for each session) in which: 1) Candidate responds to the guiding questions/ discussion prompts by synthesizing information from course texts; 2) Candidate cites *at least 2 specific points from the text(s).*	Candidate submits 1 initial posts one for each session) in which: 1) Candidate responds to the guiding questions/ discussion prompts by synthesizing information from course texts; 2) Candidate cites *at least 1 specific points from the text(s).*	

(continues)

Criteria	Advanced (3)	Proficient (2)	Novice (1)	Points
Questions posed	Over the course of 2 sessions' discussions, candidate raises *at least 3 original, insightful questions,* based upon course texts and discussion content.	Over the course of 2 sessions' discussions, candidate raises *at least 2 original, insightful questions,* based upon course texts and discussion content.	Over the course of 2 sessions' discussions, candidate raises *at least 1 original, insightful question,* based upon course texts and discussion content.	
Response Quality	1) Candidate's responses build upon other learners' perspectives/questions to deepen the discussion. 2) Candidate posts *at least 5 or more responses to other learners,* supported by evidence from course texts, and 3) Candidate offers *at least 1 additional relevant text or website.*	1) Candidate's responses build upon other learners' perspectives/questions to deepen the discussion, and 2) Candidate posts *at least 4 or more responses to other learners,* supported by evidence from course texts.	1) Candidate's responses build upon other learners' perspectives/questions to deepen the discussion, and 2) Candidate posts *3 or more responses to other learners,* supported by evidence from course texts.	
Connections	Connections to self as a teacher/student/ learner were made in *at least 3 posts.*	Connections to self as a teacher/ student/ learner were made in *at least 2 posts.*	Connections to self as a teacher/ student/ learner were made in *at least 1 post.*	
Writing Style and Composition	*All* posts are written with correct grammar, punctuation, spelling, and sentence structure.	*Most (≥50%)* posts are written with correct grammar, punctuation, spelling, and sentence structure.	*Few (< 50%)* posts are written with correct grammar, punctuation, spelling, and sentence structure.	
Total Points				/21

ACKNOWLEDGEMENTS

Special thanks to Marcella Bullmaster-Day, Associate Dean of Touro College Graduate School of Education and Director of the Lander Center for Educational Research, for developing the original NYS Framework Analysis assignment.

REFERENCES

Bakhtin, M. M. (1986). Speech genres and other late essays. In Emerson, C. & Holquist, M. (Eds.), *Speech genres and other late essays* (pp. 259–422). Austin, TX: University of Texas Press.

Bullmaster-Day, M. L. (2011). *Let the learner do the learning: What we know about effective teaching.* New York: Touro College Lander Center for Educational Research.

Bullmaster-Day, M. (2013). *Common Core Standards ELA/Literacy.* Retrieved from https://www.youtube.com/watch?v=RDeNSzwESug.

Hilburn, J., & Wall, S. D. (2011). Concept-based interdisciplinary teaching: Science and social studies teacher collaboration for the 21st century. *North Carolina Middle School Journal, 26*(1), 1–10.

Matusov, E. (2009). *Journey into dialogic pedagogy.* Hauppauge, NY: Nova Publishers.

New York State Education Department. (2015). *New York State K–8 social studies framework.* Retrieved from https://www.engageny.org/file/14656/download/ss-framework-k-8.pdf?token=LqTfBWX7.

New York State Education Department (n.d.). *New York State's FAQs about teaching social studies: Frequently asked questions.* Retrieved from http://www.p12.nysed.gov/ciai/socst/ssfaq.html.

Schwab, J. (1973). The practical 3: Translation into curriculum. *The School Review, 81*(4), 501–522.

Smith, B., & Brame, C. (n.d.). *Blended and online learning.* Retrieved from https://cft.vanderbilt.edu/guides-sub-pages/blended-and-online-learning.

Vygotsky, L. (1986). *Thought and language.* Cambridge, MA: The MIT Press.

Wiggins, G. P., & McTighe, J. (2011). *The understanding by design guide to creating high-quality units.* Alexandria, VA: Association for Supervision and Curriculum Development.

PART 4

CONTEXT

CHAPTER 35

AN HOUR IN OUR TOWN

Erin Adams

Name: Erin Adams	Audience: Undergraduate and graduate students
Affiliation: Kennesaw State University	Length: Approx. 4–5 hours
Course Title: Secondary Social Studies Methods/ Curriculum	Commonplace featured: Context
NCSS Teacher Education Standard: Element 4a. Candidates identify learners' socio-cultural assets and learning demands to plan and implement relevant and responsive pedagogy that increases candidates' opportunities to learn social studies.	

Teaching Social Studies: A Methods Book for Methods Teachers,
pages 209–213.

TASK SUMMARY

The *Hour in Our Town* activity provides an opportunity for teacher candidates to explore the local contexts in which they are learning and in which their future students may learn by visiting and analyzing two sites in their town/city/community, writing about their experiences, and preparing a community resource fair for their classmates and invited guests.

DESCRIPTION OF THE TASK

The goals of the task are to help teacher candidates explore the community by visiting sites they may not have visited before, to understand resources offered in communities and to see these resources as assets, and to consider how these sites, and their resources, offer youth rich social learning.

The Task: The assignment consists of several steps. First, candidates choose two sites to visit in town from a list of possible sites I provide. They can make these visits in pairs, small groups, or by themselves. These sites should be places where candidates can actually spend time and immerse themselves, rather than simply walk in, look around, and leave. Thus, the sites should, ideally, offer candidates something to do and should be places where the youth they will teach would access or spend time outside of school. Good possibilities include grocery stores, farmers markets, libraries, parks, malls, community centers, and festivals.

Candidates spend an hour in these two sites (30 minutes each). They have the option of taking pictures in their sites, but are cautioned to use good judgment in doing so. Candidates write a short reflection paper, which offers an opportunity to reflect on their experiences in a private way, that is, in a way that is just between the candidate and me. Some useful questions to prompt candidates include:

- What sorts of knowledge or skills would people need in these spaces?
- What does this space offer to the public?
- What kind of social learning might take place in these sites?

Finally, candidates work in pairs to create a presentation for their classmates in the form of a community resource fair. Since candidates do not visit every site, the resource fair provides an opportunity for their classmates to learn about the sites they did not visit. The assignment also allows for the simultaneous modeling of a teaching method that candidates might try in their own classrooms. To do the resource fair, candidates work with their partner(s) to create a presentation in the form of a poster or trifold board. The poster should contain a description of the sites visited, pictures of the sites (taken by the candidates or obtained online), and answers to the prompts above.

The task challenges candidates to think about *where* their students gain their social learning and *how* they learn it. Moreover, doing this assignment as an intentional class project turns the task from simply having candidates simply gaze at people and places in the community to an exploration of the rich social learning that takes place there. Thus, the task turns into an exploration of the funds of knowledge youth have and that communities offer.

While it might be too early for candidates to know about the specific youth they will teach, they can begin to engage in tasks such as this in order to develop the skills necessary to identify things such as funds of knowledge (Moll, Amanti, Neff, & Gonzales, 1992) present in communities. Moreover, the very ideas associated with funds of knowledge specifically, the study of people's social, economic, and civic activities, is incredibly relevant to social studies teaching and learning.

Assessing the Task: The task is assessed through two culminating assignments—an individual reflection paper and a group poster presentation. The two-page reflection paper allows candidates to write about their experiences, pose questions, and answer the prompts listed earlier.

The posters are assessed by the candidates, the guests who participate in the community resource fair, and by me. On the day of the resource fair, candidates set up their posters around the classroom and stand next to them. Then, I assign the group members an "A" or "B." The "A" candidates are stand next to their posters while the "B" candidates walk around the classroom to see the other presentations. After an allotted amount of time, the groups switch roles. This method ensures that at least one group member is standing next to the poster at all times. It also allows candidates to be more actively involved because they can have conversations in small groups that might be less intimidating than large-group presentations. Candidates and guests provide each group with a feedback form (see ancillary materials), which gives candidates the opportunity to practice assessing projects and giving feedback.

CANDIDATES AND THE TASK

I assign this activity in the introductory social studies education courses that I teach which is located in a diverse mid-sized city in the Southeast U.S. that has a high number of youth and families living in poverty. I want teacher candidates to venture away from the sphere of the university and into the actual neighborhoods and communities that the youth they likely teach live in. Candidates have the option of riding the city bus on a route they do not usually ride, and/or visit the local public library, the farmers market, or the flea market. I chose these sites for several reasons. First, because they are accessible, free of admission, and easy to get to by car or bus. Second, they are different enough to provide useful comparisons. However, the sites are located in very different parts of the community, serve very different populations, and are viewed differently by the political and social elite in town. Finally, these are sites that most candidates have never visited. The activity allows them to explore places in town and see these places through an asset lens.

Candidates generally enjoy the activity and gain a great deal of insight into the local community. In their papers, they grapple with big, controversial, and confusing questions about the contexts their students live and work in. For example, candidates wrote about how youth are both vendors and buyers at the flea market and that, to be successful, demands haggling and negotiation skills. Candidates who rode the bus noted that bus riders need to know geography, be able to read and understand the bus timetable and have a great deal of flexibility and patience as the bus is likely to be late.

THE TASK IN CONTEXT

The task can be assigned to teacher candidates in any stage of their teacher education program. I have facilitated this assignment, and variations of it, with candidates who were just beginning to consider a career as a social studies teacher and those who were starting to do preliminary teaching in practicum/field placement classrooms.

In exploring potential sites, consider the following:

- Accessibility
  - o Is the site safe?
  - o Is there a cost? An entrance fee?
  - o Can it be reached by car, by foot, or by public transportation?
- Appropriateness
  - o Is visiting this site unobtrusive for those that reside there?
  - o Does it enrich the candidates' understandings of the community and/or of social studies?
  - o Does the site offer a point of comparison with other sites or experiences?
  - o How familiar are candidates with this site? Does it offer something new or can the assignment offer a way to see it differently?
- Variety
  - o Are there a variety of sites to visit in terms of populations served and physical locations?
  - o Are the sites varied in terms of the considerations listed above?

APPENDIX: COMMUNITY RESOURCE PROJECT PEER & GUEST FEEDBACK FORM:

Instructors—Print on half sheets for candidates and guests to fill out during the community resource fair

Presenters _____
Reviewer _____

Please comment on the following:

1. The description of the sites visited and how they compare and contrast with each other
2. The description of how the sites relate to social studies learning

3.   The description of the knowledge teacher candidates would need to access, and/or be successful in, these spaces
4.   The quality of the insights gained from visiting these sites
5.   Presenters' quality of presentation, knowledge of subject matter, and ability to express ideas

REFERENCE

Moll, L. C., Amanti, C., Neff, D., & Gonzalez, N. (1992). Funds of knowledge for teaching: Using a qualitative approach to connect homes and classrooms. *Theory into Practice, 31*(2), 132–141.

CHAPTER 36

EXPERIENCING A DIFFERENT FIELD

Cultural Capital and the Classroom

Nick Bardo and Bárbara C. Cruz

Name: Nick Bardo and Bárbara C. Cruz	Audience: Undergraduate and graduate students
Affiliation: University of South Florida	Length: 2.5 hours of class time, 4–6 hours for field experience, 4–5 hours for written analysis, 6–7 hours for instructor feedback on analysis (depending on number of candidates).
Course Title: SSE 4380: Global and Multicultural Perspectives in Social Studies Education	Commonplace featured: Context
NCSS Teacher Education Standard: Element 5b. Candidates explore, interrogate, and reflect upon their own cultural frames to attend to issues of equity, diversity, access, power, human rights, and social justice within their schools and/or communities.	

Teaching Social Studies: A Methods Book for Methods Teachers,
pages 215–221.
Copyright © 2017 by Information Age Publishing

TASK SUMMARY

Through the comparative lens of a field experience in a context outside of their everyday lives, teacher candidates reflect on themselves as cultural beings, demonstrating an in-depth analysis of the personal values, beliefs, and ideologies they utilize every day.

DESCRIPTION OF THE TASK

The primary aim of this assignment is to push teacher candidates to seek out an environment in which their personal worldview can be cast in contrast to providing a comparative lens for analysis. The secondary aim of this project is to provide candidates with a theoretical framework for understanding how culture and power are negotiated in a diverse society and within diverse classrooms. Through a written reflective analysis, candidates delineate their own normative understandings of values, beliefs, and ideologies through comparison with what they found in the field. This assignment is important in developing what global educators such as Robert Hanvey (1976) described as perspective consciousness, the ability to acknowledge that one's worldview is not universal and is informed by the values, beliefs, and ideologies that operate on the subconscious level. The goal is to understand how these unexamined assumptions can be mistakenly projected onto others, especially in our work as teachers.

The Task: The task consists of four components each of which is described as follows:

Candidate-Centered Discussion of Pre-class reading (30 minutes): To organize the task of operationalizing and analyzing culture, Pierre Bourdieu's (1986/2011) *Forms of Capital* is assigned as pre-reading, which candidates discuss in pre-arranged learning circles. In these circles, each candidate is assigned a role for the week (discussion director, summarizer, word watcher, or connector). We operate the timer (each role is given three minutes to direct the discussion) and circulate amongst groups, noting candidates' participation and entering discussions if questions arise. After the final group member has completed his/her assigned role, the class comes together for a 15-minute Socratic seminar. We continue to operate the timer, but can also present questions when discussion stalls. Modeling these pedagogic strategies demonstrates the efficacy of dialogical discussion, introduces cooperative learning activity, and addresses formative assessment strategies as through proximity checks.

Teacher-Centered Presentation (20 minutes): Following this class discussion, a 20-minute interactive guided-note lecture on *The Forms of Capital* provides a summary of the concepts. Modeling guided notes is a way that both equips candidates with a tool for their future classrooms, and is a way to keep candidates engaged as they fill in missing words, definitions, and graphic organizers connected to the lecture on the handout.

According to Bourdieu (1986/2011), each classroom has its own rules, symbols, power structures, and culture). In the case of a diverse classroom, the teacher as authority assumes a greater degree of power. A teacher's normative conception of language, symbols, power structures, and culture may not align with the disparate familial and communal contexts of their students. To avoid later clashes, it is imperative for pre-service teachers to engage with their own normative cultural assumptions in an organized, thoughtful, and safe conceptual analysis before they are placed as authorities in classrooms.

Bourdieu (1986/2011) referred to the exchange of power within the field as capital and the worldviews and systems of perceptions that guide action within the field *habitas*, a phenomenon he said where "history turned into nature" (p. 78). This assignment, at its root, is asking pre-service teachers to trace the history of their personal worldviews and simultaneously acknowledge the history of a worldview with which they are not familiar. Through this process, candidates can begin to separate their personal conceptions of value from what they have been socialized to value.

To complement the Bourdieu reading, we bring Lisa Delpit's (1995) notion of cultural conflict in the classroom into the discussion to flesh out how teachers develop preferences for certain students' behaviors, symbols, and language as a part of their cultural socialization. During this discussion, differences related to speech patterns and communications with practical implications for diverse classrooms are targeted. Throughout this discussion, we guide the class discussion through Delpit's framework provided on the handout.

Small Group Activities (45 minutes): After the guided note lecture, candidates work with their shoulder partners to draw upon their own experiences. Shoulder partners are asked to think of examples of the three forms of cultural capital (embodied, institutional, and objectified) that were assigned different values in different fields during their lives. Candidates often cite how clothes and brands (objectified cultural capital according to Bourdieu) have different value in their home lives as compared to their schools. Others cite how degrees and certifications (institutional capital) are valued differently from one context to the next. Language is seen to have different value in schools as compared to in homes. As part of sharing out to the wider class, candidates stand and share their examples. Doing so is described to the class as another method of formative assessment. This small group discussion is often an "a-ha moment" for candidates who connect the content to their lives.

As a culminating activity for the class session, candidates complete a modified "privilege walk" (see Appendix), an activity demonstrating how certain cultures are privileged due to their access to cultural capital. This activity solidifies ideas about how power and culture are intertwined, as those with the most cultural capital are able to advance farther in relation to those with less cultural capital. The activity concludes with a class discussion debrief, where we lead the candidates to reflect on the forms of cultural capital they have been socialized to recognize as valuable. Candidates are encouraged to envision their future classrooms and to think about the diversity of cultural capital that may be represented, and how that differs from what they may see as "normal."

Field Experience (Outside of Class): After reading, reflecting, discussing and connecting the forms of capital to their lives, candidates visit a place of personal interest outside of their comfort zone. During the visit, candidates generate data through field-notes based on observations and conversations with those invested and involved in that context. Candidates utilize their field notes to describe the culture (i.e., norms, traditions, belief, values, patterns of organization, rituals, social relationships, and meanings) as they explain, compare, and contrast the similarities and differences between their own historicized cultural worldview and what they observed through the lens of cultural capital. Candidates then discuss the experience and their analysis in a way that connects to multicultural and global perspectives. Our feedback and an assessment rubric guide candidates in constructing their reflections tracing their own values and beliefs as they reflect on the experience.

Assessing the Task: Candidates are initially graded on their personal responses to the readings as part of their semester-long reading log. This evaluation is separate from the written analysis of the field experience. For the reading log, candidates write "with" the reading, describing personal lived connections to the material while synthesizing the content. We provide feedback to these written responses. Beyond this, candidates receive grades on their participation in class discussions and activities.

As related to the written component of the assignment, a rubric details the various dimensions of the analysis to be addressed. Candidates are encouraged to confer with us and submit rough drafts to get feedback before the final analysis is due.

CANDIDATES AND THE TASK

Typically, candidates are initially apprehensive about the reading due to the conceptual density and difficulty of the text. The vast majority rise to the challenge with the piece, though some might need additional support with respect to vocabulary and ideas. At the beginning of the assignment, it is apparent that a number of White candidates struggle in conceiving of themselves as cultural beings. Candidates, on the whole, have enjoyed the freedom to determine what is outside of their cultural comfort zone and the realizations that have come with it. For example, one candidate reflected on a homeless camp:

> I really enjoyed this assignment because it opened my eyes to homeless life. I felt bad and had to do some self-reflecting because many of my preconceptions were wrong. When I thought of homeless people, I just thought of high school dropouts who are drug addicts. After speaking with Jo, I know that is not the majority. My heart really went out to Jo because he is a great guy who just made a couple mistakes, and it destroyed him.

Another candidate recalled the challenge of responding to behavior different from her own:

> One must use critical thinking skills when thinking about the context of certain cultural norms that differ or go against one's own. Educators that practice multicultural education need to take this into account. A student may engage in a cultural custom that could be widely different or offensive to the teacher. The teacher must critically think about it and understand the context behind it in order to fully respect the student's culture.

Overall, candidates enjoy the project and the new lens through which to analyze culture in their lives. Anecdotally, we can report that the concepts gleaned through this project continue to impact our candidates' lives once they begin their teaching careers.

THE TASK IN CONTEXT

The task is due the fourth week of the semester-long course. After the project is graded and returned to the teacher candidates, the course continues with learning circle discussions, but class sessions focus increasingly on modeling activities and honing strategies for practical use. The cumulative project of the semester is a completed lesson plan where candidates have "globalized" or "multi-culturalized" a secondary social science lesson of their choosing. The lesson is presented to their peers for feedback. The revised, final lessons are shared with all candidates via Google Docs as a digital portfolio candidates can access and use in their future classrooms.

APPENDIX: LEARNING CIRCLE ROLE DESCRIPTIONS

Reading Role	Description	Guiding Questions
. **Discussion Director**	Your role is to identify the important aspects of your assigned reading(s) and develop questions for your group to discuss. Focus on the major themes or "big ideas" in the reading(s) and your reaction(s) to those ideas. Make sure to answer your own question. You are also responsible for facilitating the group discussion during class.	• What did the reading(s) make you think about? • What do you think the reading(s) was/were about? • What are the most important ideas/ moments in the reading(s)? Why?
Summarizer	Your role is to prepare a summary of the major elements of the reading(s). You will need to decide what you perceive to be the most important elements of the readings and explain each in a way that is easy to understand.	• What are the most important pieces of information from the reading(s)? • Why are these pieces of information important?

Reading Role	Description	Guiding Questions
Connector	Your role is to connect the reading(s) to other coursework, lived experiences, news events, political events, and/or popular trends. Make sure to provide clear and meaningful connections.	• What is the most interesting or important connection that comes to mind? • What connections can you make to your own life? News events, political events, and/or popular trends? • What connections can you make to previously learned information?
Word Watcher	Your role is to watch out for words/phrases worth knowing from your reading(s). These words might be interesting, new, and/ or important. Make sure to define each word/phrase and indicate the specific location in the reading (author, title, page or paragraph number) so the group can discuss these words in context.	• Which words/phrases are especially important to understand? • What new words are introduced in the reading(s)? • What words/phrases do you perceive to be the most interesting?

Instructions for Cultural Capital Walk:

Have teacher candidates form a straight line with plenty of space to move forward and backward as the activity proceeds. It is important to preface the point of activity, as a demonstration of how certain forms of cultural capital favor social mobility in society and education.

Read the following to participants:

I am going to read brief descriptive statements. If what is described applies to you, follow the instructions to move forward or backward. If you are not comfortable with what is being read, you are not required to move, as this is a voluntary activity. I will then read some statements aloud, pausing between each statement, giving you time to reflect and move accordingly. [NOTE: When you have finished reading the statements, have candidates note where they stand in relation to others. After this, call the candidates back for debriefing and discussion.]

Sample Statements

- If you are right-handed, take one step forward (Embodied capital).
- If English is your first language, take one step forward (Embodied capital).
- If one or both of your parents have a college degree, take one step forward (Institutional capital).
- If you rely, or have relied, primarily on public transportation, take one step back (Objectified capital).

- If your household employs help such as housekeepers, gardeners, etc., take one step forward (Objectified capital).
- If you studied the culture of your ancestors in elementary school, take one step forward (Institutional capital).
- If you would never think twice about calling the police when trouble occurs, take one step forward (Institutional capital).
- If you ever had to skip a meal or were hungry because there was not enough money to buy food, take one step back (Objectified capital).
- If you have a physically visible disability, take one step back (Embodied capital).
- If you ever tried to change your appearance, mannerisms, or behavior to fit in more, take one step back (Embodied capital).
- If you have ever been profiled by someone else using stereotypes, take one step back (Embodied capital).

Debrief Discussion Questions

1. What did you feel like being in the front of the group? In the back? In the middle?
2. What were some factors that you have never thought of before?
3. What question made you think most? If you could add a question, what would it be?
4. What do you wish people knew about one of the identities, situations, or disadvantages that caused you to take a step back?
5. How can your understanding of cultural capital and social mobility improve your understanding of your future classroom?

REFERENCES

Bourdieu, P. (1977). *Outline of a theory of practice.* Cambridge, UK: Cambridge University Press.

Bourdieu, P. (1986/2011). The forms of capital. In I.Szeman & T. Kaposy (Eds.), *Cultural theory: An anthology,* (pp. 81–93). Madden, MA: Wiley-Blackwell.

Delpit, L. D. (1995). *Other people's children: Cultural conflict in the classroom.* New York: New Press.

Hanvey, R. (1976). *An attainable global perspective.* Washington, DC: The American Forum for Global Education.

CHAPTER 37

PICTURING SOCIAL STUDIES

Kristy A. Brugar

Name: Kristy A. Brugar	Audience: Upper division, undergraduate students
Affiliation: University of Oklahoma	Length: approximately 180 minutes. (60 minutes in class, 60 minutes outside of class, and 60 minutes in class sharing projects)
Course Title: Teaching Secondary Social Studies	Commonplace featured: Context
NCSS Teacher Education Standard: Element 1a. Candidates are knowledgeable about the concepts, facts, and tools in civics, economics, geography, history, and the social/behavioral sciences.	

Teaching Social Studies: A Methods Book for Methods Teachers,
pages 223–226.

TASK SUMMARY

The *Picturing Social Studies* assignment positions teacher candidates to explore complex meanings and multiple interpretations of common social studies concepts (e.g., rights, urbanization) in multimodal ways.

DESCRIPTION OF THE TASK

The *Picturing Social Studies Project* is grounded in two over-arching understandings. The first is that classrooms are visual places. Maps, paintings, textbooks, virtual exhibits, and instructional presentations are evidence of the visual experiences for candidates: "Visual imagery saturates their [candidates'] daily existence, and they are perhaps more likely to learn about history from televisions, film, video games, and photographs than from reading" (Desai, Hamlin, & Mattson, 2010, p. 5). Second is the notion that visuals provide points of access to information as well as outlets for candidates to communicate their understandings. National and state standards documents (e.g., The *C3 Framework*, Common Core State Standards, Oklahoma Standards for Social Studies) include language about visuals and graphic representations.

With these understandings in mind, this task (spanning two class sessions and work outside of class time) asks teacher candidates to explore common social studies concepts as a means of connecting their future candidates to content. The goals of the assignment are:

- Identify common concepts in secondary social studies curricular materials (National Council for the Social Studies (NCSS), 2013, see Appendix A for examples.),
- Recognize the differing ways in which one might define, understand, and view various social studies concepts within a local community,
- Analyze and explain conceptual understandings,
- Create open-ended/discussion-based questions to further understandings and classroom possibilities around these concepts.

The Task: This assignment requires teacher candidates to explore common concepts in social studies in their local community through images. Prior to our class session, candidates receive a list of social studies concepts and select up to five that they are interested in examining beyond lists of names and dates. After previewing the list, candidates commonly select concepts like authority, citizenship, environmental consequences, globalization, and laws.

We begin with a class raffle (e.g., pulling names from a hat) to select the concept each candidate will examine for this assignment. I allow for multiple candidates to work on a singular concept individually or in small groups. After selections are completed, candidates use the next 60 minutes to explore our classroom, building, campus, community, and take pictures of their selected concept with their iPads. I have allowed candidates to use Internet sources, but my preference is that they explore and recognize social studies in their everyday experiences.

Following their data gathering, candidates organize their examples into a visual display (e.g., PowerPoint, Prezi) for a brief class presentation at our next meeting. Candidates' visual displays must include 1) an identification and definition of the social studies concept, 2) a display of at least five images that exemplify the concept, and 3) a corresponding caption for each image that explicitly connects the image and the concept. The candidates share these products with one another via our university course management system and present their work visually and verbally in class. Following the presentations, candidates re-visit their peers' products and develop at least one inquiry-based question for each concept presented.

Assessing the Task: This project is assessed in three ways: 1) the multimodal product, 2) the presentation of the product to peers, and 3) the inquiry-based questions developed around other candidates' concepts.

The multimodal product is assessed in two ways typically attributed to visual literacy: interpretation and production (Yenawine, 1997). Candidates are evaluated on their interpretation and understanding of the concept. To begin, they provide a working definition of the central concept being explored for the assignment. Is the definition accurate and thorough enough for an outside reader? Then, using that definition, candidates are evaluated on the series of images and corresponding captions used to explore the complexity of this concept and evidence of it in one's everyday experiences. In addition, candidates are evaluated on the visual display of their interpretation of the identified concept. I look for the effective use of words and images to communicate the abstract and multi-dimensional nature of social studies concepts.

The second aspect of evaluation of this assignment is the presentation of the products in class. These presentations are an opportunity for the candidates to educate their peers about a topic, make connections between and among the concepts presented, and field questions. Following the presentations, candidates upload their work to our university course management system so their peers can see it. With this access, candidates re-visit their peers' products and develop at least one inquiry-based question for each concept presented. I assess these questions on how well the author connects to the content and creates questions to facilitate discussion.

CANDIDATES AND THE TASK

Most teacher candidates are aware of social studies concepts as an aspect of secondary school instruction. However, many candidates have been taught concepts as one-dimensional, vocabulary exercises in which they repeat a definition from the glossary or a class PowerPoint. This experience influenced the ways in which they think about particular concepts and the ways in which they integrated concepts into their field-based lessons.

Upon initial introduction to this assignment, it is not uncommon for candidates to whisper, "this is easy." After completing the assignment, however, they report that the challenge escalates as they add more images as doing so pushes them beyond their prior knowledge and experience. The concepts become further complicated as candidates develop inquiry-based questions.

For example, one candidate explored the concept of citizenship. Her images included a photograph of her voter registration card and a person donating clothes at a collection center. Following her presentation, a peer asked, "how does donating clothes contribute to being a good citizen?" Other peer-generated questions included:

- What is the importance of democracy?
- Why do we say the Pledge of Allegiance?
- What could we do now to reconcile the actions of the people who came before us?

The process of gathering images for conversations as well as the inquiry-based questions was evident in the lesson plans teacher candidates created throughout the semester.

THE TASK IN CONTEXT

At my institution, teacher candidates take a series of three social studies education courses (i.e., foundations, methods, student teaching). This task is completed as part of the methods course and early in the semester (approximately week 4 of 16). Prior to this task, I introduce candidates to the scope and sequence of social studies, the *C3 Framework* (National Council for the Social Studies, 2013), as well as Eisner's (1985) conception of the explicit, implicit, and null curricula. Following this assignment, candidates explore a range of teaching strategies (e.g., discussion, inquiry-based instruction, simulations) with attention to the various perspectives and points of access for their candidates (e.g., verbal, visual) that are brought to their attention as part of this assignment.

REFERENCES

Desai, D., Hamlin, J., & Mattson, R. (2010). *History as art, art as history contemporary art and social studies education.* New York: Routledge.

Eisner, E. W. (1985). *The educational imagination: On the design and evaluation of school programs.* New York: Macmillian.

National Council for the Social Studies. (2013). *The college, career, and civic life (C3) framework for social studies state standards: Guidance for enhancing the rigor of K–12 civics, economics, geography, and history.* Silver Spring, MD: Author.

Yenawine, P. (1997). Thoughts on visual literacy. In J. Flood, S.B. Heath, & D. Lapp (Eds.), *Handbook of research on teaching literacy through the communicative and visual arts* (pp. 845–846). New York: Macmillan Library Reference USA.

CHAPTER 38

COMMUNITY MAPPING VIDEO PODCAST PROJECT

Developing Teacher Candidates' Sociocultural Consciousness

Erik Jon Byker, Amy Good, and Nakeshia Williams

Names: Erik Jon Byker, Amy Good, and Nakeshia Williams	Audience: Undergraduate students
Affiliation: UNC Charlotte UNC Charlotte North Carolina Agricultural and Technical State University	Length: Two weeks—part of the Integrated Methods Block (IMB) Clinical Experience
Course Title: Teaching Social Studies to Elementary School Learners	Commonplace featured: Context
NCSS Teacher Education Standard: Element 4a. Candidates identify learners' socio-cultural assets and learning demands to plan and implement relevant and responsive pedagogy that increases students' opportunities to learn social studies.	

Teaching Social Studies: A Methods Book for Methods Teachers,
pages 227–232.
Copyright © 2017 by Information Age Publishing

TASK SUMMARY

The *Community Mapping Video Podcast* project immerses teacher candidates in the socio-geographic fabric of the clinical schools where K–12 students are situated in order to raise candidates' levels of geographic consciousness and to report and analyze the sociocultural makeup of a school community in order to design curricula that are culturally responsive.

DESCRIPTION OF THE TASK

The *Community Mapping Video Podcast* project prepares teacher candidates in their development of sociocultural consciousness (Banks, 1996) as they explore the socio-historical geography that situates school communities. The project begins with the statement: Familiarity with the communities in which learners live helps teachers better connect with their learning communities.

The development of sociocultural consciousness of school communities helps candidates identify—and become more sensitive to—the environments where children live. A child's sociocultural environment can be deeply rooted and impact how the child approaches learning in the classroom (Dewey, 1915; Vygotsky, 1978). For example, if candidates identify that urban gardens are being planted and maintained by children and families in the school community, they can make connections to the idea of using land as a type of subsistence agriculture. The scarcity of open spaces and playgrounds, as another example, may inform how a candidate prioritizes kinesthetic learning and outdoor play.

Familiarity with the places and spaces students inhabit also equips candidates in their planning. It helps them develop what Schmidt (2011) calls "a sense of place" (p. 20). Candidates can draw on the sense of place when planning lessons, units, and homework assignments that are relevant to their students' everyday worlds. For example, a candidate could design a unit about local government that includes a problem-based learning scenario of a public issue—e.g., busing of students to schools—that is of interest to students and their families in the communities.

Socio-cultural consciousness of the community fosters meaningful home/ school and community/school relationships. Such relationships can open public private partnerships within the school community (Byker, 2016a).

The project is an introductory step to sociocultural consciousness, as candidates become visual sociologists, mapping out the social and historical geography of their clinical placement schools. The task centers around the creation of a 6–8 minute video podcast that: (a) raises levels of sociocultural consciousness about the school community, and (b) analyzes the sociocultural makeup of the clinical school's community of students from various races, ethnicities, cultures, and backgrounds.

The Task: Candidates investigate their clinical school community in virtual and physical ways. They search the school's website for data about school location and student demographics. They visit the school community and spend time walking around the community observing, taking notes, and capturing pictures of: (a) the school, (b) the surrounding neighborhood, (c) the availability of recreational facilities (e.g., parks, community buildings), (d) the types of retail places, and (e) yard signs (e.g., political signs, sports league signs). While pictures document community awareness, the photography should not be intrusive to community members.

Candidates also interview people at the school (e.g., mentor teacher, school secretary, school custodians, school principal) to find out about the surrounding community and the school's history. They then develop a 6–8 minute video podcast (e.g., YouTube video) that discusses the school community, details the socio-geographical experiences, and evaluates the utility of community mapping.

The podcast includes an examination of community intersectionality. Intersectionality is the notion that people have many ways that they identify and these identities intersect (Hancock, 2007). Community mapping illustrates the intersectionality of social studies in communities. Candidates discuss community intersectionality by addressing the following prompts in their podcasts:

Civics

- How is the school organized? Is it a public school or charter school?
- Who oversees the school? A district? A board of directors?
- Who is responsible for the school transportation and how do most students arrive at the school?

Culture

- What is the sociocultural makeup of the students?
- What races, ethnicities, and cultures are represented in the school?
- Describe your interactions with members of the community as part of the community mapping.

Economics

- How does the school receive its funding? Is it a Title 1 school?
- How many students receive free and reduce lunch service?

Geography

- Where is the school located?
- What is the neighborhood and community like? Are there residential spaces? Commercial spaces? Public spaces? Describe these places

History

- What is the history of the school's location? Whose stories are told in historical markers and signs? Whose stories are silenced?
- What will you remember from community mapping that will impact your future teaching?
- What is the impact of community mapping in developing sociocultural consciousness about your clinical school?
- How will you apply the knowledge of students' socio-geography (i.e., the communities they are from) to your future practice? Briefly discuss how you can use cultural practices and the history of communities to positively influence the lives of children in your teaching practices.

Assessing the Task: The video podcast is assessed with a grading rubric, which is based on four categories: content, mechanics, length, and presentation. Candidates share their video podcasts using the unlisted feature on YouTube so that they are viewable only by those who the candidates choose. They present their video podcasts in class, which leads to further dialogue about the racialized systems of power and opportunity—or lack thereof—that are often embedded in school communities (Howard, 2003; Milner, 2010). The content of the video podcast and their presentation are weighted higher for assessment purposes.

CANDIDATES AND THE TASK

We have used the *Community Mapping Video Podcasting* project for several years. Although teacher candidates often are hesitant about the assignment, it is usually one of the highlights of the semester. Sample comments that candidates have shared regarding the impact of the assignment include:

- Researching, interviewing and experiencing the school first hand proved to be very insightful for me as a newcomer. I am a part of the school community by proximity, but never knew how many opportunities there are within this community. I was also unaware of the size of the community as a whole.
- This assignment has helped me get to know the community in which my students live in. Through the community mapping assignment I have identified the needs and challenges that my students have due to their socio-economic status and their environmental surroundings. These challenges are also strengths as the students are connected to the rich history and culture of their community. They identify with the community and I want to be responsive to that identity.
- In the future, the assignment makes me aware that socio-geography also impacts how I will see my students' strengths, needs, and their circum-

stances. Being responsive to cultural identity will allow me to better relate to my students' everyday life experiences.

• Students look up to their teachers and value their opinions, it is important to remain open and cognizant in order to positively influence their learning. My interaction with community members during the Community Mapping assignment has been quite valuable. I will never forget the community members I met during this experience. They taught me the value of listening with open ears.

In sum, the community mapping video podcast is an example of the integration of technology for artifact creation through media authorship (Byker, 2014; Mishra & Koehler, 2009). Teacher candidates encounter—and even interrogate—their beliefs and assumptions about urban schools and communities. This includes discussing stereotypes and prejudices that teacher candidates have due to limited experiences in a variety of communities. The candidates' dialogue reflects a development of sociocultural consciousness as candidates have their eyes open in new ways to school communities (Byker, 2016b; Freire, 1998). Finally, the project is instrumental in building awareness of the geography of school communities as candidates develop a responsiveness to the children in their clinical schools.

THE TASK IN CONTEXT

The *Community Mapping Video Podcast* project is introduced early in the semester when the topic of geography is discussed. Teacher candidates, though, complete the project as an introductory experience to their two-week intensive clinical teaching experience, which happens at the semester's midpoint.

REFERENCES

Banks, J. (1996). The historical reconstruction of knowledge about race: Implications for transformative teaching. In J. A. Banks (Ed.), *Multicultural education, transformative knowledge, and action: Historical and contemporary perspectives* (pp. 64–87). New York, NY: Teachers College Press.

Byker, E. J. (2014). Needing TPACK without knowing it: Integrating educational technology in social studies. *Social Studies Research and Practice, 9*(3), 106–117.

Byker, E. J. (2016a). The one laptop schools: Equipping rural elementary schools in South India through public private partnerships. *Global Education Review, 2*(4), 126–142.

Byker, E. J. (2016b). Developing global citizenship consciousness: case studies of critical cosmopolitan theory. *Journal of Research in Curriculum and Instruction, 20*(3), 264–275.

Dewey, J. (1915). *The school and society and the child and the curriculum.* Chicago, IL: University of Chicago Press.

Freire, P. (1998). *Teachers as cultural workers.* Boulder, CO: Westview Press.

Hancock, A. M. (2007). When multiplication doesn't equal quick addition: Examining intersectionality as a research paradigm. *Perspectives on Politics, 5*(1), 63–79.

Howard, T. (2003). The dis(g)race of the social studies. In G. Ladson Billings (Ed.), *Critical race theory perspectives on social studies: The profession, policies, and curriculum* (pp. 16–26). Greenwich, CT: Information Age Press.

Milner, H. R. (2010). *Start where you are, but don't stay there.* Cambridge, MA: Harvard Education Press.

Mishra, P., & Koehler, M.J. (2009). Too cool for school? No way! Using the TPACK framework: You can have your hot tools and teach with them, too. *Learning & Leading with Technology, 36*(7), 14–18.

Schmidt, S. (2011). Theorizing place: Students' navigation of place outside. *Journal of Curriculum Theorizing, 27*(1), 20–35.

Vygotsky, L. (1978). *Mind in society.* Boston, MA: Harvard University Press.

CHAPTER 39

TROUBLING THE FAMILIAR

The Institutionalized Racism Inquiry Project

Alexander Cuenca

Name: Alexander Cuenca	Audience: Undergraduate students
Affiliation: Saint Louis University	Length: Semester-long project
Course Title: Middle/Secondary Methods in Social Studies Education	Commonplace featured: Context
NCSS Teacher Education Standard: Element 5b. Candidates explore, interrogate, and reflect upon their own cultural frames to attend to issues of equity, diversity, access, power, human rights, and social justice within their schools and/or communities.	

Teaching Social Studies: A Methods Book for Methods Teachers,
pages 233–238.

TASK SUMMARY

The *Institutional Racism Inquiry Project* attempts to trouble teacher candidates' familiarity with institutional racism by engaging in community mapping activities and lesson plan development.

DESCRIPTION OF THE TASK

The *Institutional Racism Inquiry Project* (IRIP) is grounded in the understanding that racism is embedded in the fabric of society. If social studies education is truly about preparing students for a democracy, then rooting out the inequities created by structural racism ought to be a primary objective. Moreover, because the omnipresence of Whiteness provides an *alibi of detectability*, exposing the prevalence of structural racism should be a primary objective for social studies teacher education programs.

The Institutional Racism Inquiry Project is a semester-long project that is completed in an urban middle or high school. The IRIP is intended to help candidates:

- Recognize the ways in which racism is institutionalized within the societal structures of a local community and how these permutations of racism are interconnected.
- Analyze and explain how institutionalized racism is maintained and reproduced.
- Create lesson plans that account for and interrogate the inequities created by institutional racism.

The Task: The project begins with a series of *framing readings* that elucidate the dimensions of structural racism, argue for discussing structural racism in social studies classrooms, and demonstrate how structures influence student learning (Miller & Garran, 2007). Within the context of our discussion, we visit *Racial Dot Map* (http://demographics.coopercenter.org/DotMap/) to discuss segregation in our region and visit *The Geography of Race* website (http://www.umich.edu/~lawrace/index.htm) to discuss the economic consequences of segregation.

Teacher candidates then turn their attention to the ways in which social studies education tends to reproduce the status quo (Brown & Brown, 2010; Howard, 2003). The final set of readings that prepare candidates for the IRIP demonstrate how students' encounters with the structures of society shape their responses to social studies instruction (Gillen, 2014; Rubin, 2007).

The IRIP is conducted in three phases, with target completion dates throughout the semester. Overall, the project requires candidates to observe for patterns of discrimination and inequality in eight community institutions:

1. Housing patterns
2. Zoning laws
3. Businesses

4. Transportation
5. Environmental quality
6. Schools
7. Spaces for civic expression
8. Media representations

First, candidates engage in community mapping activities for the local community. Considered both a process and a product to help candidates understand community resources, for this project, community mapping is more intentional—to interrogate the racialized structures and lived experiences within a community. In essence, candidates interrogate the ways in which Whiteness is maintained in everyday institutions. Candidates focus on Tatum's (1997) definition of racism—"prejudice plus power." During the project, candidates face the question: how is Whiteness controlling access to social, cultural, political, economic, and geographic resources and decision-making?

With that introduction, I pair up candidates in dyads and give them four weeks to engage in the following activities:

Demographics. Candidates gather demographic information about the schools and surrounding community focusing on U.S. Census Bureau and the state board of education data for the local area.

Scouting. Candidates generate a map (usually via Google) and drive through the community. They identify places such as businesses, parks, bus stops, libraries, subdivisions, community organizations, and public institutions and journal their initial impressions.

Community Engagement. After the scouting trip, candidates spend significant time engaging with the systems, structures, and people within the community. They observe patterns such as the movement of people, interactions between people, the composition of people in various spaces, similarities and differences in neighborhoods/subdivisions, visible geographical demarcations, public and private signage, and the usage and upkeep of public resources (e.g., playgrounds, basketball courts). Candidates also enter libraries, grocery stores, and businesses, and identify possible informants for the next stage of the project. During these visits, candidates jot down their impressions about the community.

Artifact Collection. Candidates return to the locations they identified and collect artifacts (e.g., photographs, documents, and interviews with informants) from the neighborhood. They must interview at least five members of the community from three different institutions. These short interviews (five minutes or less) are designed to capture thoughts on the history, contemporary issues, and existing inequities within the community, and the ways in which various institutions intersect to sustain inequities.

Media Analysis. Candidates conduct keyword searches in local and regional media sources for mentions of institutions within the community. Candidates catalog differences between the media representation of the community and their experiences with the community. This analysis helps candidates explore how the community is constructed through the media.

During the four-week community mapping activity period, the candidate pairs submit weekly electronic progress updates. Each update includes a written summary of the activities and an upload of the jottings, drawings, reflections, and/or artifacts collected.

The second phase of the IRIP is a multimodal presentation of the operation of racism within a local community. This presentation synthesizes the experiences and activities conducted during the community mapping experience. Candidates visually organize the information, artifacts, and experiences to illustrate the interconnectedness between the different kinds of institutions (e.g., residential, educational, employment, environmental, media) and how these interconnections sustain oppression. Typically, I ask students to return to the Miller and Garran article in order to revisit the ways in which institutions are mutually reinforcing in maintaining inequity. What must be clearly communicated through the project is how the words and images being presented expose the visible, yet invisible operation of racism within a community.

The final phase of the IRIP is the generation of three inquiry-based lesson plans that utilize the knowledge developed from the community-mapping experience. Lessons must focus on how institutional racism operates using the disciplinary lenses of history, geography, economics, and/or civics. Candidates develop these lessons individually, but in consultation with their dyad partner. Candidates follow the Inquiry Design Model (IDM) blueprint (http://www.c3teachers.org/inquiry-design-model/), which helps them build lessons that encompass the entirety of the C3 Inquiry Arc. The inquiry-based lessons provide an opportunity for candidates to draw directly from the social milieu that surrounds teaching and utilize this milieu as a scaffold for critical and justice oriented social studies teaching.

Assessing the Task: The assessable products of the three phases of the IRIP are: 1) the four weekly progress updates, 2) the multimodal presentation, and 3) the inquiry-based lesson plans. Each of these products has two distinct targets. For the weekly progress updates, I look for a) fidelity to the activities within the timeline and b) development of candidates' abilities to surface how patterns of how racism is normalized.

For the multimodal presentation, I look for a) the richness of the words, images, and experiences communicated during the presentation and b) the degree to which candidates are able to construct connections between and across the different institutions to illustrate the operation of racism within a community. Drawing on the definition that racism is "power plus prejudice," presenters must demonstrate how different institutions work together to control access to social, political, economic, and geographic resources in ways that create racial inequities.

Finally, in the inquiry-based lesson plans, I look for a) how well candidates execute the components of the IDM and b) their ability to interrogate institutionalized racism within a community and adapt the skill of interrogation and the outcome of that interrogation into social studies lessons.

CANDIDATES AND THE TASK

Most candidates are aware at a basic level of the concepts of institutionalized racism, Whiteness, and privilege. The community-mapping phase of the IRIP provides tangible evidence of the institutionalization of racism and its everyday operations. For candidates, observing the lack of basketball hoops in spaces for recreation, the physical separation between White and Black families at playgrounds, or the lack of grocery stores within a walkable distance became important and observable lessons beyond readings and discussions. Interviews with community members shed light on a discriminatory criminal justice system that perpetuates poverty and disrupts acts like voting, since the only voting precinct in the community is at the police station. These experiences translate directly into the inquiry-based lessons that candidates produce. Candidates have developed inquiry-based lessons on food deserts (geography), problems with the municipal court system (civics, government, economics), and redlining (history).

The IRIP is not a panacea. Some candidates resist the opportunity to make the invisible visible. Yet, the problems within a democracy provide some of the most salient lessons for social studies classrooms. Therefore, preparing candidates with the capacity to inquire into societal inequities and to make those observations into meaningful lessons may be one of the most important contributions of social studies teacher education programs. If K–12 social studies classrooms cannot afford to be silent on the inequities caused by institutionalized racism, then neither can social studies teacher education classrooms.

THE TASK IN CONTEXT

Teacher candidates are introduced to the IRIP at the beginning of the semester and are prepared for the project by the framing readings referenced above. During the first two phases of the project, teacher candidates are simultaneously engaging in their community inquiries and learning about various methods such as questioning, deliberation, or historical thinking in order to help them generate inquiry-based lessons that tie community and social studies teaching and learning together.

REFERENCES

Brown, A. L., & Brown, K. D. (2010). Strange fruit indeed: Interrogating contemporary textbook representation of racial violence toward African-Americans. *Teachers College Record, 112*(1), 31–67.

Gillen, J. (2014). *Educating for insurgency.* New York: AK Press.

Howard, T. (2003). The dis(g)race of the social studies. In G. Ladson Billings (Ed.), *Critical race theory perspectives on social studies: The profession, policies, and curriculum* (pp. 16–26). Greenwich, CT: Information Age Press.

Miller, J., & Garran, A. M. (2007). The web of institutional racism. *Smith College Studies in Social Work, 77*(1), 33–67.

Rubin, B. (2007). "There's still not justice": Youth civic identity development amid distinct school and community contexts. *Teachers College Record, 109*(2), 449–481.

Tatum, B. D. (1997). *"Why are all the black kids sitting together in the cafeteria?": And other conversations about race.* New York: Basic Books.

CHAPTER 40

A "LIVED-IN" SECONDARY SOCIAL STUDIES METHODS COURSE

Brad M. Maguth

Name: Brad M. Maguth	Audience: Undergraduate and graduate students
Affiliation: The University of Akron	Length: Semester-long
Course Title: Secondary Social Studies Methods & Field Experience	Commonplace featured: Context
NCSS Teacher Education Standard: Element 4a. Candidates identify learners' socio-cultural assets and learning demands to plan and implement relevant and responsive pedagogy that increase students' opportunities to learn social studies. Element 4d. Select, create, and engage learners with a variety of social studies instructional strategies, disciplinary sources and contemporary technologies, consistent with current theory and research about student learning. Element 5a. Use theory and research to continually improve their social studies knowledge, inquiry skills, and civic dispositions and adapt practice to meet the needs of each learner.	

Teaching Social Studies: A Methods Book for Methods Teachers,
pages 239–243.

TASK SUMMARY

A "lived-in" model to social studies teacher preparation embeds teacher candidates in 10th grade U.S. History classrooms in an urban school whereby they take over instructional planning and implementation responsibilities, in consultation with a cooperating teacher and their methods professor, for the semester.

DESCRIPTION OF THE TASK

The lived-in model to social studies teacher education is grounded in 20–25 preservice social studies teachers, enrolled in a six-hour social studies methods block, being placed in supportive social studies classroom environments that allow for the building of relationships with students and teachers. All course sessions meet on-site at one area high school, and all candidates are initially assigned to one of two experienced U.S. History teachers for sixteen weeks (10–12 candidates per class). Candidates meet at the school for class Monday through Friday from 12:50–3pm.

Every day during this time, the candidates mentor, tutor, and teach two periods of 10th-grade high school students, all identified as the school's most academically vulnerable youth. For the first two weeks of the semester, candidates spend half of their time (12:50–1:43pm) observing their assigned teachers and working with pre-selected students in small groups for guidance, instruction, and mentorship. Candidates interview their assigned 10th graders and report on their socio-cultural assets and learning demands. During the second half of the class (1:46–3pm), candidates meet with me and their cooperating teachers to discuss theory and practice in social studies. As a class we review the school's state report card (including test scores in U.S. History), NAEP U.S. History findings, state and local district social studies standards, and classroom textbooks and materials. We connect these readings to issues surrounding the "state of the social studies."

The Task: Drawing from assigned course readings, their interviews, and observations of school-based social studies practitioners, and the needs and interests of youth, candidates work in small groups to plan and pitch their units to their peers. All units must promote student inquiry (aligning to the *C3 Framework* and using the Inquiry Design Model Template). Before implementing their units, candidates must submit draft materials to me, their cooperating teachers, and peers for written feedback. Once approved, they upload materials into a secure online learning management system.

Starting in week three, candidates, under my and their cooperating teachers' supervision, implement their approved, inquiry-oriented U.S. History units. Each class implements five to six units, and most units last around two weeks.

It is important to note that even though groups take turns planning and implementing their units, every candidate is expected to teach and engage youth on a daily basis through inquiry stations, preparing for debates, grading their work, drawing conclusions based on analyzing student data and implementing enrichment and remedial interventions. Since the 10th graders are identified as academically vulnerable, candidates frequently pull students out of class to make-up work and offer layered interventions. These tasks require that candidates review and understand daily planned lessons and activities before coming to class.

I provide instruction and supervision at the high school where I am present, visible, and available on-site. Outside of working with candidates to design and implement strong inquiry-oriented units, I float between the two 10th grade U.S. History classes to supervise and observe. Drawing from the "flipped classroom concept" in teacher education, candidates learn the bulk of prescribed course content online in modules, reviewing and critiquing assigned readings for homework (Marks, 2015). During class, I expect candidates to apply disciplinary and pedagogical concepts and strategies for hands-on learning in classrooms. At 2:30pm (when the final period ends) candidates from both 10th-grade classrooms meet for reflection in our dedicated classroom around the following questions:

- What went well? How do you know this?
- What didn't go well? How do you know this?
- Drawing from theory and practice in social studies, how do you plan to adapt your practice in the future to better meet the needs of learners?
- How did this unit encourage civic learning and engagement? In particular, in what ways did you and/or youth take informed action in schools and/or communities and serve as advocates for learners, the teaching profession, and social studies?

After groups from both classes share their responses to these questions, I invite candidates in the non-planning groups to share what they observed and learned from the day's activities. We then move to discuss the upcoming teaching schedule, and resources, materials and supplies methods students must review before our next class.

Assessing the Task: Outside of planning and implementing an inquiry-oriented unit in 10th grade U.S. History, candidates must complete a written reflection on the overall quality of the unit just implemented. This reflection requires candidates draw from their teaching experiences while reviewing the students' submitted work for patterns, themes, and discrepancies in order to draw conclusions about the quality of their learning.

Assignments completed and submitted by the group planning instruction include:

- The successful completion and posting of a C3 Unit Plan (group assignment) w/all final supplementals.
- Written reflection (individual assignment) in which candidates draw from their experiences implementing their unit and discuss the quality of student learning based on a review of student work and grades.

Non-planning group members individually complete the following assignments:

- Provide written feedback on the C3 Unit Plan and accompanying supplementals before its implementation, and the overall quality of unit implementation and its impact on student learning. In particular, candidates outside of the planning group are asked:
  Before (Due 7 days before unit implementation)
  - How well does this unit align to cited standards?
  - How consistent with social studies research is this unit in presenting and engaging learners with a variety of social studies instructional strategies, disciplinary sources, and contemporary technologies?
  - How well does this unit encourage civic learning and engagement?
  After (Due 7 days after unit implementation)
  - In general, how well did 10th graders learn unit objectives; including applying disciplinary content knowledge to argue a position? How about the group of students you've been specifically assigned to work with?
  - How well did this unit encourage civic learning and engagement? How do you know this?

CANDIDATES AND THE TASK

Before entering this course, teacher candidates have limited experience teaching and mentoring youth: They complete general coursework with no more than 10–30 field hours in the broad areas of planning, assessment, and inclusion. Although many have completed micro-teachings in front of university peers on campus, few have had the opportunity to teach whole social studies units to multiple sections of high school students under direct, semester-long supervision. Through this "lived-in" model to teacher preparation, candidates gain experience (over 150 hours) learning the importance of flexibility, adaptability, and developing strong relationships with youth. Moreover, candidates benefit from sustained on-site supervision in order to plan and implement inquiry-oriented units. This on-site supervision and strong collaborative partnership with cooperating teachers limits the traditional discrediting of university methods learning commonplace in traditional social studies methods courses and field placements (Adler, 2008; Fehn & Koeppen, 1998).

Outside of benefiting candidates, this clinical model employs an all-hands-on-deck approach to differentiating instruction and engaging academically vulnerable youth in an urban school. In a lived-in model, social studies teachers, methods faculty, and candidates work together in order to ensure a high-quality social studies experience for the students. Research conducted by an outside external evaluator found that participating 10th graders enhanced their attitudes and perceptions towards school and demonstrated statistically significant gains in overall GPA versus non-participating 10th graders (Maguth & Deevers, 2014). The high school students often approach me to tell them how a candidate inspired them, taught them, and made a difference. With so many trained, competent, and caring adults in the room, youth look forward to coming to class and note how they feel special with all the individual attention they receive.

A lived-in secondary social studies methods course provides the next wave of social studies teachers with hands-on experience connecting theory and practice and provides youth with individualized instruction in a supportive, caring, and differentiated learning environment. Cooperating teachers appreciate having the extra supports (candidates and faculty) to help engage learners in doing and learning social studies. I benefit from being on-site in order to help candidates better connect theory to practice and to cultivate numerous social studies research opportunities.

THE TASK IN CONTEXT

Students complete this six-hour-methods block the semester before their full-time, semester-long student teaching.

REFERENCES

Adler, S. (2008). The education of social studies teachers. In C. Tyson & L. Levstik (Eds.), *Handbook on research in social studies education* (pp. 329–351). New York: Routledge.

Fehn, B., & Koeppen, K. E. (1998). Intensive document-based instruction in a social studies methods course and student teachers' attitudes and practice in subsequent field experiences. *Theory & Research in Social Education, 26*(4), 461–484.

Maguth, B., & Deevers, M. (2014, November). *"Lived-In": The results of embedding pre-service social studies education in a 10th grade U.S. history classroom to enhance student learning.* Presentation at the annual conference of the College and University Faculty Assembly of The National Council for the Social Studies, Boston, Massachussets.

Marks, D. (2015). Flipping the classroom: Turning an instructional methods course upside down. *Journal of College Teaching & Learning, 12*(4), 241–248.

CHAPTER 41

MENTORING, PUBLIC OUTREACH, AND SOCIAL JUSTICE ISSUES

Ingredients for a Powerful Professional Partnership

Joe O'Brien and Tina M. Ellsworth

Name: Joe O'Brien and Tina M. Ellsworth	Audience: Undergraduate students
Affiliation: University of Kansas	Length: Semester-long project
Course Title: Advanced Practices in Teaching Middle/Secondary Social Studies/Kansas University Council for the Social Studies	Commonplaces featured: Context
NCSS Teacher Education Standard: Element 5c. Candidates take informed action in schools and/or communities and serve as advocates for learners, the teaching profession, and social studies.	

Teaching Social Studies: A Methods Book for Methods Teachers,
pages 245–250.
Copyright © 2017 by Information Age Publishing
All rights of reproduction in any form reserved.

TASK SUMMARY

Teacher candidates collaborated with the Dole Institute of Politics on the development of instructional materials for an online exhibit of the Americans with Disabilities Act that in-service teachers then field-tested.

DESCRIPTION OF THE TASK

We design professional learning experiences for our teacher candidates, which are dependent upon mentoring relationships and partnerships (see Figure 41.1) that better enable them to understand the importance of furthering student learning and of contributing to the larger profession. We place candidates in mentor-mentee relationships to empower them as professionals. Although we pursue this endeavor through a student-run organization, the Kansas University Council for the Social Studies (KUCSS), what the candidates have accomplished is feasible in a methods course.

Annually, candidates involved in KUCSS (2015) choose to work on two curricular projects. In 2015, they selected the social justice implications of the American with Disabilities Act (ADA) and the chance to work with content experts and a digital archive of primary sources related to ADA's passage and to field test their work in an urban high school. Candidates developed material for the Dole Institute's online exhibit for the 25th anniversary of the ADA's passage (http://dolearchivecollections.ku.edu/collections/ada/), some of which they field-tested with Kansas City teachers (http://dolearchivecollections.ku.edu/collections/ada/classroom/). The experience resulted in greater insight into the unique needs of those with disabilities as well as a subtle, but substantive shift in the mentoring relationships (see Figure 41.2) as the candidates became the authorities and presented their work to content experts and teachers.

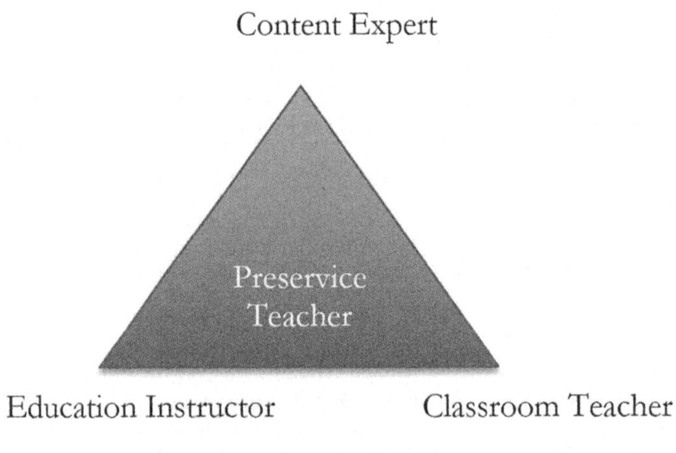

FIGURE 41.1.   Mentoring Relationship

Content Experts   Classroom Teachers

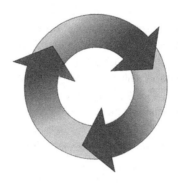

Education Instruction   Candidates

FIGURE 41.2.   Mentoring Relationship With Candidates as Instructors

In this task, we follow Schwab's (1983) suggestion to give equal weight to all of four commonplaces: teachers and teaching, learners and learning, subject matter, and context. The goals of this project are to help candidates:

- engage in the professional work of teaching through design and field-test of instructional materials
- forge collaborative partnerships among candidates, social studies-related content experts, and in-service teachers in the creation of instructional materials
- deepen candidates' content knowledge
- promote social justice through creation and presentation of ADA materials to classroom teachers, social studies professionals, and students.

The Task: The semester-long project requires a two-track approach. First, we explain how to design and field test the instructional material. Second, we handle the logistics associated with the project, such as partnering with classroom teachers and with a program that has a public outreach mission:

1.   *Find an educational partner.* Identify a social studies-related program in need of strengthening its educational outreach program. Invite a representative of the organization to collaborate on a project by serving as a content knowledge expert providing content assistance and content validation throughout the project.
2.   *Establish professional mindset and autonomy.* Explain to candidates that they will design, field test and publish and/or present instructional ma-

terial of their choosing. Having the program outreach person involved adds validity to the work, particularly if the person indicates what the program intends to do with the material.

3. *Explore and decide upon project's purpose(s) and outcome(s).* Guide the candidates' discussion about possible projects. In our case, although the Dole Institute's representative wanted to post instructional material on the planned online exhibit for the ADA, she did not suggest what material to develop. The Dole Institute representative offered her content knowledge and expertise and referred candidates to suggested online resources to research. Ultimately, the candidates focused on how the built environment prior to the ADA prevented equal access to those with a disability.

4. *Create a project plan.* The plan is pivotal for two reasons. First, shifting the focus from an academic project to a professional one proves troublesome for candidates. Typically, they possess little professional experience or awareness of how an audience like the Dole Institute, professional educators, and the public creates higher expectations and more demands on their time than coursework. Second, the plan reassured us of the candidates' ability and willingness to undertake the project.

5. *Select collaborative workspace(s).* Candidates establish a collaborative online place for them to gather with all members of the collaborative: the methods instructor, the program outreach person, and the classroom teachers. The ADA group used Schoology and Google Docs to coordinate their activities and to involve the teachers and content experts.

6. *Research and compose instructional material with publication and/or presentation as a goal.* Candidates need to realize they are writing to multiple audiences: the students for whom the material is intended, a content expert who likely knows little about pedagogy, classroom teachers who likely know little about the intricacies of the ADA, and the general public. Doing so can prove challenging. For example, as they considered the material in light of a teacher audience, they needed our guidance on what information about the ADA to offer teachers. They sought ways to embed information about the ADA into relevant parts of the instructional material without appearing to insult teachers' intelligence. Trying to appear as content experts when they just learned about the ADA themselves placed the candidates in a delicate professional position.

7. *Field test and revise the material.* Distinguish this project from a typical lesson plan assignment. For example, in-service teachers provide input on the Schoology site during the development process and then provide a critique after field-testing the material after pedagogically validating it, which they support with student work. Candidates read the comments

and revise the material accordingly. The content expert then critically reviews the work prior to agreeing to post the material online.

8. *Situating the candidates' final work in a professional setting.* Ultimately, we want candidates to make a professional contribution beyond a typical course assignment. Those involved in KUCSS have instructional material available to educators on three separate university program websites and a published lesson plan and have been presenters in 10 national presentations.

Assessing the Task: There are three phases to the assessment: 1) Research, composition, and expert review of instructional material with publication and/ or presentation as a goal; 2) field test and revise the material; and, 3) situate the candidates' final work in a professional setting. During the first phase, along with the content expert, we assess the quality of the lesson plan's content and pedagogy. During the second phase, in-service teachers field-test the material and the candidates revise the lesson plan. Last, students prepare their work for publication in a professional setting. In this instance, Dole Institute staff reviewed and revised the material for publication on the Institute's website and for presentation at a national conference.

CANDIDATES AND THE TASK

Simply put, the experience proves empowering and exhilarating, yet humbling, for the teacher candidates. They routinely acknowledge how the collaborative nature of the KUCSS project benefits them by participating in professional learning communities during their first year of teaching and establishing relations with their peers, content experts, and "experienced and world class teachers." As one candidate noted, we "spent a lot of time reflecting and tweaking the work," which led to a deeper understanding of issues like those surrounding people with disabilities and to a realization of "how difficult it is to develop truly meaningful lessons for students." Given that they are novice professionals, we try to impress upon candidates that the development and sharing of instructional material on persons with disabilities is a form of social advocacy. We hope that with more time and experience they will use such professional opportunities as means to further their peers' ability to promote social justice in their classrooms.

THE TASK IN CONTEXT

This task is currently situated as a project for an extra-curricular organization, the Kansas University Council for the Social Studies (KUCSS), to complete in a calendar year. The organization is made up of undergraduate social studies education majors who seek further professional development, which includes partnering with other organizations and designing instructional materials for them to be used with wider audiences. This project would also fit in a methods course prior to student teaching, and would be carried throughout the entire semester to allow time for curricular development, field-testing, and feedback from the classroom, and revision before preparing for publication.

REFERENCES

Kansas University Council for the Social Studies. (2015a). *Bipartisanship and the ADA: Past, present, and future*. Robert J. Dole Archive and Special Collections at the Robert J. Dole Institute of Politics. Retrieved from http://dolearchivecollections.ku.edu/collections/ada/classroom/

Kansas University Council for the Social Studies (2015b). *Senator Bob Dole & 25th anniversary of the Americans with Disabilities Act*. Dole Archives: WWII Letters. Retrieved from http://dolearchivecollections.ku.edu/collections/wwii_letters/

Schwab, J. J. (1983). The Practical 4: Something for curriculum professors to do. *Curriculum Inquiry, 13*(3), 239–265. doi.org.www2.lib.ku.edu/10.2307/1179606.

CHAPTER 42

TRACKING IN SCHOOLS

Candidates Map Their Placement Context

Alexander Pope

Name: Alexander Pope	Audience: Undergraduate and graduate students
Affiliation: Salisbury University	Length: Two full days in placement plus write-up time; one class session (75 minutes) for discussion
Course Title: Social Studies and Reading in Secondary Schools II	Commonplace featured: Context
NCSS Teacher Education Standard: Element 4a. Candidates identify learners' socio-cultural assets and learning demands to plan and implement relevant and responsive pedagogy that increase students' opportunities to learn social studies.	

Teaching Social Studies: A Methods Book for Methods Teachers,
pages 251–255.
Copyright © 2017 by Information Age Publishing
All rights of reproduction in any form reserved.

TASK SUMMARY

In their placement schools, teacher candidates map student interactions, shadow one student throughout the school day, and track teacher interactions with students during classroom instruction.

DESCRIPTION OF THE TASK

The student and teacher tracker assignments occur during the semester prior to full-time student teaching. At this point, teacher candidates are familiar with writing objectives, lessons, and unit plans; identifying relevant standards; selecting materials; and developing assessments. They have designed and delivered at least one C3-based inquiry lesson in the field. The tracker task is part of a semester focus on social justice pedagogy. Candidates probe the context of their assigned, one-day-a-week placement.

The task directs candidates' attention to specific aspects of how middle or secondary students experience the school context and how teachers impact classroom context via their interactions with students. Through written responses and in-class sharing, examinations ground deeper critiques of how and where teaching and learning are constructed.

The Task: The student and teacher tracker tasks each consist of three smaller parts, an overall written reflection, and class discussion.

Student Tracker: The student tracker focuses candidates' attention on two dimensions of students' experiences: 1) the macro experience of student groupings in the building generally and the cafeteria in particular, 2) the micro experience of one student across his/her school day. Each of the three parts, detailed below, includes instructions for analyzing gathered data. After completing the parts, candidates submit an overall reflection.

Part 1: Student Mapping: Our candidates complete at least one full day in placement each week. Our program promotes a "whenever your teacher is in" approach as it more closely mirrors the reality of teaching as a profession requiring more than 40 hours per week.

Candidates arrive at least 20 minutes before the first bell. Working with a map of the school, they note where students are located, if there are demographic distinctions (e.g., cliques), and whether certain areas feel safer to them than others and what that means. This task prepares candidates to examine aspects of their placement they otherwise miss. It focuses their attention on what students might feel and how they position themselves as they wait for classes to begin. Candidates are immediately drawn to questions of access and whether the building or faculty welcome students.

Part 2: Student Arrangement: The second part requires candidates to attend a lunch period. Candidates map how students arrange themselves by ethnicity, gender, and grade level during one of the limited free-choice times in the school day. Identifying ethnicity and gender can be fraught with problems (Davenport, 2016), and we discuss those before and after this assignment. For example, students and teachers do not approach a table and ask the ethnicity of every student; they behave based on appearance and this is how candidates are asked to proceed. It is more important to observe patterns in seating across the cafeteria than to specifically identify every student in the space.

This task primarily focuses candidates' attention on how intraschool grouping during lunch might highlight important patterns that could impact the classroom experience. Candidates have another opportunity to consider the sociocultural realities of their placement. They consider for themselves, and then discuss with our class, how those realities might suggest strengths or challenges within a school. For instance, class discussions regularly touch on a responsibility to promote intercultural dialogue, and how that can be both more important and more challenging when students self-segregate outside the classroom.

Part 3: Student Shadowing: Candidates are skeptical of the final part of the student tracker, at least until they begin. They are required to shadow a student for a full day, attending all classes, and sitting with the student at lunch. Candidates can ask permission from any student they wish but are encouraged to reach out to students who they do not know well. More than any other part of the task, student shadowing brings attention to the school context as actual students experience it.

During the day, candidates chat with the student about school generally, what students do outside of school, or goals after graduation. Candidates are typically either juniors or graduate students; they have been removed from middle or high school long enough to forget the realities of a full school day. Candidates are not asked to transcribe the full day but should seek insights about what a student experiences across a day in that school.

This assignment also forces candidates to move beyond basic activities like "10 Things About Me" worksheets. The student shadowing is paired with an introductory reading on "funds of knowledge" (Moll, Armanti, & Neff, 1992). I remind candidates that students are complex individuals; a quiet or disengaged social studies student may an active leader in another context.

Teacher Tracker: The teacher tracker assignment focuses candidates' attention towards how faculty shape school context. Through three parts, candidates examine discrete but potentially hidden aspects of classroom practices. Candidates map teacher movement and verbal exchanges with students to assess student-teacher interactions, and time how much the teacher talks during the lesson to assess one type of teacher control. Candidates also reflect on their learning by referencing the collected data in an overall written response and class discussion.

Part 1: Teacher Movement: The first part of the teacher tracker considers how and where the teacher moves in the classroom. Over the course of a period, the candidate traces the teacher's path around the room, never removing pen from paper. The resulting jumble of lines depicts the teacher's foot traffic.

Teachers often favor certain areas of the room over others. Patterns in teacher movement may or may not relate to where particular students sit, but are worth noting. Candidates must account for the type of lesson being delivered. This observation suggests how a teacher does or does not use physical presence as pedagogy.

Part 2: Teacher Recognition: Building on teacher movement in the room, candidates next focus on whether the teacher is equitable in student recognition. Over the course of a full lesson, candidates note every interaction between teacher and students. They note the gender and ethnicity of involved students, and the type of recognition.

With whom and how the teacher interacts are important aspects of the classroom context. Candidates hypothesize why the teacher calls on some more than others do, or how to elicit greater participation. The recognition tracker privileges verbal interactions, but resulting discussions explore options for non-verbal interactions. This part provides a rich visual of how the teacher organizes the interpersonal context of his/her classroom.

Part 3: Teacher Talk: In the final part, candidates run a stopwatch whenever the teacher talks (e.g., delivering instructions, asking or answering a question). Candidates make a basic computation of what percentage of the class time was occupied by the teacher's voice.

Teachers have underestimated the dominance of their voices in social studies classrooms (Parker, 2006). Candidates must recognize how easily a teacher can control vocal interactions. Candidates must judge whether the teacher talks an appropriate amount. Doing so requires further consideration of the role of verbal communication in the classroom context.

Assessing the Task: Parts of the task, such as mapping the school, are graded on a completion basis. Written analyses are graded according to the following categories:

- Sociocultural aspects—Does analysis address sociocultural difference in the school or classroom?
- Impact on learning—Does analysis consider how school context impacts the potential for learning?
- Professional dispositions—Does analysis suggest ways to challenge or enhance observed qualities?
- Clarity/polish—Are analyses well written, such that others can assess the claims?

Candidates also share their observations and conclusions as part of regular class discussion.

CANDIDATES AND THE TASK

Teacher candidates are broadly skeptical about both tasks. They believe the student tracker assignment is like stalking one of their students. They worry about recruiting a student. They wonder about behavior in other classrooms—should candidates answer content questions from the teacher?

Candidates are less concerned about the teacher tracker assignment. Observing the mentor teacher is familiar. Candidates are still reluctant, however, to label students' perceived ethnicity or behavior. Candidates sometimes resist critiquing the mentor teacher based on this small sample of observations.

Candidates are generally surprised that the tasks are quite feasible. Students are often happy that a "teacher" shows an interest in their life outside the narrow band of a single class. Students feel important when a college student follows them around. Candidates are rarely surprised by the typical ethnic and gender segregation in the school and cafeteria. They are familiar enough with varied self-segregation.

Similarly, candidates are at first unmoved regarding potential racialized patterns in the mentor teacher's interactions with students. Candidates argue the teacher "calls on the ones who know" or "corrects the trouble makers." Only after sharing their results in class do they see how pervasive and consistent the patterns are. Candidates then consider more pernicious explanations. But on the whole, the most illuminating piece is often finding out how much of a class their teacher talks.

THE TASK IN CONTEXT

Approximately 2–3 weeks apart, the tasks are key parts of an ongoing social justice inquiry. Before the tasks, teacher candidates complete journal entries about their placement and practice "writing for social justice" (Christensen, 2000). Between the tasks, candidates study funds of knowledge and select topics for a larger inquiry project. Following the tasks, candidates revise a curriculum to address a relevant social justice issue.

REFERENCES

Christensen, L. (2000). *Reading, writing, and rising up: Teaching about social justice and the power of the written word.* Milwaukee, WI: Rethinking Schools.

Davenport, L. D. (2016). The role of gender, class, and religion in biracial Americans' racial labeling decisions. *American Sociological Review, 81*(1), 57–84.

Moll, L., Amanti, C., & Neff, D. (1992). Funds of knowledge for teaching: Using a qualitative approach to connect homes and classrooms. *Theory Into Practice, 31*(2), 132–141.

Parker, W. (2006). Public discourses in schools: Purposes, problems, and possibilities. *Educational Researcher, 35*(8), 11–18.

CHAPTER 43

ACADEMIC PROFILES

Connecting Kids, Data, and Practice

Kent Willmann

Name: Kent Willmann	Audience: Undergraduate and graduate students
Affiliation: University of Colorado	Length: 3–5 week span in a clinical setting
Course Title: Methods and Materials in Social Studies	Commonplace featured: Context
NCSS Teacher Education Standard: Element 4a. Candidates identify learners' socio-cultural assets and learning demands to plan and implement relevant and responsive pedagogy that increases students' opportunities to learn social studies. Element 4b. Candidates use knowledge of theory and research to plan and implement instruction and assessment that is relevant and responsive to learners' socio-cultural assets, learning demands, and individual identities.	

Teaching Social Studies: A Methods Book for Methods Teachers,
pages 257–262.
Copyright © 2017 by Information Age Publishing

TASK SUMMARY

Academic Profiles is an exercise intended to help teacher candidates form productive academic relationships with a broad range of students by collecting a variety of academic and other data about five students and proposing instructional decisions designed to meet those students' learning needs.

DESCRIPTION OF THE TASK

The ability to form productive and positive academic relationships with a variety of students is one of the most challenging aspects of teaching. *Academic Profiles* is designed to both instruct and assess teacher candidates' ability to target and differentiate instruction. Candidates use a variety of academic data, including interviews, to explore students' abilities, challenges, interests, and preferences. Then candidates employ learning theory and research-based practices to design instruction to meet student needs. In the process of completing the task, candidates and students build relationships that can lead to improved student performance. The task reflects components of the edTPA that challenge candidates to identify and serve individuals and groups of students with similar learning needs, citing theory and research as the basis for the choices.

The Task: *Academic Profiles* asks candidates to select five diverse students from their clinical setting and prepare a one- to two-page academic profile that includes a data-based portrait for each student, along with a set of possible instructional choices based on that profile. The profile may include examples of academic successes and struggles, preferred learning methods, extra-curricular activities, socio-economic & cultural background, academic history and plans, grades, testing information, favorite and least favorite classes, and teachers.

To create a diverse group, candidates are required to select at least one student with an IEP/504 and one ELL student. Moreover, at least one student must represent a non-dominate race and/or ethnic group, non-dominate social/economic status, struggling reader or writer, ADHD, Asperger's, gifted and talented, LGBT/Gender expression, or from a clique (e.g., honors, jocks, band). The other two students are up to the candidate.

Possible sources of data on the students include:

- Student interviews
- Teacher interviews
- Observation and shadowing of students
- Student cumulative folders with standardized test results
- IEP/504/GT/ELL status and associated documents
- Attendance information
- Grades, classroom assessment/test scores & homework completion rates
- Parent conference notes
- Class participation rates & discussion contributions

- Work samples
- Student perception survey results

Candidates then suggest instructional choices based on the information collected supported by from pedagogical theories and methods. Considerations include:

- What modifications are required?
- What culturally responsive, differentiation and motivational techniques are appropriate?
- What kind of assignments, topics, scaffolds, and assessments would work best?
- What feedback on assignments and assessments is likely to help the student?

To support their choices, candidates reference key authors and the learning/developmental theories discussed in this course and others.

What follows is a list of the considerations I have found useful in setting up the task:

1. Introducing this assignment early in the methods course is crucial. It takes significant time in the clinical setting to identify students for the profiles. Once the students are identified, it takes additional time to conduct interviews and collect data. All this must be done and the profiles written so that the information can be used later in the clinical experience to focus instructional planning, practice, and assessment.

2. Informing the Cooperating Teachers (CT) about the task is helpful in identifying students, accessing records, and providing opportunities for interviews and data collection.

3. Sharing samples of previous candidates' academic profiles is often the most successful way to provide clarity for the assignment. (For examples, please contact the author at: Kent.Willmann@colorado.edu.)

4. When providing models, highlight low inference reporting of what is learned about a student. For instance, it is better to use observation notes to state, "I have noticed on three occasions that student X tends to become off task during activities that require independent reading" than to write that a "student X is not motivated."

5. Candidates should be reminded of their mandated reporter responsibilities. While the task is focused on academic performance, students may share confidential information that requires reporting. In addition, much private student data (IEPs, test scores) is often shared. Candidates should be reminded of privacy requirements. Real student names should not be used.

6. If conducting the task as a combined assessment with a differentiation and/or other methods related course, frequent communication among

university instructors in task development, assignment dates, and grading responsibilities lead to success.

7. When reviewing learning theories, research, authors, researchers, and leaders during the course, sharing specific classroom-based practices and connecting them to typical students provides clear modeling. Among the authors and theorists commonly used are Brown (2007), Gay (2002), Marzano (2007), Tomlinson & Strickland (2005), and Wormeli (2011).

8. A broad net is cast when selecting authors, theorists, researchers, etc. Making connections to earlier education courses is encouraged. Candidates may use university professors, cooperating teachers, special education teachers and other educational voices that have influenced their choices.

9. If one's institution uses edTPA making direct connections between the two tasks can lead to better performance.

Assessing the Task: I actually enjoy and look forward to grading this task; it is like watching a candidate working individually with a student and the session ending with the two sharing a high five celebrating an academic achievement. Broadly, the candidates receive feedback on the diversity of students selected, on the quality and quantity of information collected about each student, on the use of learning theory to target teaching choices and in communication skills. (See the rubric in the Appendix.)

Often my feedback reflects on candidates' relationships with students. Those candidates who struggle to connect with students or who display biases toward sets of students can be identified and provided with supports. Those who excel can be steered towards developing and targeting their skills.

Typically due dates have to be adjusted due to clinical scheduling issues. Interim due dates are established for student selection and data collection.

CANDIDATES AND THE TASK

Many teacher candidates describe the task as their favorite, despite sometimes struggling initially to identify students. A few illustrative candidate comments follow:

> So often it is easy to interact with the excelling students, but this activity forced me to interact with those who had learning differences and it helped me learn how to differentiate between them in the classroom.

> One student I interviewed was a bright young man on the [autism] spectrum. I was fascinated by what he knew, how passionate he was, and although we had very different interests, my interview helped me relate to him as a person. I realized that he had specific needs as well as the ability to thrive, and that it took effort on my part to develop the understanding I needed in order to be an effective teacher for him.

Knowing as well that M is separated from his family has led to some interesting conversations and insights on how to support students. The only time I've seen him look sad was following the revelation that his father had died; I sat and talked with him for a bit about how he was feeling, how he was coping at home, and how I or Mr. H could help. We gave him some extensions and exempted him from a few assignments to give him time to adjust and to keep moving on. To be honest, this experience was an exercise for me in seeing how you change things to match what your students' need in that moment. Ninety percent of the time, M needs rigor and motivation; he works well when we place the responsibility for his learning on him. At this time, though, he needed a break, so a break is what he got. This is a confirmation for me that a part of teaching is asking the students what the feel they need to be supported. They are the expert on themselves, and so they are the first people to consult when we're trying to help them.

THE TASK IN CONTEXT

The task is often given as a cooperative assignment in a methods and a differentiation course, although it works well in a stand-alone methods course. Teacher candidates use information from both courses to identify key learner characteristics and to make targeted teaching choices, practicing what they will do every day as a teacher. This assignment is given early in the semester so that candidates can identify and collect information about the five students they profile, although, it is not turned in until the middle of the semester. Candidates are then expected to use the information about the students as they develop and implement lesson plans in their clinical settings during the rest of the semester. They also use their findings as they prepare a draft of edTPA Task 1.

Acknowledgments: Like all quality-teaching tasks, *Academic Profiles* has been a collaborative endeavor influenced by esteemed colleagues. University of Colorado colleagues contributing to the effort include Alison Boardman, s.j. Miller, Amber Kim, and Sara Staley. Credit must also be shared with the many cooperating teachers, teacher candidates, and the profiled students themselves. Wormeli suggests a similar task in the work referenced below.

APPENDIX

Academic Profiles Rubric

Criteria/Score	Incomplete 5–6 I/F/D	Partially Proficient 7 C	Proficient 8 B	Advanced 9–10 A
Student Selection	Little or no diversity. Didn't follow selection guidelines	Missing one or more required element.	All selection requirements met.	Selections highlight key differences in instructional choices.
Student Characteristics	Student learning characteristics based on severely incomplete or inaccurate data/	Limited set of data used to identify student learning characteristics.	Clear data used to identify student learning characteristics	Broad and varied set of data used to identify key learning characteristics.
Teaching Choices	Teaching choices not discussed or are disconnected or unfocused on learning characteristics	Teaching choices not included for all students or are mismatched with learning characteristics.	Teaching choices based on key learning characterizes	Teaching choices targeted for individuals and groups of students, based on characteristics and teaching goals.
Learning Theory	No attempt to identify learning theorists.	Less than 2 theorists identified or significant errors in interpretation.	2 or more research/ learning theorists identified and correctly attributed	Choice of research/theories enhances your profiles.
Writing Style	This is nearly unreadable and requires significant editing.	Unclear communication and/or significant errors hamper message.	Clear communication style with few errors.	Communication style and choices enhances your message.

REFERENCES

Brown, M.. (2007). Educating all students: Creating culturally responsive teachers, classrooms, and schools. *Intervention in School & Clinic, 43*(1), 57–62.

Gay, G. (2002). Preparing for culturally responsive teaching. *Journal of Teacher Education, 53*(2), 106–116.

Marzano, R. (2007). *The art and science of teaching: A comprehensive framework for effective instruction.* Washington, DC: Association of Supervisors and Curriculum Developers.

Tomlinson, C., & Strickland, C. (2005). *Differentiation in practice: A resource guide for differentiating curriculum, grades 9–12.* Alexandria, VA: Association for Supervision

Wormeli, R. (2011). Differentiated instruction: Setting the pedagogy straight. *Middle Ground, 15*(2), 39–40.

BIOGRAPHIES

S. G. Grant is Professor of Social Studies Education in the Graduate School of Education at Binghamton University in Binghamton, NY. His research interests lie at the intersection of state curriculum and assessment policies and teachers' classroom practices, with a particular emphasis in social studies. Grant served as senior consultant and writer on the *College, Career, and Civic Life (C3) Framework for State Social Studies Standards* and as the project manager for the New York Social Studies Resource Toolkit project. In addition to publishing six books, his publications have appeared in *Theory and Research in Social Education, Social Education, Teachers College Record,* and the *American Educational Research Journal.*

John Lee is Professor of Social Studies Education at North Carolina State University. His scholarly work focuses on curriculum design, standards, and the uses of digital historical resources in learning and teaching. He is also interested in theory and practice related to new literacies and global learning. Lee is an author of the *College, Career and Civic Life (C3) Framework for Standards in Social Studies* and co-founder of the C3 Teachers project (c3teachers.org). He also directs the Digital History and Pedagogy Project (dhpp.org). He is the author of Visualizing Elementary Social Studies Methods.

Teaching Social Studies: A Methods Book for Methods Teachers,
pages 263–264.

Kathy Swan is professor of curriculum and instruction at the University of Kentucky. She is co-author of the book *And Action! Doing Documentaries in the Social Studies Classroom* and the children's series *Thinking Like A Citizen* and co-editor of the book, *Teaching the C3 Framework: A Guide to Inquiry Based Instruction in the Social Studies*. Swan served as the project director and lead writer of the *College, Career, and Civic Life Framework for Social Studies State Standards* and is a co-founder of C3 Teachers. Her recent work focuses on the Inquiry Design Model and its use in pre-service and in-service teacher education.

Made in the USA
Coppell, TX
09 January 2020